An Only Child and Her Sister

An Only Child and Her Sister

A Memoir

Casey Maxwell Clair

ISBN-13: 9781532910494
ISBN-10: 1532910495

For my sister, Christine.
Finally.

CHAPTER 1

———————— ✺ ————————

I GOT MARRIED when I was thirteen years old.

People are understandably shocked when they hear this and always ask "Why in the *world* did you get married at thirteen?" And I always answer, "I don't know, I guess the right guy just hadn't come along till then."

✺

The year was 1962. It was a small affair; just the groom, myself and my mother. The wedding was held in the absolute very best corrugated aluminum structure in all of Ensenada, Mexico. The ceremony, and I use the word loosely, lasted a little over eight minutes and we were all back home in Los Angeles the same night.

Throughout my life, I've usually been the one to deliver the news that I was pregnant and married only a few short months after formally entering my teens. People always have a hard time believing I'm from a big city like Los Angeles, California. The assumption is that I must have been raised in a polygamous sect hidden in the wilds of Utah or, barring that, misspent my youth somewhere south of the Mason Dixon line. I've heard myself referred to as the "Loretta Lynn of Sherman Oaks" on more than one occasion. These days it's not quite as shocking to hear about a thirteen year old getting "in the family way," but in 1962? Trust me; I was the first on my block.

Because it was such a shameful and embarrassing story, and I'd had so many horrible reactions to it over the years, I learned to tell it on myself right away in order to give people a chance to retreat if they couldn't handle it. I suppose it was a little like quitting before you're fired. These days I've found a much happier balance, I don't feel I have to confess my life story to every person I come in contact with. But for many years, if anyone asked how I was doing, whether it was the check-out clerk at the market or the ticket taker at the movies, I would feel compelled to joke that I was "doing okay for someone who got married in the eighth grade."

And if we got past the first question, the next question was invariably "Why on *earth* would your parents *allow* you to get married that young?" The answer to that one always gets 'em.

It was my mother's idea.

―⤶

By late December, 1962, I was thirteen and a half years old and had been sick with the stomach flu for a few weeks. I would throw up in the morning and then I'd feel okay the rest of the day. One morning as I was coming out of the bathroom after a particularly vocal "concert at the bowl," as my mother phrased it, she called me into the living room and told me to sit down. That instantly made me nervous; my mother wasn't the kind of woman to initiate a heart to heart with me. We didn't even like each other much at this point. In fact I had run away for over two weeks with my eighteen year old boyfriend, Don; but that had been almost three months earlier.

My mother lit a cigarette and took a deep drag. I took one of her cigarettes from the pack and lit up along with her. I had been smoking with her permission for about a year at this point. How could that be? Well, when I was eleven she had caught me with a cigarette, but instead of promising never to do it again, I made a passionate case for why I should be allowed to indulge in the habit.

"You know, Mom, I don't even really like cigarettes," I told her. "I think the biggest reason that I want to smoke is that it's forbidden.

If I were *allowed* to smoke I bet I'd lose interest in the whole idea. After all," I went on, "you allow me to swear and say 'fuck' whenever I want, but I hardly ever do." It was true. I'd realized at about age eight that from the first time I tried swearing I got no reaction from my mother or my father and it had soon lost its appeal.

Mom was very impressed with my logic and even more impressed that I had the guts to try to run a scam on her. It was a dangerous game with few survivors. But at age twelve I had gotten into the ring with her and she had agreed to let me smoke; her only rule was that I had to buy my own. But here I was a year later, *still* smoking, *and* smoking one of *her* cigarettes. And she wasn't mad. Clearly something was very wrong. After a few awkward moments of each of us puffing away she broke the news.

"You're pregnant."

"Pregnant?" She might as well be telling me that I was the Empress of China, that's how unbelievable this was for me to hear. "How could I be pregnant?"

Mom sighed and took another drag on her cigarette. "Oh please, we don't have to have *that* conversation, too, do we?"

Not that we had ever had *that* conversation. Never once had my mother sat me down and, awkwardly or otherwise, spoken a word about what it meant to be a teen-aged girl on her way to becoming a woman. Not that she was shy about such things. My mother, Eve Whitney, did not have a shy bone in her body. In her entire life I don't think she ever experienced a moment of hesitation when it came to doing or saying whatever came into her mind. I never once saw my mother have what most people would call feelings of guilt. And as for maternal instincts --- well, the truth is that my mother didn't like children, and I happened to be one at the time.

Occasionally I'll catch a documentary on PBS that shows a female tiger in the jungles of wherever, nursing a baby monkey, orphaned by the tiger just hours earlier. The tiger's maternal instinct is so strong that she is willing to nurture what would ordinarily be dinner. My mother somehow skipped that evolutionary

3

link in the chain. And the truth is, everything in my life has been affected by that fact, whether I realized it at the time or not.

"I'll take you to a doctor to make sure, but it sure looks to me like you're knocked up."

Not an ounce of concern; not a whisper of compassion. Not even anger or frustration; that would have at least been a sign that the two of us were connected somehow. No, this was simply information that I, at thirteen years old, was somehow supposed to process and then come to a decision. No discussion about what that decision might mean to the rest of my life.

And while such behavior might be understandable if my mother had been severely lacking in intelligence or education, such was not the case. Extremely smart, very well read, politically active and up on all the latest news stories, my mother could hold her own in a conversation with anybody about anything. She simply didn't give a rat's ass about her daughters.

Of course, I loved her madly. I didn't know I could do anything else. She was the only mother I had and I longed for her approval, yearned for a kind word, dreamt of the day when she realized what a good little girl I was and got down to the business of loving me back.

Having found none of the above in the first thirteen years of my life, I had turned to the first nice boy who had shown an interest in me. He was eighteen years old, his name was Don, he bought me a hot dog and – this was the clincher - he actually smiled and asked me how I was doing. Maybe it wasn't love at first sight, but it was more attention than I had received in years; and so, about two weeks later, I managed to convince my new best friend, Don, that the best possible idea in the whole wide world was for the two of us to run away together. Just get in his car and go. Whatever happened, I figured it couldn't be any worse than the life I was living. And besides, maybe if I just disappeared, then even my mother would have to take notice, right?

"If you *are* pregnant," my mother said, lighting a new Winston with the remains of the one she was smoking, "then you basically have three choices; you can give it up for adoption, you can get an abortion, or you can get married."

I'm pretty sure I didn't know the word "surreal" at the time, but "surreal" is absolutely the best word to describe the conversation I was having with my mother. The manner in which she listed my three options didn't imply that one choice was any better than another. True to form, her voice very clearly conveyed the message that it really didn't matter much to her which option I choose. She had better things to do than to be stuck having this conversation in the first place.

In stunned silence, I looked around my mother's apartment. The water in the kitchen sink had a thick layer of grease riding atop the week's dirty dishes. Open containers of food were scattered along the counters. Cat droppings decorated the carpet. A half dozen or so ashtrays were overflowing with spent butts. My mother's face glared at me with a familiar mix of impatience and annoyance and all of a sudden the idea of marriage landed on my newly adolescent brain like a butterfly; all bright colors and flights of freedom. Not that I had any real idea of what marriage meant, but if it would get me out of this apartment, away from the icy glare of my mother, then it sounded pretty good to me. My sister, Chris, had made her getaway the year before, spending most of her time ditching school and looking for trouble with a group of neighborhood bad boys, spending only the occasional night at the apartment when she needed a place to crash.

And Chris was my *younger* sister, by fifteen months.

"I'm going to take you to a doctor to be sure," said my mother again in her gravelly baritone from behind a cloud of smoke, "but I'm sure."

How could she be sure? I wasn't even sure that what Don and I had had was real sex, so the idea of my being pregnant hadn't even entered my mind. But if I knew precious little about such matters, I knew that my mother was well versed. Many was the night she had entertained a "friend" in her bedroom, one thin wall away from

5

mine. I knew the sounds, the rhythms of sex, but none of the particulars. But mom was saying I was pregnant, so what was I going to do?

One more look around the apartment, my eyes coming to rest on my mother's look of impatience.

"I want to get married," I said meekly.

"Fine," she said. And then, nonchalantly, "Are you sure that what's-his-name is the father?"

Could this be any more humiliating? "Don's the *only* one," I managed to answer.

"Good, that makes it easier," she replied.

Mom took me to the doctor that day and he confirmed that I was three months pregnant. She wanted to meet with Don's parents right away. Don and I hadn't talked much since we'd returned from our two weeks on the run and he didn't yet know that I was pregnant.

Here's the sad truth; I didn't even know where the father of my baby lived. After we had met at North Hollywood Park, Don would come over and keep me company during those many days and nights that my mother was either working or out on a date. And keeping me company is pretty much how I got pregnant.

Mom threatened to call Don if I didn't so I made the call and a short time later we were sitting in Don's spotless, perfectly ordered living room facing his folks. His mother, Elsie, was a thin, tense, hand-wringing ball of anxiety; his father, Don Sr., a quiet and stoic man. It was a weekend and yet his dad was wearing a tie with a cardigan sweater buttoned up, just like Ozzie Nelson on *The Ozzie and Harriet Show*. My mother got right to the point. She told them that I was pregnant and that Don was the father and that we needed to get married right away. Don went pale. His father cleared his throat. His mother let out an involuntary shriek and then called my mother crazy. She said I was trying to ruin Don's life. Don Sr. tried to remain calm and reason with my mother; his son had just graduated from high school and was supposed to be starting classes at USC very soon. He couldn't just let his son get married and destroy his life. Surely, there must be another alternative.

Mom shrugged and we stood to leave. "I can think of one," she said. "I could have your precious little son arrested for statutory rape. He was an eighteen year old taking a thirteen year old across state lines. How's that for ruining his life?" And just like that they saw things her way.

CHAPTER 2

⁂

THERE ARE NO excuses for my mother's behavior during my childhood, but there are, perhaps, reasons. Her own childhood was a nightmare of secrets and lies. Eve Whitney grew up in Denver, Colorado with her sister, Margaret, who was three years older. They lived with their father, Joe, a weak and ineffectual man; and their domineering grandmother, Grandma Whitney. The girls were told that their mother had died when they were younger, but they weren't given any of the details, just that they should be glad she was out of their lives. When Eve and Margaret were seven and ten, Grandma Whitney told them they were too much to handle and sent them off to live in an orphanage run by a Catholic order of nuns.

It was not an easy life for Eve. She was a spirited and scrappy kid and the convent was not a place that honored that kind of spunk and individuality. When Chris and I were growing up, Mom loved to tell us horror stories about the cruelties she suffered at the hands of the nuns. She was beaten, deprived, neglected, always hungry and repeatedly shamed; she was never hugged or kissed as a kid and, as a consequence, she was very uncomfortable with any kind of touching or affection. Eve frequently ran away and would just show up at her father and grandmother's house begging them to let her stay. But they would just pack her right back off to the convent and then she would be punished all the more for having run away. For reasons I never learned, Eve's sister, Margaret, was allowed to return home. As a result of my mother's mistreatment at the hands of the Catholic Church, she grew up hating the Catholic religion and everything to do with it. And even though it wasn't Margaret's fault that she was allowed to leave the convent while Eve wasn't, Eve grew up disliking her sister as well.

But instead of simply dealing with her pain and her disappointment, Eve developed a strange pride about having gotten through that rough part of her childhood; she felt that it had toughened her up. And tough, for Eve, was a damn good thing.

When she was fourteen years old Eve got news that would change her life forever; still living in the convent/orphanage, she was told that her Grandma Whitney had died. It wasn't that Eve would miss "the old bitch" because she wouldn't, but news of the woman's death had brought an unusual visitor. A woman named Rilla showed up at the convent claiming to be Eve's mother. She calmly told Eve that she was there to take Eve, as well as her sister, Margaret, to live in California.

Eve's initial shock was replaced by skepticism. She knew her mother was dead, she had always known it, so who was this person and why would she want to take Eve anywhere? Up until now no one had wanted her; no one had showed the least interest in her life, including her own father. This well-dressed woman who wore her dark hair in a stylish wave seemed sophisticated, worldly. At fourteen, Eve was a skinny kid with big brown eyes and mousy hair pulled into braids. Eve scanned the woman, searching for similarities, but she didn't see much resemblance and didn't believe that this could really be her mother. But in the end she didn't care who the hell this woman was; she looked like more fun than the nuns, and leaving this place with a complete stranger was a damn sight more appealing than staying here with people who beat her and humiliated her in the name of Jesus.

"I'll get my sweater," she told the woman. And as simple as that Rilla, Eve, and Margaret drove to California. According to my mother, Rilla was completely unapologetic about her long absence. Rilla told the girls their father had been a worthless mama's boy and that the only thing he ever did that took any balls at all was to marry her and have two kids. But Rilla and Grandma Whitney had battled constantly over who would boss Joe around the rest of his life and Grandma Whitney had won. She'd offered Rilla two thousand dollars cash as an incentive to leave town and Rilla had taken it. Rilla told her daughters that she believed she had done them a favor by leaving them because she "wasn't much good with kids." But now Grandma Whitney was dead and the girls weren't kids anymore, so she thought it was time to come and get them. End of discussion. Eve and Margaret could either accept Rilla's story without a word of protest, or go back to their former accommodations at Our Lady of Pain and Suffering.

Their new home was a modest little bungalow in Gardena, California where Rilla lived with her common law husband, Tony, a bald man with a fat cigar and a big smile. Rilla turned out to be quite a flamboyant and edgy character; she and Tony had run a speakeasy in the late 1920s and early 1930s until prohibition ended. Now "Uncle Tony", as the girls were told to call him, bet the ponies all day and Rilla had a little beauty parlor in town. Rilla and Tony were raucous and fun, unless they'd been drinking too much, which was often, and then Rilla was loud and Tony was mean. They fought big and several of their battles ended with one of them in the hospital.

The warfare between Rilla and Tony was contagious; the girls were glad to be away from their old life but not happy to be sharing time or a room. One big bone of contention was that Eve was in awe of Rilla and admired her spunk and individuality while Margaret was much less enamored. In fact, Margaret was becoming more and more resentful of the fact that Rilla had abandoned them in the first place. Eve and Margaret battled constantly. Just as Eve, years later, seemed to enjoy it when my sister Chris and I were at each other's throats, Rilla encouraged the fights between her two daughters. What a lovely family tradition to initiate.

By the time my mother was sixteen she had filled out in all the right places and had grown into a traffic stopping beauty. Tony was still gambling for a living and not doing very well, and Rilla had grown tired of running a beauty parlor. Rilla recognized an opportunity when she saw one and she took Eve to a photographer friend and had some shots taken. Soon Eve was getting modeling work and helping out with the bills. Things went so well that Rilla thought Eve should try it full-time and encouraged her daughter to quit school. Rilla acted as Eve's manager and by the time Eve was eighteen she had landed a contract at MGM Studios. That meant she'd be getting a steady paycheck from now on, so Rilla sold her salon and it fell to Eve to support the household.

It was the early 1940s and musicals were popular. Big productions, casts of hundreds, this was a good time for Eve to be under contract at the studio; it almost guaranteed that she would get cast in small parts in the dozens of movies that MGM was cranking out back then. There was always a demand for beautiful girls to decorate the background of those big, glitzy production numbers and Eve worked constantly. It was all new and very exciting to her; she was meeting important people and beginning to date a variety of men. Rilla controlled that part of Eve's life as well, giving her heartfelt, albeit unsavory advice on how to get gifts and money out of men. Once when Eve was invited to spend a weekend on a yacht with a much older man, Rilla instructed Eve to say that she couldn't go because she'd miss out on several hundred dollars' worth of film work. Of course, the man offered to reimburse Eve for her lost income. Next Rilla told her to tell him that she had nothing suitable to wear for such a glamorous weekend. As Rilla predicted, the man offered to send a check and a car so Eve could go shopping. I'm sure that Rilla would describe what she was doing as "career advice." I think the phrase "pimping your daughter out" is a more accurate term. If Eve developed a thick skin and a cynical attitude about the world in general and men in particular, perhaps she had cause.

What always surprised me was the sincere admiration in which Eve held this woman who called herself "mother." Whenever she would tell me stories about Rilla, she never failed to say how much she respected the woman. Once, when I was an adult myself, I asked her just what the hell she admired so much about a woman who had abandoned her until she was fourteen and then practically turned her out as a prostitute. My mother said she liked Rilla's gumption and outspokenness. She took pride in the fact that Rilla had been a tough broad who didn't take shit from anybody. Not exactly the all American definition of "mother" that most girls grew up with in the fifties and sixties. And so it came to pass that Eve Whitney ended up being one tough and outspoken broad who never took shit from anybody.

Trust me; it's overrated.

Over the next few years Eve appeared in dozens of movies, "Ziegfeld Follies," "DuBarry Was a Lady," "Joan of Arc." She became what was then known as a "Petty Girl." George Petty was an artist who was famous for his illustrated pin-up girls of the 1940s. There was even a movie made about him in 1950 called "The Petty Girl" starring Robert Cummings. Eve also posed for Vargas and was Miss January in a "Vargas" calendar for the War Effort edition in 1942. One of the duties of a showgirl under contract to the studios was to serve coffee to the servicemen at the Hollywood Canteen, a diner near the studios that was opened by Bette Davis and John Garfield during the war, and that's where my mother met my father.

⁓

My father, Eddie Maxwell Cherkose, was born and raised in Detroit by his mother, Mimi. Eddie never knew his father who had died of pneumonia a few months before my dad was born. As a result of that loss, his mother was extremely over protective of him as a child. Luckily for my grandmother's nerves, from the time my father could form a sentence, all he ever wanted to be was a writer; not a terribly dangerous pastime for a child. He wrote songs and plays and performed them for his family. His aunts, uncles, and grandfather were a great audience for young Eddie and they encouraged his creative side. At age twelve one of his songs was published in the local newspaper and he officially became a paid writer. When Eddie was old enough to leave home he made his way out to Hollywood to break into the entertainment business as a song and gag writer.

L.A. in the 1940s was a magical place. For the lucky and the talented it was a town filled with opportunity. Eddie got a small apartment in Hollywood *with* maid service for six dollars a week. He did his homework and found out that many actors, agents, managers and producers lunched daily at the famous Brown Derby restaurant in Hollywood. My dad went there every day for a month and had himself paged to the telephone. It seems corny now, the stuff of sit-coms, but back then Hollywood was a touch more innocent and pranks like that actually worked. His ingenuity finally paid off when he landed an interview with an agent who remarked, "Good to meet you, Eddie, I've been hearing your name around town." Soon my dad was working steadily writing gags for the comedy singing quartet, The Yacht Club Boys. Eddie was paid $25 a week to write jokes for them. They all worked in a hotel room at the famed Garden of Allah in Hollywood. The group was staying there while they worked on "Pigskin Parade" at Twentieth Century Fox with Judy Garland. After that, my father was signed by Fox to write material for the Ritz Brothers picture "On the Avenue." He also worked at MGM, Republic, and Paramount where he wrote songs for many of the Gene Autrey and Roy Rogers pictures.

Eddie's next job as a writer came when he enlisted in the Army in 1942; he was assigned to the newly formed F.M.P.U. which stood for "First Motion Picture Unit," also known by its acronym "fumpoo." The unit was formed to produce training and propaganda films for American servicemen. The first F.M.P.U. production, "Winning Your Wings" is credited with generating 150,000 new recruits. The unit was stationed at Hal Roach Studios in Culver City, California, known affectionately at the time as Fort Roach.

Though most of the group were exempt from basic training, the soldiers were still required to sleep at the studio and so several soundstages were converted to barracks with rows and rows of army cots. Some of the famous people in the movie unit at that time were Ronald Reagan, Frank Capra, Clark Gable, Jimmy Stewart, John Huston, George Reeves, William Holden, Alan Ladd and Theodore Geisel, better known as Dr. Seuss. My father got to know them all and had marvelous stories to tell when I was growing up. When I was little I asked my father if he had ever done anything heroic during the war, he responded that he had been "awarded the Typewriter Ribbon for crossing Washington Boulevard against a red light!"

My dad was a handsome and dashing figure in his studio-tailored army uniform. With his dark hair and trim mustache he looked like a cross between Clark Gable and Errol Flynn. One night my dad and some of his army buddies went to the Hollywood Canteen for a couple of beers, and that's where he first saw Eve. He was smitten the minute he laid eyes on her and he told his friends that he had absolutely, positively just met the girl he was going to marry. Even though Eddie was thirty at the time and my mother was just nineteen, Eve accepted his request for a date.

Eve was attracted to Eddie's marvelous sense of humor, and she thought he was a talented writer but, at nineteen, she wasn't looking to get married and so she continued to date other men. I think what she liked most about Eddie was that he could take a joke on himself as well as anybody. And Eve was more than capable of delivering a wicked aside that might have withered someone less clever or confident. If there was one word that could be used to describe both of them, it was "irreverent." Nothing was sacred to either of them. If there was a good laugh or a biting turn of phrase to be had, then anything was fair game. Another thing that Eve and Eddie had in common was their mutual disdain of any type of organized religion. My father had been raised strictly Orthodox Jewish, his grandfather had been a Rabbi and one of his uncles ran a Shul, a Jewish synagogue, so Eddie's young life had been dominated by religion. And Eve had spent her childhood in a Catholic convent/orphanage and had no warm memories of those days. As an adult Eddie had come to the conclusion that he liked being Jewish for the culture, the humor, and the food. On one of their first dates he took Eve to Canter's, a Jewish delicatessen in L.A. My mother, ignorant of such exotic delights, took one look at the menu and promptly ordered a bowl of "Kerplash" soup. It would be many years before she could pronounce the word "Kreplach."

Eddie was falling in love and he didn't want to go there alone. He was determined to win Eve over and pulled out all the stops to charm her. He wooed her with songs he wrote especially for her, often sending her on clever scavenger hunts of song titles that would spell out secret love letters. Because it was war time, there was a shortage of many items and the government was rationing products such as gas, butter, and sugar. They also limited the use of some forms of communication to official business. One time my father, illegally using official army equipment, telegraphed a series of letters of the alphabet in a message to Eve from Fort Roach. It didn't seem to spell anything and Eve was confused until she showed it to a musician friend who figured out that the letters were musical notes; when he played them on the piano the tune was "You'd Be So Nice To Come Home To." That's the song that won Eve over; they were married on my father's birthday, May 25, in 1944.

⁓

Eddie was still reporting for duty at Fort Roach and Eve was working steadily at MGM. Things were very, very good. Eve had moved into Eddie's Hollywood apartment with Eddie and his mother, Mimi, who kept the place spotless. And, even though the "husband/wife/mother- in-law" combination is famous for being poisonous, the three of them got along quite well. These were absolutely, positively, the best of times for them both.

15

When Eddie was discharged from the army, he got steady work writing songs for movies, special material for Eddie Cantor's radio show as well as comedy sketches for Abbot and Costello, Bob Hope, Danny Thomas, and Henny Youngman. In 1947 my father wrote one of his most popular songs, with music by Jules Styne, called "Pico and Sepulveda." It was performed by Freddy Martin and his Orchestra under the name "Felix Figueroa." Famed L.A. radio show host, Dr. Demento, used it for many years as an official theme song.

After a few years Eddie went on the road with Spike Jones and his band "The City Slickers" writing gags and novelty songs for Spike's radio show. They traveled all over the country by train because Spike didn't like to fly. The show was broadcast live from wherever they were performing on their cross-country road tours of one-night stands. Spike had trouble sleeping at night so there were many 3 a.m. writing sessions on the train, most of which took place in the men's lavatory -- as did the poker games. One of my favorite of my dad's songs was written during one of those late night sessions. Spike did the music and my dad wrote the lyrics for "Pal-Yat-Chee" a parody of the opera "Pagliacci." This version was sung by Homer and Jethro and was accompanied by the trademark "Spike Jones" collection of bells, whistles, and burps.

When my mother wasn't working she often accompanied Eddie on the road. It was an exciting, chaotic life and the two of them couldn't get enough of it. Eddie remained absolutely crazy about Eve and when they did have to be separated because of work, he continued to write her dozens upon dozens of love songs and poems. During these years they truly did make each other better people than they had been. Eddie's romantic view of life softened some of Eve's cynicism; and Eve's absolute belief in Eddie's talent helped to give him the confidence to write as well as he did.

But like many young marriages, there was an invisible bubble around the two of them. They lived in their own special world. Hollywood was then, and still is, a very narcissistic town. And the truth is that Eddie and Eve were two very charming, very beautiful and talented narcissists working in a famously narcissistic business. Not that they didn't socialize. It was the era of the nightclub and Eddie and Eve were often spotted at Ciro's or The Trocadero with the likes of Groucho Marx and Rudy Vallee. But their hearts were reserved for each other.

After five years of this love-fest, Eve became pregnant with me and everything changed pretty quickly after that. They went from a vagabond life in Eddie's furnished apartment to buying a little house in the San Fernando Valley and attempting to keep normal hours for the first time in their lives. Eve stopped working and Eddie tried to get writing jobs in L.A. In the whole time they'd been married my grandmother had kept the apartment clean and saw to it that there was always food in the fridge and a meal on the table. But recently she had moved to a hotel in Venice Beach. Without his mother there to cook and clean, Eddie could see for the first time what a truly atrocious housekeeper Eve was; I guess "home-economics" wasn't on the training schedule for contract players at MGM in the 1940s. And, just to complete the scenario, Eve didn't know, and didn't *want* to know, the first thing about cooking.

It didn't matter; he was still crazy about her. None of it mattered to Eddie.

CHAPTER 3

───── ✍ ─────

I WAS BORN two days shy of my dad's thirty-eighth birthday. His wedding anniversary was on his birthday and he really hoped that I'd wait two days so we'd share that day as well. That way he'd only have to remember one date for everything. Even with the huge adjustment of a "normal" family life routine, Eddie and Eve reportedly still had fun playing house for the first year. I've been told that I was a good baby; which was important since my dad was now working at home. I think I knew instinctively, almost from birth, that always being a "good little girl" was the key to making my mother and father happy. And I knew that always "making my mother and father happy" was the key to a happy home.

Fifteen months after I crashed the party that was my parents' marriage, my sister Christine was born. She was such a pretty baby with huge, turquoise eyes and curly blonde hair. She certainly didn't look like trouble when she first arrived. There have been countless studies backing up the theory that "latter borns" are more likely than "first borns" to act out and cause trouble. Statistically they are the rebels of the family. Maybe Chris was just fulfilling her role in the family order, or maybe she was just born with a nasty case of colic, but she somehow succeeded in annoying my parents, especially my father, from the very beginning. Even as a young child I could feel the tension in the room every time Chris entered. My dad showed more affection to our boxer dogs, Slugger and Nicky, than he did to Chris.

Dad was getting enough writing work that after a couple of years we were able to afford a nice, two-story house in a pleasant neighborhood called Sherman Oaks. It was around this time that my father officially dropped the last name of Cherkose and began using his middle name, Maxwell, as his new last name. Maxwell is the name that I grew up with and I never knew that Cherkose had even been my name until I saw my birth certificate as an adult.

For our first Christmas in the new house Eve and Eddie went all out decorating for the holidays. My dad even put a big Santa Claus on the roof. Unfortunately it was still there when they sold the house a few years later. "Handyman" was never a word used to describe my father's talents. Unlike most writers, Eddie had never had another job in his life.

We got a beautiful Christmas tree that we all helped decorate and my dad topped it off with a Jewish star made out of aluminum foil. That small nod to each faith was pretty much the sum total of our religious instruction to date.

Slugger and Nicky, our two boxers, had lived long, loving lives before my sister and I came along, but they had gotten sick and passed away within two months of each other, so on that Christmas I got a new Boxer puppy in my stocking. We named him "Slugger" after the first one. My dad always referred to him as my "brother" and I would always include Slugger when people asked how many were in my family. It would be many years before I looked back on that Christmas and realized that something wasn't right. The puppy was in *my* stocking, not my sister's. I don't even remember what she got, but I can tell you it wasn't anything as special as a puppy. Even at ages two and three, my father had somehow decided that Christine was a second class citizen as well as the cause of whatever problems he might be having at the time. My mother had at least been consistent in her disdain of both Chris and myself, but my father had his clear favorite and it was me. At the time it seemed like a pretty decent deal; what little girl doesn't long to be the apple of her father's eye? It didn't occur to me what this arrangement was doing to my sister's young heart.

And, as if fulfilling my father's worst fears, Chris would often have a way of saying or doing the wrong thing at the wrong time. One occasion sticks in my mind to this day. My father was writing on a television show for Spike Jones and that meant he had to go to the studio and keep fairly normal hours. One day he took Chris and me to the set to meet the cast of the show. One of the stars was Billy Barty who was a wonderful actor and comic. He was also what we now refer to as a "little person." Fearing we would say something to embarrass him, my father took Chris and me aside. "Now when you meet Mr. Barty," said my dad, "I don't want you to say, 'look at the little guy,' or 'look at shorty' or 'Daddy, is he a dwarf?' Do you understand what I'm saying?"

My sister and I nodded and then the door opened and Billy Barty came out of his dressing room. My sister immediately blurted out, "Look at the midget!" Then she looked up at my dad who was obviously furious with her. Terrified, Chris innocently and honestly replied, "But you didn't tell us not to say 'midget,' Daddy." Any kid could've made the same mistake, but Chris had a knack.

Luckily Mr. Barty took no offense. He thought Chris was cute, which was nice because my dad sure didn't.

It was at this time that my mother took her last acting job. Lucille Ball had asked her to appear in an episode of "I Love Lucy." Eve and Lucy had become friends years before when Lucy was filming the movie "Du Barry was a Lady." Lucy wanted Eve to play a model in the episode and she would even get to use her own name: Eve Whitney. The episode is called "The Charm School" and the situation is that every time Lucy and Ricky have a party, the men end up in the living room talking sports and the women end up in the kitchen gossiping. But when an attractive woman, Eve, shows up, the men fall all over themselves offering to light her cigarette and take her coat. Eve extends her hand to each person as she is introduced and in a deep, breathy voice utters the phrase, "How do you do?" Lucy and Ethel are fit to be tied; they don't like the attention their husbands are showing to Eve. The next day Lucy and Ethel are recounting their annoyance and Lucy laments, "What's that Eve Whitney got that we don't?"

To which Ethel replies, "Nothing. We just have more of it in all the wrong places."

And that very day Lucy and Ethel sign up for charm school.

My mother never auditioned for another role. She had become bored with acting and, truth be told, she was never much more than adequate. "As an actress your mother was a wonderful model," my father used to say. And he was madly in love with her!

It was around this time that my father's career began to falter. The kind of comedy and "specialty writing" that Eddie excelled at seemed to be falling out of fashion. Eddie was having trouble finding work, and it didn't help that he did not want to work for anyone younger or less experienced than himself. This was the mid 1950s and a lot of television executives were young and inexperienced. Having been a successful writer from the age of twelve did not create fertile ground for humility, and outright groveling (coin of the realm in Hollywood, then and now) was not in my father's vocabulary.

This situation was made even worse by the fact that so many of my parents' friends were still among the rich and famous in Hollywood. I remember when my sister and I were taken to a birthday party for "Little Lucie" at Lucy and Desi's house on Roxbury Drive in Beverly Hills. This party was like nothing we'd ever seen. Even compared to today's over-the-top extravaganzas, this party was something else. The backyard was transformed into a carnival. There were magicians, horses, clowns, cotton candy venders, a hot dog cart, and a real Ferris wheel. My father had written material for Desi over the years; he and Desi had even co-written the song "There's a Brand New Baby at Our House" that Ricky sings to Lucy when Little Ricky was born on "I Love Lucy." Now Eddie was struggling and here we were at a child's birthday party that probably cost more than he had made all year. I must've been a strange kid because the most thrilling part of the birthday party for me was when the Ferris wheel reached the tippy top and I could see over the wall and catch a glimpse of Jack Benny's house next door! At eight years old I was a huge fan of Mr. Benny's and watched his show every day without fail.

My mother never lost confidence in my father's raw talent, but she was beginning to lose patience with his moods as well as his inability to cope with the situation. It was around this time that my father began taking "bennies," which were amphetamines or "uppers," to deal with his frustrations. They were very popular in the creative community at the time, nobody fully realized the long term side effects of such drugs, and the little white pills enabled my dad to change his entire schedule; he began sleeping during the day and working all night. The worst side effect of the pills, of course, was that they made him extremely moody and cranky. Any little sound would set him off and we soon learned to watch our every move.

I was much better at this game than Christine was; every time she would accidentally let a screen door slam or knock over a book by mistake she reinforced Eddie's feeling that Chris was a thorn in his side. No matter how hard she tried, Chris never seemed to get it right as far as my father was concerned. She would go to give him a hug and somehow poke him in the eye with her elbow. She'd crawl up into his lap and manage to knock his typewriter off his desk. Looking back on it now, it was clearly a case of trying too hard; a little girl desperate to be loved. Lord knows we weren't getting much attention from our mother who showed less and less interest in the idea of spending time with her daughters. My father continued to pull farther and farther away from Chris, and closer and closer to me. I became his "favorite" and he had no problem saying so, even in front of Christine. He took to calling me his "FBI," his "First Born Infant." And when Chris asked if she could be his "Second Born Infant," his "SBI," she was told there was no such thing. How much of this cruelty came from the drugs and how much was from my father's heart, I have no idea. What I do know is that I was caught between the guilt of seeing my sister hurt, and the thrill of a young girl's pride in being her father's "favorite." I carry that guilt with me to this day and probably always will. I know that it was my father who put Chris and me into this impossible position. He created an environment that pitted us against each other, that forced me to shut her out in order to become his partner in a cruel game of "keep-away" with my own sister. I know that if I had gotten in between my father and my sister all I would have accomplished would have been to incur his anger and join Christine in exile. So I did little but watch as my father included me more and more, and excluded Chris every chance he got. It was a slow process and I certainly didn't analyze it all those years ago the way I have since. But even as a child I could feel the balance shifting as I learned to be the best little "FBI" that I could be.

And then there was my mother. Why didn't she step in and set things right? No matter what my father was going through back then; the drugs, the frustration over work, the depression, he never stopped loving my mother. One word from her and he would have taken another look at his behavior, even if only to make Eve happy. But Eve was liking the title "mother" less and less and I don't remember one instance when she stepped in and defended Chris from daddy's wrath. To the contrary, she seemed to be coming around to Eddie's point of view.

My father became convinced that "all the trouble" in his life started the day Christine was born. He became fixated on the idea that somehow things would have stayed the way they were when he and Eve were the happy couple-about-town, if only Christine hadn't shown up to spoil everything. It wasn't that he was physically abusive to her; it was more that he was dismissive of her. Still, if we had to choose between his unpredictable behavior and our mother's reliable lack of warmth, both Chris and I would pick daddy every time.

CHAPTER 4

MY FATHER STARTED taking more and more of the pills, and, of course, the more pills he took, the worse things got. Sometimes he would stay up for several nights in a row. And then he would crash and sleep for a couple of days. And if he was sleeping through a lot of days, then he wasn't out there looking for work. It was a dangerous cycle and he was falling deeper and deeper into depression. The confusing part was when he was in the "up" phase of this cycle. Few people knew terms like "Manic Depression" or "Bi-Polar" back then, but I'm pretty sure my father would have fit the diagnosis. When he was "up" and "feeling positive," he was his old wonderful, creative, incredibly loving self. At least he was to me. Chris was shut out of even this passing mood swing of affection. But then he would "crash" and he would become a dark, scary presence.

As things continued to deteriorate, my mom and dad started to argue constantly. Both of them were screamers so the fights got loud and sometimes dangerous. And as fighting became the favored mode of communication in our house, Chris and I joined in, going at each other almost as much as our parents. One time, I got so mad at my sister that I took a high heel shoe of my mother's, which for some reason I called "darlings", and I struck my sister right in the head with it. I hit her so hard that the heel didn't come out of her head after I hit her. She was screaming at the top of her lungs. I tried to pull the shoe out of her head but it was stuck in there good. I was scared to death of getting in trouble, but she wasn't bleeding so I picked her up and set her in a chair with the green satin "darling" still sticking out of her head at an odd angle. I left her there and went outside and began to jump rope in the front yard. How could they suspect me of plunging a shoe in my sister's skull when here I was playing outside without a care in the world? When my mother went inside and found Chris, she grabbed her and me and we rushed to the emergency room with the shoe still implanted in Chris' head. The doctor removed the shoe, stitched her up, and we went home. I was never punished. I wasn't even spoken to. Even my sister forgave me completely.

How is it possible that I wasn't punished for such a thing? My best guess is a total lack of concern on both my mother's as well as my father's part. Looking back, I'm surprised my mother even bothered to make the trip to the hospital. It wasn't really her style.

Like our father's roller coaster mood swings, Chris and I would be at each other's throats one moment, best of friends and comrades-in-arms the next. There are some very cute pictures of my sister and me when we were very little, "before the fall" so to speak. In most of those pictures we're wearing beautiful matching outfits and smiling happily. We look clean and cared for; we look like loving sisters. The smiles are so genuine that I know we must have had some good times in our young lives. Maybe that's why it hurt so much when things began to fall apart. When I think about those times, there is a knot in my stomach that tightens as I realize how Chris and I were completely abandoned, even though both of our parents were in the house. My father drifted further and further into drugs and began to disappear from our lives. I don't remember any sit down meals with either of my parents. My father was usually asleep and my mother had stopped even trying to prepare meals. Chris and I ate a lot of peanut butter and canned beans on our own back then. We didn't complain. Somehow we knew it wouldn't do any good and a cross word would only make things a lot worse. We weren't bathed or shampooed unless there was an event we had to look pretty for, such as those cute photos I mentioned. In fact, one day my mother took Chris and me to a barber and had our beautiful long hair cut really short because she said she was tired of grooming us and combing out tangles. I have no memory of her doing either.

It was about this time that I first met Corley, my imaginary friend. My feelings about my sister were so guilt-ridden and confusing, my connection to my parents so fraught with fear of abandonment, that it was just easier to invent someone who would stick around. But you'd think that as long as I was dealing with make-believe, I'd create a loving and accepting imaginary friend. But Corley was a moody one, and would go long stretches without talking to me or playing with me at all. Most little boys and girls invent an imaginary friend at some point in their life. Who invents one who won't speak to her?

Chris and I weren't really aware of how dysfunctional our family was. We had become accustomed to a "good" daddy and mommy and a "bad" daddy and mommy. It was the only reality we knew and so we didn't feel particularly deprived. I learned how to adapt and accommodate to whichever personality I was dealing with; again, this was something I did much better than my sister. How could she ever improve her social skills when she knew from the get-go that she would lose? We all need to win a few before we can learn how to cope, how to put things in perspective.

One argument that my parents had stands out from the others, not because it was the worst one but because it was after this argument that I realized for the first time that I had a way to cope, and it was called a sense of humor. My sister and I were probably about seven and eight. Our parents had gotten into a huge fight and my mother had grabbed the car keys and slammed out of the house. My father stormed up the stairs and into his office. Chris and I were on our own for the next several hours. My father came downstairs sometime later that afternoon when he got hungry. He saw us playing and it should have occurred to him that he'd forgotten all about us, but clearly that wasn't what was occupying his mind. He couldn't believe that Eve still wasn't home. He sat himself down in the big wingback chair that faced the front door, folded his arms, and waited. And waited. Finally, about two hours later, the door opened and in swept my mother. You could tell she was still really mad because she slammed the door when she saw him waiting with a look of challenge on his face. Chris and I froze.

"Where the hell were you?" my father demanded.

Eve took a defiant stance, crossed her arms and snarled, "I went to the bank, Stupid!"

Eddie grunted and without missing a beat said, "Yeah... and you came back the same way."

It was quiet for about thirty seconds. Then all of a sudden I started to giggle. Somehow I knew that what my father had said, however outrageous, was funny. And then my mother started to laugh. Really laugh; which made my dad laugh and pretty soon they were laughing so hard they were crying. Chris started to laugh too, but she looked to me and shrugged a questioning shrug. She didn't get why everybody was laughing; she was just glad the fight was over. But I have never forgotten that day. It was the day I learned a lesson that probably saved my life in a million different ways over the years.

There were a lot more bad arguments after that, but few with a funny ending.

As a couple Eddie and Eve still had plenty of social invitations but my dad was becoming increasingly unsociable and started turning everything down. He preferred his cave and we barely saw him at all. My mother must have been very lonely although she never shared her feelings with us. Who knows what might have happened if they could have actually communicated with each other. But my father was operating in a drug induced haze, and my mother was so invested in her "tough" persona that she was incapable of reaching out to him with anything resembling tenderness.

And so one day my mother simply walked into Eddie's office and told him that she had filed for divorce.

"If I'm going to live alone I may as well be single," she said. And she walked right back out again.

Eddie, crazed and sleep deprived, wasn't thinking clearly as he tried to reason with her. It was too late, she said; she'd already been to an attorney. At first, Eddie thought she was joking. After all, Eve was famous for starting things she never finished and he chose that moment to give her several examples: How about the time she knitted him just one Argyle sock? Or the time she signed up for a real estate class and only went once? And how about when she was going to learn to cook and ordered that brand new set of pots and pans that never made it out of the box? She assured him that she intended to go through with the divorce. Once he realized she was serious, he begged her for another chance. To this day I remember his pleading; "Just give me one more chance, Eve. Can't you please...?" I had never heard such pain in my father's voice and it cut deep into my heart. He was the closest thing I had to a loving parent and here I was witnessing his agony. I wanted to scream at my mother to change her mind, to give him "one more chance." But it really was too late. Eve's mind was made up. When she refused to even try to work it out, he accused her of having an affair and the fight turned ugly; and then it turned physical. In a rage, my father struck my mother. She managed to lock herself in the bedroom and called the police. Chris and I cowered in the corner as my father tried to break down the door. Just as the hinges began to bend, the police arrived. They wrestled him away from the door and put him in handcuffs. As the police were about to take my father away he asked for a moment alone with me. Not Chris, not both of us, just me. He knelt down and told me that he was going to jail and would have to live on bread and water and he wanted me to know that it was all my mother's fault. He added, matter-of-factly, that she was a "mother-fucking whore," and then he hugged me one more time before being led away to the police car.

CHAPTER 5

—⸱♆⸱—

THE DAY AFTER Daddy was taken to jail, my mother took my sister and me on a three day train ride to visit her sister, Margaret, in Houston, Texas. It was our first real trip and we were very excited, having no idea that our lives were about to fall apart. Aunt Margaret was a lot different than our mom. She sewed clothes for her kids, cooked real meals; her husband even had a normal job. Her house was neat and orderly, and her children, Terry, a girl about my age, and Donnie, a sweet, gentle boy, a few years older, were both very well-behaved. Chris and I weren't used to having real meals served at a table and I guess we must have really chowed down because Aunt Margaret never missed an opportunity to call us fat, undisciplined, little slobs. Even so, I appreciated the order and the "normalcy" of the home. Hours and hours, even entire days would go by without some kind of an emotional hurricane. It was a foreign rhythm to me, a rhythm I could grow to like. But it was a short visit and then it was time to go back. On the train home I closed my eyes and hoped that maybe my mother had felt the same thing I had; the comfort and security of an ordinary home life.

When we returned home our mother gave us the news that we were going to be attending a new school. But not just any school; this was a wonderful place, a camp of sorts, she told us, with a swimming pool and horses... and how lucky and special we were to be able to stay there for a while. We were thrilled about the pool and the horse part, but we were not too happy about the 'staying there' part. We wanted to wait for our daddy to get home but Mom said that we had to go now and that Daddy wanted this for us too.

The "camp" turned out to be a Catholic boarding school and orphanage in the hills of Burbank, California called Villa Cabrini. For us to be going to a Catholic school of any kind seemed odd to Chris and me since the only thing we knew about religion was that our parents were passionately against it. We knew that our mother was born Catholic and that our father was Jewish, but Chris and I were completely ignorant about the details of either religion and had been discouraged from learning even the most basic bible stories. And now, all of a sudden, we're being dumped at this Catholic boarding school and orphanage.

What a strange and frightening word for an eight year old to hear:

Orphanage.

I had a mother, even if she was totally lacking in maternal instinct. She was alive and healthy. There was no reason she couldn't care for her children, except perhaps that she didn't want to.

I had a father, whom I loved and adored, but who seemed to be falling apart right in front of my eyes. Even so, I would have gladly spent my days and nights with him even if it meant dealing with his outrageous mood swings.

But I was being deposited, along with my sister, into the hands of strangers; nuns who were, back then, clothed in the black and white "habit" that successfully removed any hint of softness in their appearance. It took just a few minutes; my mother filled out some paperwork, reminded us of how lucky we were to be here, and then left.

As Mother Superior led us down the empty hallway I could feel the knot of fear and panic tightening in my chest. It was the first time in my life that I was aware of finding it difficult to breathe. Why couldn't I catch my breath? Everything was spinning and I was afraid I might faint and so I concentrated on the details of my new "school." The green linoleum floors were polished to a high shine. The yellow hue of the lights produced a strange wave of nausea that I remember to this day. Everywhere I looked, there were statues and crucifixes of Jesus and assorted saints looking down on us. Chris and I had been in a church only once or twice, to attend baptisms. We'd gone to a Jewish temple with our grandmother a few times for a wedding or a bat mitzvah. Up until now we had never been forced to choose a religion, but the truth was that I secretly leaned much more to my Jewish roots. The jokes were certainly funnier. And whenever we went somewhere Catholic it seemed like you were on your knees, on your feet, on your knees, on your feet, over and over like a tiresome game of 'Mother, May I?" It was all very somber and mostly in Latin. Whenever we went somewhere with my Jewish grandmother, however, someone was sure to feed you. It was all about the food, specifically comfort food. It definitely seemed like being Jewish was the way to go. But now I was being led down a series of cold, stark corridors lined with graven images of Jesus and the Saints. And for me at least, there was no comfort there. Every inch of this place felt foreign and frightening to me. And it didn't help that the Mother Superior's voice was stern and flat and had not an ounce of warmth in it.

It is perhaps ironic that the first real prayer I remember ever saying in my life was in the hallway of Villa Cabrini Catholic Boarding School and Orphanage. "Dear God, please take me away from this place."

It was especially alarming considering all the horror stories our mother had told us about her own experience in just such a place; how badly she was treated by the nuns when *she* was in the convent. How could she *choose* to send us to any place even remotely similar? And how could she do it without so much as a word of explanation? *Her* mother hadn't come back for her until she was fourteen. Is that how long we'd be here? Would she come and visit? "Dear God, *please* take me away from this place!"

It was a Saturday afternoon when we arrived and the facility was mostly empty. A few other nuns were present but most of the children were home with their families for the weekend. Chris and

31

I were given two sets of uniforms each, navy blue for everyday and white for Sundays and special occasions. We were uncharacteristically quiet as the orientation continued. The buildings felt medieval and intimidating even though they'd been built in the early 1900s. The interiors had a very cold, industrial feeling. Everywhere the walls were chalky green enamel, and those glaring yellow-white light fixtures hung naked from the ceiling every few feet. My dormitory was a large, open room with about thirty metal-frame, single beds in rows of three. It was very sparse with identical thin, white blankets stretched tautly and cornered over each and every bed. Right away I knew I was in trouble. I'd never even seen a bed made like that. My mother didn't give a rat's behind if Chris or I ever made our bed. And my father rarely got out of his bed so I don't think I ever saw one properly made. If "Bed Making 101" was looking like a challenge, God knows how the rest was going to go.

Because I was starting fourth grade and Chris was starting third, we were assigned to different buildings. So not only were we being taken out of our home and put into this cold, awful place, we were now going to be separated from each other as well. Do you suppose the nuns, the guardians of our welfare, might have thought to let two sisters room together? Maybe we could've bonded, even if it was the bonding of two kids stuck in a horrible place with only each other. But nobody thought of that.

Ironic, then, that we were instructed, in no uncertain terms, to always refer to the nuns as "sisters."

―ᥫ―

I was lonelier and more frightened than I had ever been in my life. And on that first night there were no other girls in the big, empty dorm. As I lay there staring into the dark of the room and the dark of my life, I felt a gnawing feeling that was growing inside my chest. It began that night at Villa Cabrini and it stayed with me throughout much of my life. I didn't know until years later that it was called anxiety and that most people don't feel it on an ongoing basis. I would describe it as a "low hum of fear," running inside me like the drone of an air conditioner. I wouldn't have dared ask any of the nuns, and certainly not my mother, what this feeling was all about. I just kept it to myself and assumed that it was a part of growing up. I would almost forget it was there until someone or something made me feel particularly frightened, and then the low hum could turn into a throbbing, painful pounding; as it did this night. I cried for my mom and dad, I cried for my sister. I cried for myself until I fell asleep.

It was still dark when an unfriendly nun harshly woke me up that very first morning. I understand now, and I think I understood even back then, that the business of educating and caring for dozens of girls is not an easy job. If the nuns of Villa Cabrini had merely been "serious" and "joyless," I think my memories of them wouldn't be quite so toxic. But they were not merely serious and joyless, they were mean and cruel.

Not one memory do I have of a smile, a gentle hand, or an understanding tone. If I ever needed a lesson in the Catholic concept of Original Sin, I got it in spades from the nuns of Villa Cabrini. Every instruction was delivered as if I had already screwed up the job six times from Sunday and needed to be chastised for doing so. Every opportunity to create a feeling of warmth and safety was abandoned to their need to establish control.

And so on this, my first morning, I was roughly shaken from sleep and told to dress for church. Chris was already seated in a pew when I got there and I was never so happy to see her in my whole life. We were both wearing the dress white uniforms with the white beanies. For my sister and myself to be dressed alike reminded me of all the smiling photos of us wearing matching outfits – only this was not one of those happy moments, not for me anyway. The church itself was, of course, awe inspiring in its beauty and its architecture, the better to fill the pews with frightened, awestruck and obedient children. And if I thought my rude awakening was an exception to the rule, I could see that the entire front section of the church was filled with an army of black and white uniformed nuns wearing the same dour expression on their faces as the grouch who woke me up; I was scared to death. I wanted to stand up and run full speed out of the church.

The priest performed the entire Mass in Latin and it was terribly confusing for two little girls who didn't understand a word of what was being said. And sure enough, just as I had remembered, there was a lot of standing, sitting, kneeling, and repeat. Chris and I tried to stay in sync with the nuns. If this is what church was all about I could understand why my mother was so against it.

After Mass there was breakfast in the Dining Hall. There were about twenty tables, but it was still the weekend, so the hall was mostly empty. Breakfast was oatmeal and a cup of hot chocolate with a thick, gelatinous layer of skim on top. I'm not sure if the milk had gone sour or my stomach was just so tied in knots that I couldn't keep anything down, but that layer of skim floating on the top made me sick to my stomach. Still, I was not allowed to leave that dining room until I had finished every morsel, whether I liked it or not, including the skim on the hot chocolate. Why were they doing this? Why were they torturing me? What awful thing had I done to deserve ending up in this place? I was still young enough to think that if "grown-ups" were in charge, then there must be a good reason. And the only good reason for any of this to be happening was that I was indeed, a bad girl. Maybe I didn't understand the details of what I had done, but I must have done something, and it must have been terrible. Otherwise, none of this made any sense.

To this day I cannot drink hot chocolate.

After eating we were escorted back to our own dorms to change into the navy blue uniforms and blue beanies. Then Chris and I were given a complete tour of the school grounds and that's when we realized that my mother was wrong or, more likely, lying. There was no swimming pool, no horses, no "fun activities," just cold, intimidating buildings surrounded by high wrought-iron gates. It felt more like a prison out of a Gothic novel than a school -- and nothing at all like a summer camp.

That night, after dinner, we were all sent to our respective buildings. Several girls at a time were ushered off to the bathroom. A huge, cavernous room, it had a long, trough-style sink with several faucets that lined one wall. Along the other side, there was a row of toilets and a number of stalls with doors; each stall housed an old, claw-foot bathtub. The door didn't go quite all the way down to the floor so a nun walking by could tell if you were in the bathtub or not by whether your feet showed. Years later, as an adult, I read a terrifying book by Stephen King called The Shining. In it a young boy is trapped in a dank, sprawling inn that has somehow robbed the adults of any warmth or reason. The book itself was wonderfully written, but I know I brought my own childhood experience to the page as I trembled with fear with each chapter.

Over the next few days and weeks my feelings about Villa Cabrini intensified. I kept waiting for someone to smile, someone to show the least little bit of tenderness. I was used to bad moods; my father's moods had been a roller coaster of highs and lows since I was a young child. But he would bounce back, exhibiting days and sometimes even weeks of enthusiasm and downright glee. These nuns were something else, and the deep sense of loneliness I experienced in my soul as I watched my mother drive away only grew with each passing day. I hated this place with every fiber of my being.

My mother finally picked us up on Friday afternoon and I told her how much I hated it and how I didn't want to go back. She said she didn't care if I didn't like it and that I was indeed going back. My nights were interrupted by a recurring nightmare; in it my family was traveling in my mother's green Ford convertible. She was driving and Daddy was riding shotgun. Chris and I were in the backseat, fighting. We were so busy hitting each other and arguing that when we looked up, we saw the two front doors were wide open, our parents were gone and the car was just barreling down the road at full speed with no one at the wheel. I don't think we need to bother Dr. Freud on this one. I'm pretty sure my dog could figure this one out.

My loneliness only grew deeper as time went by. I tried to conjure up my imaginary friend, Corley, but she was having none of this place. This was not an environment that inspired my creative side; too much fear, too much anxiety. The dorm was cold and the girls unfriendly and vice versa. Having to get up while it was still dark in order to go to church everyday seemed cruel. Where was it written that God was an early riser?! I still didn't understand anything that was going on in church so I got no comfort from being there.

But something else was going on, something that made absolutely no sense to me whatsoever; my sister was enjoying this place. Chris embraced Villa Cabrini and the whole Catholic experience. Because we were in different buildings I would wonder with envy what her building was like and why she found comfort here while I only felt the full weight of God's cold shoulder. Maybe she had nicer nuns; that must be it! The truth was that, no matter how cruel or cold the nuns were to Chris, they were probably still nicer to her than her own parents. Even if they were critical of her behavior, at least they were paying attention! No wonder she felt welcome here. Chris threw her little self into the spirit of the school and was thrilled when she was asked to sing in the choir. She had always had a wonderful voice and now she was being recognized for it. Although I'm not sure how happy the nuns would have been if they had heard her clearly, as I did, sing the words "Oy Vey, Maria" instead of the more traditional "Ave, Maria". This is the kind of thing that can happen when you start letting (half) Jews into the choir lofts.

One Friday afternoon, Chris and I waited for our mother to pick us up. We waited and we waited with our little bags packed and we watched as, one by one, all the kids left for the weekend. It was getting dark out as Chris and I sat on the steps of the school. One of the nuns, a particularly nasty one, finally came outside and escorted us back to our separate dorms.

"You two must be very bad children for your mother to forget you like this," she said. I guess Chris and I just weren't feeling bad enough for her taste. I begged to stay with Chris that night. I was still thinking that her dormitory had to be a happier place than mine. And it doesn't take a genius to figure out that two sisters who had just been so completely disregarded by their mother might want to take some comfort in the company of the other. That simple request was denied.

Up until that night, I had simply hated this school. But after that incident my sadness became anger. And not knowing the first thing about how to express anger, I simply took it all out on myself. Somehow my rage and my disappointment were transformed into a complete disregard for my own well-being. I refused to brush my teeth, bathe, or even go to the bathroom. I came up with the most devious ways in which to avoid being clean. I would wet my toothbrush, squeeze toothpaste on it, and then clean the sink with it. The bathroom stalls were the only place I could actually be alone without the fear of a nun barging in with an accusing eye. I would hide there, removing my nightgown and straddling the tub, balancing each leg so as not to get wet or let my feet show. I'd make splashing noises and squeaky sounds on the porcelain to fool the "monitors," but all that got wet were my feet. It was a lot of trouble to go to just to avoid taking a bath, but I was determined to act out in some way, and I guess this was the best I could do. Looking back on it now, I can see how my options were limited. Expressing anger in a healthy way is a learned skill, but where was I going to get that kind of experience? I wouldn't dream of risking my relationship with my father by getting angry with him. My mother would have done little more than laugh if I ever thought to be angry with her. And my position as FBI, First Born Infant, meant that I set the terms with my sister, so there wasn't that much need of anger there. I think my behavior at Villa Cabrini was a way of exercising some control over my otherwise out of control life. Refusing to "do what I was told" regarding my bathroom habits was my own pathetic rebellion.

These little games, if you could call them that, were my only joy. Strange as it sounds, the bathroom became my "Alamo," my last stand for independence. Looking back on that time I can see the desperation in my acts. I did pee, I couldn't help that -- but I stopped "going to the bathroom" at Villa Cabrini. I would wait as long as I could before "going." My goal was to "hold it" until Chris and I went home for a visit but, needless to say, that didn't always work out. Of course, in the end, I developed a constipation problem that lasted for the next forty years. That'll show 'em!!

CHAPTER 6

ON THE WEEKENDS that mom did pick us up, there was never an apology or an excuse for the fact that she had "forgotten" the previous week. My mother was very much of the school that said "never let them see you sweat, and never, EVER apologize." One weekend visit brought a real shock with it. Instead of going to our home, mom drove us to an apartment building in North Hollywood and said that this was where she lived now. Then she added, matter-of-factly, "Your father and I got a divorce."

Divorce?! Sure, my parents fought, but they had always fought. And then they would make up and be back to poking irreverent fun at everything and everyone, including and especially themselves. The truth was that Chris and I didn't really understand the full meaning of the word. Divorce was still rare and somewhat shocking in 1957 and I didn't really understand how it worked. We just knew it was bad. Mom's new apartment was full of boxes, some half-empty. We recognized a lot of furniture from our old house now crammed into this much smaller place. There were two bedrooms, one for mom and one for us. Where was daddy now, we wanted to know? We missed him, and we missed our dog, our "brother." She told us that our dad lived in another place with Slugger. And then she added, matter-of-factly, that daddy had been very sick for quite awhile and we'd see him when he was better. End of discussion.

When I stepped into our new bedroom, I saw that our beds were there but all of our "stuff," our toys, our games, our clothes, was gone. Mom said she'd had to leave a lot of our things because there wasn't room for it all and she didn't think we'd need many clothes since we were now wearing uniforms at school. Chris and I never thought to ask what happened to our old house or our old life for that matter. One day we lived in a house with two parents and our beloved Slugger; and the next day we lived in a Catholic boarding school/orphanage. And now our mother lived in a small apartment with no room for any of our things. And we had no idea where our father lived. As frightened and confused as we were, we didn't ask about any of this because it was certain that we'd get no answer. Questions annoyed our mother and we knew it.

Mom needed money to live on so she got her first "real" job, as a bookkeeper for a mortgage company. "Your dad's not working and that damn school is costing me a fortune," she said. Excited by my own eight year old brilliance, I told her that I had the absolute perfect solution to her dilemma. I reminded her again how much I hated Villa Cabrini and then I explained how she could save all that money if Chris and I could just come and live with her. Then she wouldn't have to work so much and she could stay home with us. It was perfect, wasn't it? "Forget it," she said. "I have to work, you have to stay at school, and that's that." And back we went to Villa Cabrini.

A few weekends later Chris and I were taken by mom to see where our father was living. Mom drove down a narrow, little street in North Hollywood called Satsuma. The street came to a dead end at a row of warehouses just before the railroad tracks. Dad's place was definitely on the wrong side of those tracks. We pulled into the driveway and there was a small, dreary square building the size of a bedroom. It was terribly dark and depressing even from the outside. Right behind it was another box, slightly smaller, that looked even worse. *That* was my dad's place. Inside was a small kitchenette and a bathroom, but basically it was a one-room apartment decorated in an oppressive mix of gloom and despair. I had always looked up to my fabulous father, and now I hated myself for feeling pity.

We were glad the place had a little bit of yard for Slugger and a garage for my dad's one material treasure on earth; his 1955 salmon pink Cadillac convertible. My mother had dropped us off and said she'd be back in an hour or so. She told us she'd honk the horn and that we should come to the car because she wouldn't be coming in.

At least at our mother's apartment Chris and I had a real bedroom to share. Here there was no bedroom whatsoever, our dad's couch was his bed and that was it. How could this have happened? My father was a handsome, witty, successful writer, working for some of the biggest stars around. My mother was a beautiful starlet, friend to movie stars and television personalities. Now they lived in two separate places and neither place felt like home.

The man sitting at the desk in the corner of the room seemed like a stranger. We didn't talk about the last time we saw him which was when he was on his way to jail. We didn't talk about why he was living here. He asked how we were doing at Villa Cabrini and we both said we were fine. I didn't think he was in any shape to hear how much I hated it there. Even then I took care of my father's feelings. And if he needed me to try and cheer him up, then that's what I was going to do. But it wasn't going to be easy. This funk was beyond the understanding of an eight year old girl, no matter how much I wanted to make things better. Chris and I petted Slugger and sat there uncomfortably. Thankfully, after a few moments of awkward silence, Dad turned on the TV. A little while after that we heard mom's horn.

On the drive back to Villa Cabrini I don't think Chris or I said one word. Once I was back in my designated bed in the dorm, I tried to figure out what had happened to my life. I felt that gnawing pain in my chest. I worried what would become of Chris and me. Maybe we'd just live in this hell hole forever. That thought made me cry and this time I couldn't stop. I just cried and cried and cried, throughout the night. Believe it or not, I missed my mother; and, of course, I *really* missed my father. I missed my brother, Slugger. I missed my room at my old house, and my toys, and my friends from the old block.

As the months passed Chris and I ended up spending a lot more weekends at Villa Cabrini instead of going home. On many of the weekends that my mom did come and get us she started leaving us home alone while she went out. We were still just seven and eight years old and we begged her not to go, but she said the weekends were "her time off, too!" and she deserved a break as much as anyone. She said she couldn't afford a babysitter so she'd either have to trust us or leave us at Villa Cabrini more weekends. That was all it took for me to behave. We didn't get into trouble, we didn't do anything wrong, we just watched TV and went to bed. At least we had each other during that time. After a while we were introduced to different "friends" of mom's. Whatever her failings as a mother, she was still a very bright, clever, extremely beautiful woman and she had absolutely no trouble attracting men when she wanted to. Occasionally, for some unknown but welcome reason, she would take us with her on a date. These nights were a mixed blessing for us; while it was strange and disconcerting to see our mother with another man, at least we got a decent meal on those nights. My mother had still not bothered to learn how to cook or to shop for food, so when Chris and I came for a visit there was never much to eat and we were always hungry.

Other than a few short day visits we didn't see our Dad much during this time. It became apparent that whatever had happened between them, our parents were no longer speaking to each other at all. It also became clear that whatever had happened to my father, it wasn't getting any better. We didn't even see him on our birthdays that year when Chris turned eight and I turned nine. When we did see Daddy he would grill us about what Mommy was doing and who she was doing it with. The questions were completely inappropriate but I didn't know that at the time. I had no idea that "Find out who your mother's fucking" was perhaps not a normal question for a father, even a divorced father, to ask his daughters. Mom's instructions to us couldn't be clearer: "Don't tell that son of a bitch one damn thing about my life, *especially* about who I'm screwing."

I saw no way out of this lonely life. I cried all the time. I cried in bed. I cried in class. And it only made me cry more that Chris seemed so happy. She *loved* Villa Cabrini. She *loved* church. She *loved* the nuns. She *loved* singing. She *loved* Jesus. Even the school part wasn't fun for me anymore – and I had always loved school. Everything about the Villa Cabrini experience seemed punishing to me. Eating was a cold, tasteless, silent affair. The classroom was a serious, anxiety producing hell. So much of the class work had to do with religion and I was completely ignorant in that area. I didn't fit in and I didn't stand out. I was a sad glob of self-pity in a starched blue uniform.

The nuns failed to see the charm in all this and they eventually called my mother and asked her to come in to "discuss a few issues." They let it be known, even to me, that they preferred talking to her rather than my Jewish father. I'm sure that suited my father just fine.

The first area the nuns wanted to address was my artwork. I was very fond of drawing profiles of women and, for my age, I was actually quite good at it. The problem was that I always drew my females naked from the waist up and with large, pointy breasts. This made perfect sense if you knew that the walls of my father's office at home had been covered with photos of his favorite pin-up girls. The nuns considered my portraits to be dirty-minded and dangerously sinful. I braced myself for the worst, but I have to say that my mother came to my defense on this issue. Having been a Vargas pin-up girl herself, and having been a part of boosting morale as well as enlistment in the armed forces during World War II, all with the help of her own perky breasts, she disagreed quite vocally with their assessment and did everything but threaten to report them to the House Un-American Committee for treason. She told them that, while I may be one big pain in the ass, I was also "one hell of an artist" and she refused to reprimand me for my work and neither should they. Next question! The Sisters tentatively moved onto their second problem: my questionable grooming habits. I knew that my mother wouldn't be too upset about this one since she was the one I had learned my "questionable" grooming habits from in the first place. Once she stopped modeling, my mother became completely disinterested in all the care and primping that went with that job. She shrugged and lit a cigarette and so the nuns moved on to what they considered the biggest issue, which was my incessant crying; it had to stop or they'd be forced to expel me. This one pissed my mother off big-time.

That weekend at her apartment she warned me that I damn well better stop crying like a baby, or else. She meant business and I would have stopped if I could have. I really wasn't using the tears to manipulate my mother, I think it was just the only way I had of dealing with the disappearance of any and all happiness from my life. I wanted so much to be a good little girl; for my mother, for my father. I believed that if I could just be a little bit better, a little bit cuter, a little bit smarter, then that would somehow magically fix whatever it was that had shattered our family. But the tears just flowed, whether I liked it or not. Things went on this way for a few more months. The nuns were getting more and more frustrated with me and it seemed like my mother never stopped being furious. I don't have one memory of any of the nuns actually talking to me about what might be upsetting me. I knew I wasn't going to get that from my mother, but these "Sisters" kept talking about the compassion of Jesus and so I hoped that one of them might want to do more than talk about it.

I think Chris felt guilty that she *didn't* feel bad about Villa Cabrini. Compared to her life at home, this place was Shangri-La.

Everything came to a head near the end of my fourth grade semester at Villa Cabrini. One day the Mother Superior called my mother in and delivered the news that I could no longer remain at the school, my uncontrollable sobbing was too upsetting to the other children in the dorm and they thought it best for everyone involved if my mother found someplace else for me. My mother ranted and raved and tried to threaten the Mother Superior but, in the end, I was escorted out of Villa Cabrini right then and there with my little travel bag. I had once referred to my travel bag as a "pushky" which is a Yiddish word for "little bag" that my Jewish Grandmother had taught me. Now *that* got the nuns' attention. I've often wondered whether, if my tears had been one hundred per cent Catholic tears, I would have been asked to leave. I certainly wasn't the only "resident" who cried herself to sleep every night, but during my time there, I was the only one "expelled." At any rate, they were glad to be rid of me, and I sure the hell was glad to be leaving.

My sister didn't come with us.

My mother didn't talk to me the whole drive home. She just swore to herself and smoked one cigarette after another. I was surprised when we drove right past her street and kept going. Eventually we pulled up at my dad's house instead. She snatched me out of the car and dragged me to the door. No words, nothing. Then she drove away. I knocked on the door and waited for my father to answer, but the door remained shut. I knocked again. Nothing. Was he home? Had my mother even let him know she was leaving me here? After what seemed like an eternity I nervously turned the doorknob. It was open. I stepped into the room. My dog, Slugger, was there and he was thrilled to see me. He practically knocked me over, jumping up and kissing me, dancing with joy. But it was so dark inside the room that it took a while for my eyes to adjust. The blinds were drawn and the place was completely in shadow. It smelled musty and sour. My dad was sound asleep on the couch/bed but after a few moments the commotion that Slugger created finally woke him. He looked terrible, frightening even. I hadn't seen him in a few months and he was almost unrecognizable. He hadn't showered or shaved in days, his hair was a mess, and he'd put on a lot of weight. At first he didn't seem to recognize me or know what was going on. I didn't know what to say; he didn't seem to know why I was there and he certainly wasn't very glad to see me. I told him that I had been kicked out of Villa Cabrini for crying too much. I told him my mother had dropped me off and he was suddenly furious that my mother might have seen him looking like this. I told him she hadn't come in; that she'd just dropped me off at the door. Finally, he opened the blinds a crack to let in a little light. That's when I saw that most of the wall space was covered with pictures of naked and half-naked women. That wasn't such a shock; he had always had them pinned to the walls in his office back at the old house, hence my admirable expertise in drawing the nude female figure. But these photographs were different; various photos of my mother's head were pasted over each one's face so it looked like a room full of naked Eve's. The really strange part of this story is that I don't remember it disturbing me all that much at the time. Weird, certainly, but not all that disturbing considering everything else that had been going on in my life.

Once my dad was fully awake and aware, he told me that I couldn't stay with him. It was, after all, a one-room place and there was nowhere for me to sleep – or even sit for that matter. He said that my mother would just have to figure it out. As I stood there, "pushky" in hand, he tried calling her on the phone but couldn't reach her. The longer he waited for her to answer, the madder he became, swearing and storming around the cramped quarters. I tried to stay out of his way as he ranted, taking one step this way and two steps that way as he paced in anger, but the room was small and there was no place to duck and hide. Finally he made a call to the neighbor across the street. Mrs. Raufman had been very nice and welcoming when my dad had first moved in and had even brought him a casserole. She had a daughter, Cissy, who was my age and we had played together a few times when Chris and I were visiting. My father explained the situation and Mrs. Raufman offered to let me spend a few nights at their house. I wanted to cry again, but I was afraid it would send my father into another rage.

I loved Cissy's house. Mrs. Raufman was a stay-at-home mom and she kept her house very clean; better yet, there was always food there. After a few days of staying with the Raufman's, my dad called and said I could come back to his place. I didn't know what to expect. As I walked up the driveway I could see the blinds were open and when I entered the apartment was actually light inside. He had attempted to decorate somewhat, replacing some of the "Eve" naked pictures with movie memorabilia that had hung in his office before. The room was now reasonably neat, my dad was showered and clean shaven, and he was in a good mood. This was the daddy I remembered; bright-eyed, funny and warm. The frightening man who was passed out on the couch when my mother dropped me off was gone for the time being.

There was now a green army cot in the corner of the room with a pillow and a blanket. There was a stack of cardboard boxes that were turned sideways to hold my belongings. He said that I would be staying there with him, at least until something else could be figured out.

CHAPTER 7

ON MY FIRST night there with Dad, he was in a very upbeat and playful mood. He made some knockwurst sandwiches on rye with Dr. Brown's cream soda for dinner. I was in bliss. I was so incredibly happy. This is what I wanted. This is what I needed. This would be my new life and I was thrilled. A few days after I officially moved in, my father enrolled me at Lankershim elementary school in North Hollywood to finish fourth grade. I found out years later that Marilyn Monroe had attended the sixth grade there in the 1930s. Even though it wasn't ideal to be starting school at the end of a semester, I was a very happy kid because enrolling in school meant I *lived* there. And I already had a friend my age right across the street, *and* we would be in the same class. Cissy and I would walk or ride our bikes to school together, do our homework together. When I got "home" the first day of school, Daddy was at the typewriter working, his pipe positioned in the corner of his mouth, and the heady combination of cherry tobacco and drug store cologne filled the air. The duplex had no air conditioning and so my dad had a cooler going in the middle of the room. It was an odd type of device you had to pour water into and then let the air pass over, thereby cooling it. Only instead of pure water my dad would add a huge bottle of Jean Nate cologne to the mix. It was probably a horrible smell but I absolutely loved it. It smelled like heaven to me. Daddy actually seemed happier with me there and it made me feel important, as if my presence was making a positive contribution toward his improved mental and physical state. He had even been to the store and stocked the fridge with his idea of nourishment;

doughnuts, Twinkies, m&m's, whipped cream, watermelon, and Bubble Up (a 1950s version of 7-Up or Sprite but with more sugar). When I arrived home, he presented me with a huge bowl of m&m peanuts topped with a mountain of whipped cream that he christened the "Maxwell Special." There would be many of those over the years. Everything I said and did those first few days was adorable. Everything made him smile or laugh out loud. Life was good.

One morning I awoke for school and my dad was still working at his chair. He hadn't gone to bed. He seemed happy and energetic and very glad to see me. This was such a stark contrast to life at my mother's, not to mention life at Villa Cabrini, that I barely thought about the fact that I hadn't seen my mother in weeks. And if my sister was having a grand old time back at Villa Cabrini, well, goody for her. I got daddy.

He even drove me to school that morning, and I remember I had an excellent day in class. I actually loved school again. In addition to Cissy, I met lots of other kids and it seemed to me that my life was bordering on normal.

When I got home that day Daddy was still at his typewriter. I played outside with Cissy and my friends until it was dark. He was still working away when I came in. He wasn't hungry so I made myself a "Maxwell Special" for dinner, watched The Jackie Gleason Show on TV and put myself to bed. Being in one room I found it a little hard to get to sleep with the light on but the sound of dad's typewriter lulled me to dreamland.

When I awoke the next morning Daddy was *still* in his chair working. He hadn't slept, or showered, or changed clothes. He didn't pay much attention to me as I ate doughnuts and drank Bubble-Up for breakfast, and he only grunted a distracted "goodbye" when I left for school. He was still at it when I got home, but his mood was now dark and he seemed cranky and irritated. I tried to do everything exactly as I had done it the day before when it had all been adorable, but today it didn't work. I grabbed a snack and tried to stay out of his way. But as I was setting up to do my homework, one of my school books slipped out of my hands and onto the floor. Daddy exploded. All of a sudden he started screaming at me at the top of his lungs. I apologized immediately and repeatedly, but it didn't do any good. He just screamed louder, a steady stream of curses that included calling me a "big, fat pain in the ass." Then, without so much as a pause, he moved on to my mother. He called her every name under the sun, and plenty more I'd never heard. She was a slut, a whore, a cocksucker. A what? Isn't a cock a rooster? He said he wished that she were dead. Then he said, "No – *worse*, I wish she were fat so no one would love her!" And then he looked at me mid-Twinkie and called me fat. I didn't understand what was happening. Why was he being so mean to me? The low hum of fear in my stomach, the one that had first appeared at Villa Cabrini, was kicking into full throttle. I went to my cot in the corner of the room and buried my head in a pillow. I knew that crying would just make matters worse so I learned how to cry myself to sleep without making a sound. Slugger licked my tears and I held him close until I finally drifted off.

Daddy was still in his chair when I got up the next morning. He looked like a crazy person. His eyes were glazed and he was writing furiously. He ignored me completely and I left without him even saying goodbye. I was beside myself with worry all day. Clearly I was irritating him and I feared that soon I'd have to go somewhere else to live, maybe even back to Villa Cabrini. My mother had never told me anything about my father's problems with drugs. I didn't even know what they were. So the only possible cause for daddy's ferocious mood swings was... me.

Cissy and I walked home from school that day. She peeled off to go to her house and me to mine. I walked slowly up the driveway and saw that the blinds were all drawn and the door was closed. My heart pounding in my chest, I entered cautiously. The room was dark and dank as it had been the first day my mother had dropped me off. I instinctively knew to be quiet; even Slugger knew. He wagged his tail and greeted me in silence. When my eyes adjusted I could see that my dad was asleep on the couch. Not so much asleep actually, more like "passed out," his breath heavy and labored, his body draped over the edge. I turned on the TV in the corner of the room to watch my favorite shows, "Jack Benny" followed by "Burns and Allen." I didn't know it at the time, but I was acquiring an addiction of my own; comedy. Laughter as celebration when things were going well, laughter as an escape on days like today, I turned the volume on the TV so low that I had to imagine a lot of what the actors were saying. With dad passed out on the couch, I made no noise when I laughed, just the face that makes a laugh. I didn't know much about what was going on with my father, but I knew to keep the place dark and quiet. I had a couple of dough-nuts and a Butterfinger and tried to lose myself in Jack Benny's world. It wasn't the first night I fell asleep with the television on.

In the morning Dad hadn't moved. I had some candy for break-fast, grabbed some change to buy lunch, and went to school. Daddy was still asleep when I got home that day but he was beginning to stir. But even in his sleep he seemed annoyed with me, yelling at me to turn off the damn TV even though it was on the quietest setting there was. Having no room of my own to go to, I went outside and sat in the yard, leaning against the wall. I sat there with Slugger for hours just wondering what to do with myself. When it got dark I went inside. I got a couple of candy bars from the kitchen and took them into the bathroom to unwrap so it wouldn't make noise. I ate them in the dark and went to bed. As I lay in my cot that night I was filled with anxiety and kept tossing and turning. Every time I changed position my army cot creaked. After this happened a few times my father got up from his bed and charged towards me. Because it was dark I didn't see him until he was looming over me. He scared me to death, screaming that if I moved one more time he'd kill me. You can bet I didn't move – but I didn't sleep either.

I had no idea what to expect when I got home from school that next day. I approached the house with fear and dread. To my surprise, I saw that the blinds were up, the door was open, and the aroma of cherry pipe tobacco and Jean Nate once again filled the air. Dad was showered, shaved, and hard at work in his chair. And he was thrilled to see me. And that's when I realized that there was a cycle to my dad's moods and the trick was going to be to learn them. Never once did it enter my mind that there was something wrong with a man screaming at his daughter that he was going to kill her if she so much as moved a muscle in her sleep. That's not the way my mind worked. Whatever my father's moods, whatever my mother's failings, I still loved them both and was totally convinced that I had the power to "fix" them if I just set my mind to it.

I simply did my very best to anticipate daddy's frame of mind and stay out of the way when it was bad. Not an easy task when you're both living in one room.

When daddy was on an upswing, occasionally he would go to someone's office or home to write and I would get to go with him. One of my father's army buddies, David Rose, was a very well-known composer. Among his biggest hits was the "The Stripper." He also wrote the theme music for the TV show "Bonanza." David had been married to Martha Raye and to Judy Garland before meeting his third wife, Betty, a lovely woman who was always very nice to my sister and me. Before my parents divorced, we had gone to the Rose's estate in Sherman Oaks many times where Chris and I would get to swim with their two daughters, Melanie and Angela, who were our same ages. Each girl had an enormous bedroom with toys lining the walls like a toy store. They shared a Jack and Jill bathroom that had been completely scaled down to their sizes like a dollhouse. The bathtub, sink and toilet were just their height. But the most amazing thing about their house was that David, a huge train fanatic, had installed a miniature train with about eight cars that ran all around their property. Whenever there were kids visiting, David would gladly put on his engineer's cap and give us all rides.

But as wonderful as a trip to the Rose's was, it was hard not to feel the disparity between their mansion and our one gloomy room. And I know it bothered my father much more than it did me.

_____ ᘒ

Daddy's "up" moods would sometimes go on for a week or so, but I had learned that I couldn't trust them to last. I would try to image his good moods as balloons that I could keep inflated a little bit longer if I just kept him laughing. I listened, *really* listened to the jokes he told and the witty observations that seemed to keep him temporarily out of the doldrums. I learned how to feed him straight lines and deliver whatever punch lines he needed to make him feel like he was going to get through the day. That walk up the driveway after school became a nerve rattling guessing game for me. I'd take bets with myself on which one I was going to get that day. If the blinds were up, that meant that he was up and working and I got the best daddy in the whole world. If they were down, then it was going to be a day, or perhaps a week, of tiptoeing around the apartment and getting myself to school. But despite my dad's erratic behavior I loved it there. And, even better, I was doing well living there. I did well in school, earning straight A's. I had friends, both real and imaginary. I had Slugger. On the "up" days I felt like everything I did was just right. Daddy would laugh at my jokes and tell me I was funny and smart. Some summer nights he'd come outside and toss a softball with me. When he was stumped on a script or a lyric, he'd even ask my opinion or get my reaction to something he was writing. I felt like the most important person in his life, and isn't that the dream of every little "Daddy's Girl?" Sometimes I would think about Chris, away at Villa Cabrini, and sometimes I would miss her. But even as a young child I worried that my parents' fears about her were justified; that everything she touched went to hell in a hand basket. Life with my father was so precarious that the truth was I didn't want to add anything or any-one, even my own sister, that might disrupt that fragile equilibrium.

Occasionally Daddy needed a break and I got to stay at Cissy's house across the street. I think Mrs. Raufman liked feeding me; I was always so incredibly appreciative. At home my father fed me so many sweets — breakfast, lunch and dinner — that I was thrilled to be eating real food. A baked potato was a treat and carrots were rare delicacies. Mrs. Raufman might have had trouble getting Cissy to eat her vegetables, but not this kid.

There was another part of my father's personality that I was exposed to during this time that wasn't always easy for me to deal with. My father's obsession with my mother had grown more and more intense and it was threatening to take over his life. At nine years old I had no idea what "appropriate" emotions looked like, and that included grief. I knew my father was grieving the loss of my mother and I understood that. What I didn't know at the time was that, had it been twenty years later, his actions would have gotten him arrested for stalking and harassment. Many was the night he would announce that the three of us, my dad, me, and Slugger, were going to spend the evening cruising the boulevards of Los Angeles in search of my mother. It was presented as a grand outing. Bologna sandwiches were made, a thermos of lemonade was prepared, and we were off until the wee hours of the morning. We'd cruise the parking lots of all the restaurants and night spots my mother was known to frequent, drive by apartments of suspected boyfriends, and when all that failed, we'd just drive around with the top down keeping our "eyes peeled" for the woman who drove my father absolutely crazy. Eventually Slugger and I would fall asleep in the back seat. I never told my father, but I always loved falling asleep in the car because the back seat of his Cadillac was so much more comfortable than my cot.

There was a popular song at the time, made famous by Frank Sinatra, called "All the Way." The lyrics include the lines:

"...When somebody loves you, It's no good unless they love you, All the way." My father became fixated on that song. He would break down and sob every time he heard it. In his mind my mother

54

hadn't loved him *all the way* and so it really hit him hard. When the song would come on the radio I just knew that it was my job to comfort him. I would put my arms around him silently as he wept and just be there until it was over. I felt really important and needed during those times. Some days were worse than others. Some days the cries were more of a wail and that was very hard on me. It scared me to see my father in such pain. Many times I'd find him holding a ring that my mother had given him when they were dating. It was a thick gold band with their names, Eve and Eddie, engraved in script on the surface. It was his proof that she had once loved him enough to have it made for him. Why didn't she love him anymore?

"Why wouldn't she give me just one more chance?" he'd moan over and over again. I felt helpless and it made me hate my mother at those moments. When the song was over he would either continue to weep until it was out of him or he'd get furious and go into a tirade about what a slut she was. This "slut" was the same woman who could make him happy if only she would "give him one more chance." It was like living with Jekyll and Hyde, and Daddy could turn without a moment's notice. It was a strange, roller-coaster existence but, given the alternatives, it was still where I wanted to be.

CHAPTER 8

———— ⁓ ————

IT MAY SEEM odd, but there were moments when I really missed my mother. I had memories of a different time, whether they were real or imagined doesn't make that much of a difference; a time in which I was part of a family that laughed, and loved, and enjoyed at least the appearance of normalcy. I missed that terribly. It was the fifties, the families were nuclear, divorce was rare, and mothers stayed home and took care of their kids. This was many years before "Kramer vs. Kramer" and fathers almost never got custody of a child. But here I was living with my dad, having little or no contact with my mother even though she lived only a couple of miles away. And I had a sister who lived in an orphanage despite the fact that both her parents were alive and well. It was all pretty embarrassing for a nine year old girl and I did my best to pretend that things were not what they really were.

One week everyone in my class was supposed to bring in something about our mothers for "show and tell," so I brought in the only thing I could find; a set of publicity glamour photos of my mother looking sultry in her bejeweled gowns slit up to her waist. My father had a drawer full of them and, well, it seemed like a good idea at the time. I'm sure it seemed pathetic, not to mention odd, to my teacher and classmates, but I was so desperate to be proud of her the way the other kids were proud of their mothers and the one thing I knew, the one thing that everybody agreed on, was that she was incredibly beautiful. Looking every bit the movie star, she seemed like this stunning creature that I had the good fortune to be connected to. And if she was more like a famous acquaintance than a real live mother? As I said before, it was better than nothing. Some of the kids in my class didn't believe the woman in the photograph was my mother. After all, no one at school had ever actually seen her; she'd never come to any school events or parent/teacher meetings. My guess is that the school assumed she was dead and that I just didn't want to accept it.

I didn't tell my dad that I took pictures of mom to school. Even though her face had been plastered all over the naked pictures in the apartment, I knew not to mention her.

Occasionally, when he was on a high, he'd get a burst of creativity and enter one of the many jingle and slogan contests that were popular in the 1950s. He was extremely good at it and was always winning something. No matter how bad things got, as long as he was coherent, my father always had an incredible talent with words. One time he won a "Trans-solar" radio that was powered by the sun, which was pretty amazing back then. Even the light from a lamp was enough to generate it. That Trans-solar radio made me very popular for a while and I think that was when I began to realize that words, put together in a clever way, had their benefits. Mostly Dad won free meals and candy, which was helpful because he didn't cook and, as far as he was concerned, candy was all three food groups. Once we won a year's supply of a candy bar called "Butter Brickle." We were over the moon with joy; a *year's supply!!!!* Week after week we waited patiently for our truckload of Butter Brickle to arrive, but when our "prize" finally showed up, there was one medium sized box containing three dozen candy bars. This wouldn't last the two of us a week! How ludicrous, we thought, that someone could possibly think that puny little box would last anyone a year?!

One Saturday night I took a chance and called my mother's house to say hello. There was no answer, but I could tell that the call had upset my dad. I worried that my attempt to reach my mother, albeit unsuccessful, was going to send him spiraling into a terrible funk. But instead his response was to announce another "reconnaissance" tour. He and I, along with Slugger of course, were going out for an adventure. We took some of our "year's supply" of candy and out we went out into the warm San Fernando Valley night. He drove around until the wee hours of the morning, but he didn't find her, not that time. Perhaps stranger still was the fact that I thought that what my father was doing was romantic. I was, after all, nine years old, and I figured that this is what love looked like. I enjoyed those long nights of driving aimlessly if only because my dad and I and my "brother" were together out in the world.

Some nights weren't "reconnaissance nights," some nights were just "keep daddy distracted" nights. He would get desperately lonely and he'd do everything he could to keep me from going to sleep – even if it was a school night. He'd pay me to stay up late just to watch television with him. Back then we didn't have all the TV channels that we do today and most of them signed off at midnight or earlier. But there was one local channel that had an all-night amateur show. This was fifty years before "American Idol" and the talent pool was much thinner, but it was the only thing on at that hour. Those nights, the strain to stay awake for my father, the pain in his eyes, remain fresh in my mind to this day. I remember that the show we watched was called "Rocket to Stardom" and was sponsored by the Yeakel Brothers Oldsmobile dealership. The continuous talent acts went on all night long, and the later into the evening, the more amateur they became. My dad and I especially loved the really bad ones at 2:00 a.m. You might see a guy playing a saw like a violin, twins twirling batons, plate spinners, and bad mime artists. No, I mean *really* bad mime artists. I remember being amazed that I was the only kid who knew about this program, but of course I was probably the only kid who was allowed, encouraged, and sometimes even *paid* to stay up and watch it.

There was one outing my dad and I would take that had nothing to do with my mother. Once in long while we'd visit "Gummy," my grandmother, in Venice Beach, a wonderfully bizarre beach community with a boardwalk and a row of old hotels housing mostly older Jewish retirees. That's where Gummy spent the last ten years of her life. She'd had one lung removed due to cancer and she also struggled with emphysema, so the beach air was what she needed. She seemed very old to me and she tired easily, but her face lit up whenever she saw me and that was enough to make me look forward to our visits. Most times we'd pick her up at the beach and drive around Santa Monica, Beverly Hills, and Brentwood in the Cadillac convertible for a couple of hours and then we'd have lunch, usually at Junior's Deli. That was one of the joys of living in Los Angeles in the 1950s and 1960s, miles and miles of roads and thirty cent a gallon gasoline meant that you could drive around all day just for the sheer pleasure of it.

As we'd drive down Sunset Boulevard my grandmother would spot a restaurant or a nightspot. "I remember when that was the Trocadero," she'd say.

Or "Remember when Ciro's was over there?" On and on they would go for the next hour pointing out missing landmarks. To me, it seemed like a waste of time to try and remember what used to be where and when, but now, to my own children's chagrin, I do the same thing. "Hey, you know what used to be here before the Beverly Center? Kiddieland! It was a little amusement park, it had a rollercoaster and pony rides for the kids, and..."

Occasionally I'd get an overnight visit with Gummy. She always gave me at least one complete scrubbing when I arrived; she'd scour my nails with a brush and complain the whole time, "Doesn't anyone ever wash you? When was the last time someone shampooed your hair?" She obviously didn't consider the local swimming pool a good substitute. By the way, the old hotel where Gummy lived all those years is now a very fancy, very trendy hotel called Shutter's.

Gummy's hotel was a wondrous place for a kid to wander and explore. It had a ballroom, an indoor pool, a hotel switchboard, and lots of older people. I was quite a hit with some of Gummy's chums who played cards because I knew how to play Hearts, Pinochle, and Casino and could hold my own at any table.

My grandmother's temple was just a block away and she had several friends in the building who walked with her to services. On the way back she would slow way down when we reached "Muscle Beach." It was a section of the beach set up for weight lifters and wrestlers and there were always plenty of young, fit men working out and showing off. I didn't know it at the time, but I think this was my sweet grandmother's guilty pleasure. It was a thrill for her to be on a first name basis with famous wrestlers like Freddie Blassie and Gorgeous George, big stars at the time. And I think they enjoyed her as well. She would bring them all a "nosh" and they would gather round and flirt with her.

A lot of my memories of those visits revolve around food. And this *was* my Jewish grandmother, after all. She made her own chopped liver with hard-boiled eggs and red onion, which is still the best I've ever tasted. My favorite breakfast that she made for me was a nice, fresh Kaiser roll topped with strawberry jam. Oh, and beautiful memories of pastrami on rye, a nice, crunchy dill pickle from the corner market – which is *now*, by the way, an over-priced restaurant on the strand.

When I reflect on those visits with Gummy, it's like a warm embrace that soothed and nurtured me during my early child-hood. Hopping aboard the open tram that took us down the Venice boardwalk for a nickel, "people watching" the "beatniks," as they were called back then, shopping for inexpensive pieces of jewelry that made me feel like a little grown up girl, trips to a wonderful amusement park called "P.O.P.," for Pacific Ocean Park, which had a roller coaster that hung out over the ocean, the beautiful carou-sel on the Santa Monica Pier, bingo for hours in the grand lobby of Gummy's hotel; all bright spots of warmth and love that helped me keep my heart in one piece at a time when I could have easily given up on life and love and dreams of any kind. When I got older I always had the impression that there were dozens and dozens of those trips to Gummy's, but the truth is that I only visited her about a half a dozen times before she passed away. Such was the power of her sweet attention.

_6

CHAPTER 9

———————— ⌒ ————————

THINGS SETTLED INTO a routine over the next several months and I really started to feel relaxed and secure living with my dad. Granted it was *his* routine. I had no inkling that a family's priorities might ever revolve around a *child's* needs. And that ignorance contributed greatly to my happiness back then. Best of all, I seemed to be dealing with dad's erratic behavior pretty well.

But then the first summer came. Dad explained that with school being out and me being there all the time he wouldn't be able to get any work done so my mother was coming to get me, *that day!* She pulled into the driveway and honked. I got into the car with a little sack of clothes. Chris was in the car already and, at first, we were like strangers. Our lives had already begun to take different paths and it took a while before we were comfortable with each other again. My mother drove us to Hody's, an upscale coffee shop in the valley. The children's menus doubled as clown masks so it was fun for kids, and they had a reasonably priced full bar so it was even more fun for the adults.

Over lunch, I learned that Chris had finished third grade at Villa Cabrini and was looking forward to continuing there, but mom told her that was out of the question. She was short of money. Years later Chris and I learned that a boyfriend of my mother's had been footing the bill for the boarding school so the two of them wouldn't be bothered with children afoot during their fling. But now the fling was over and so were the tuition payments. Halfway through dinner at Hody's a *new* friend of mom's joined us. His name was Abel and he was a real peach. Chris and I had been introduced to a few of our mother's "friends" in the past and had found none of them particularly nice, but Abel was in a class by himself. He never once even acknowledged our existence; never spoke to either of us. Instinctively Chris and I knew that it was not going to be okay if we talked, or laughed or did much of anything that might interrupt our mother's "date," so we both just finished our meal in silence. All in all, it was a hell of a reunion.

A few days later my mom announced a new summer plan for Chris and me. Because she had to work and couldn't be home to watch us, she was going to treat us to a new, fun place for the next two months: a real farm in Blythe, California. We would get to ride horses and swim all the time. Well, we'd heard that one before. But hope springs eternal, especially in young girls, so Chris and I spent that night pretending that this "plan" was going to be just wonderful.

It took about four hours to get there and it was still oppressively hot at ten o'clock at night when mom pulled her convertible onto the dirt road that led to a little farmhouse. She woke Chris and me up and the three of us walked to the door and knocked. And knocked. Finally an older woman answered. She looked tired and worn, and appeared to be about sixty. We found out later she was thirty-two years old. Blythe, it seems, is nobody's idea of a health spa. She seemed surprised to see us, and not pleasantly so, especially not at this hour. This was a farm, after all, and people get up early on farms. My mother asked if she was Irma. She said she was and cautiously invited us in. Inside the house was rundown and sparse, but clean. My mother refreshed Irma's memory with the story of how my mother worked with a woman named Barbara whose gardener, Julio, had a brother Juan, who worked on Irma's farm. With me so far? Back in L.A. Eve had mentioned to Barbara, the woman she worked with, that she was looking for a place to send her two daughters for the summer. Nothing healthy or normal like, say… a summer camp. No, Eve was looking for something more affordable, so she came up with the brilliant idea of sending her eight and nine year old daughters off to stay with complete strangers! Once Barbara got the gist of what Eve was looking for, she mentioned it to Julio, her gardener, who asked his brother, Juan, if the man he worked for, Ray, who was Irma's husband, if they would be interested in making a few hundred dollars taking in a couple of kids for the summer. Ray asked his wife Irma and they had agreed that they could use the money and it would be something to consider. But Ray had forgotten to tell Irma that he had said yes and even cashed the check already. So here we were.

Irma didn't seem all that thrilled with the plan but she showed Chris and me a little room with one twin bed to share. I guess they must've worked everything out because in the morning when we got up, our mother was gone. Irma let us know that we'd have to get ourselves on a different time clock. Things started really early on the farm. Irma had been up since 4:00 a.m. and was about to serve the mid-day meal. It was 9:00 a.m.

Chris and I went outside to check things out. It was already over 100 degrees and climbing. In the light of day we could see how big the farm was. Ray and Irma probably had fifty acres of land. There were rows and rows of corn fields that were at least five feet tall. They had a variety of vegetables: carrots, tomatoes, cucumbers, lettuce, and tons of watermelons. We couldn't get it through our heads that everything just grew out of the ground like that; we'd never seen a real farm before. In about twenty minutes the temperature had risen to 110 and we were ready to go back home. We wanted to be somewhere where we could ride a bike, visit a friend, see a TV show or a movie. But we were stuck, and we were stuck for the whole summer.

There were several workers picking the fruit and vegetables and an older man wearing overalls was driving a tractor. This turned out to be Ray, Irma's husband. There were chickens and pigs running around and a whole pasture full of cows. After a while Chris and I went looking for the swimming pool and the horses. Guess what? No pool, no horses. I have to say that if I'd spent as much time on a horse as I was promised by my mother, I'd have a wall full of blue ribbons by now.

Even though there was no pool, they did have several twenty-foot wide irrigation ditches. And with temperatures inching close to 120 some days, those irrigation ditches started looking a lot like swimming pools to Chris and me. We had no idea how dangerous they were; we could've easily been sucked into an irrigation pipe at any time and that would have been the end of our ongoing series of "World's Greatest Summer Adventures." But we were oblivious to any danger and those ditches were the best part of our afternoons.

We were very lucky, fortunate, blessed --- pick your own word --- that nothing bad happened to us while we were there for those two months. My mother didn't know these people from Adam and yet she had just dumped us off without a word. Luckily Ray and Irma weren't bad people; we were never abused or molested. But they weren't nice people either. They didn't really ever talk to us or play with us. They didn't have a TV. No toys, no games, nothing that a couple of young girls might have amused themselves with. But they fed us well and we had the cows to play with, the irrigation ditch to swim in, and we had books to read. Once a week when the family took some of their produce to town, they'd let Chris and I go to the little library and check out some books. Ray and Irma went to bed at around 7 p.m. each night. We were expected to go to our room as well. There were two lamps in our room and we would cover them with a pillowcase so the light wouldn't disturb anyone, then we would lay with our heads at opposite ends of the bed and read until we fell asleep. Plus, during the day, we had the outdoors to explore, acres and acres of open land. The San Fernando Valley looked nothing like this. To city girls like us, anything other than a cat, a dog or a goldfish was like something out of National Geographic. We grew to love the cows; we even took them up as pets and gave them names. Mine was a lovely redhead named Kelly; my sister's was a pale yellow cow which she named Blondie. Our big activity of the day, after our swim in the ditch, was to crack a watermelon and feed it to our pals, Kelly and Blondie. Cows, by the way, absolutely love watermelon.

The only traumatic event at the farm in Blythe was when we witnessed a farmhand snap a chicken's neck. We had named that chicken Charlie. And that night Charlie was dinner. Neither Chris nor I could eat Charlie. And then we stopped naming the chickens.

So, to review: up at four in the morning, catch a chicken execution or two, afternoon swim in a potentially lethal irrigation ditch, split a few watermelons for the livestock, bed by seven o'clock. But the truth is; we had a pretty good time. At least this summer had allowed Chris and me to spend it together. We had no one but each other, no parents to compete for, no "FBI" monikers to brandish, just a long, hot summer in which to bond and be sisters. I'll bet Chris would remember this summer fondly as well.

The weeks and months passed and one day our mother came to get us. We told her all about our summer on the drive home but I don't remember any reaction other than annoyance that summer was over and we were once again in her charge. When we arrived back at her apartment it was a complete disaster. She had always been a messy housekeeper but without my dad around to nag her, she had really let things go. There were dirty dishes, pots, pans, cups and glasses, all piled high in the sink. And there were more dirty dishes on the coffee table, on the floor, in the bedroom, bathroom, everywhere. None of it bothered my mother one bit. On the contrary, she got royally pissed off if anyone even attempted to clean up. The odor of overflowing ashtrays mixed with the smell of rotten food permeated the air. There were random items of clothing strewn wherever, and trash scattered throughout the apartment.

One of the reasons my mother didn't mind the mess was that she was rarely there. It was a funny quirk in her character; so tough, so independent and opinionated, and yet my mother didn't like being alone. If she wasn't working, or on a date, then she was at her cousin Jane's house. Since leaving my dad and moving closer to Jane, they had reconnected. It was good for me and Chris because she would actually take us with her. Jane was married to a man named George Selleck. They had two little boys together, Doug and Gregg. And Jane had another son, John, from a previous marriage. Chris and I loved going to Jane's. They always had food in the house and they lived on a big cul-de-sac with tons of kids and an empty field at the end of the street. Perfect for Hide and Seek. Most of the time when we visited, the other cousins from the Selleck side of the family would also come over: Bobby, the oldest, Tommy, Danny, and sister, Marty. Tommy grew up to be Tom Selleck and starred in a television show called "Magnum P.I.", a huge hit throughout the 80s, and then went on to headline another hit TV series, "Blue Bloods."

CHAPTER 10

⁂

AFTER MUCH THOUGHT (my guess would be somewhere around ten minutes) Mom decided our fate for the coming school year: I was going back to my dad's to start fifth grade, Chris would be staying with her and going to elementary school. There was no talk of Villa Cabrini and I was incredibly relieved about that. I was also a little torn that Chris would have mom all to herself. Hard to believe that a steely mix of neglect, impatience and a total absence of nurturing skills would inspire me to envy my sister's access to my mother, but I was still a little girl with a little girl's belief in her power and responsibility to win over her one and only mother. Maybe Eve hadn't given Daddy "one more chance" but I certainly wouldn't be guilty of that sin of sins: I was determined to give her all the chances she needed. But I also knew that the amount of time Chris really got to spend with mom "all to herself" wouldn't be very much, so I didn't object to the plan.

On my last day with Mom, she had planned to get us some new school clothes and shoes. It had been months since we had gotten anything new and both of us were looking pretty rag-tag. As we were about to leave to go shopping, one of her boyfriends, Doc, showed up and offered to escort us for the day. We all drove in Doc's Lincoln to Sak's Fifth Avenue on Wilshire Boulevard in Beverly Hills. Chris and I looked like refugees in Buckingham Palace, but mom wasn't going to pass up an opportunity to soak a "mark." It's what *her* mother had taught her, and mom had learned her lessons well. Instead of looking at school clothes, we went directly to the "Special Occasions" department and Mom picked out two really elaborate party dresses for us to try on. Even then I remember being blown away that the price tags read $100.00 each! Doc insisted on paying for them. Then we went to the shoe department and Doc paid for two pairs of patent leather Mary-Jane's. Afterwards, Doc took us all to The Tail 'o' the Cock restaurant on Ventura Boulevard in Sherman Oaks. We had steak, Shirley Temples, dessert, another dessert, another Shirley Temple. What a meal! All told I figure old Doc spent around $400.00 in 1960 dollars. And I don't want to know what my mother did to make him forget that he spent it on two little girls under ten years old.

Chris and I were certainly happy with our beautiful designer dresses and our fancy shoes; the only problem, of course, was that we *still* didn't have any proper clothes or shoes to wear to school.

⁓

Daddy and Slugger were very happy to see me. Although I hadn't talked to Dad on the phone all summer I felt like I'd been missed. How strange it is to read that last sentence back to myself. My father didn't call me; his daughter, his "FBI", all summer, yet I felt loved and missed and held in high regard. As a mother now myself, the thought of going an entire summer without calling my children is incomprehensible. Dad had sent us a few letters and a few self-addressed, stamped postcards to send back to him and we had. Now it felt like "home" to be back with him. It's interesting that after my parents divorced I never referred to either of their residences as "my house" or "my home" for the rest of my childhood. It was always "my mom's apartment" or "my dad's place." So, here I was, back at "dad's place" and happy to be there. The shades were up and things were pretty normal, if you don't count the naked pin-ups or the scent of Jean Nate wafting from the air cooler.

Junk food in all its fructose glory was still a staple at dad's house, but he had recently added some canned goods; mostly items that you could eat straight from the can without any bothersome heating up or time consuming preparation. And even if a particular item called for it to be heated, we would *still* eat it straight from the can. Needless to say, there was no "fancy" equipment in my father's kitchen, not even a toaster. If we wanted toast we fried bread in a frying pan. We both loved watermelon so we ate a lot of it when it was in season. Dad would take the melon and slice it across the middle making two equal halves; the halves then served as bowls when you turned them upright. It was brilliant. No dirty dishes. This was a passion with my father, figuring out ways to eat an entire meal while dirtying the least number of dishes possible; zero being a perfect score. For instance, if you wanted a salad you would take a head of lettuce and a bottle of dressing and hold them both over the sink and pour the dressing over the bites you wanted. No dirty dishes. Pretty clever! There was a reason for this economy with dishware: we only had three dishes, three forks, three spoons and only two knives. Why only two knives? Because dad didn't trust Chris with a knife. He was convinced she'd do damage, either to herself or him. But his aversion to ever washing a dish inspired a series of wonderful labor saving ideas. One such practice yielded three uses out of a single paper plate. First use: you put a piece of waxed paper *on* the paper plate and put your food onto the waxed paper. Second use: turn the waxed paper over and dish up your food onto the clean side. Then the third use: just go ahead and use the actual paper plate.

Another area where we got a lot of bang for the buck was my wardrobe. Besides my hundred dollar party dress, I had two skirts, a couple of tops and one pair of saddle shoes. My only option was to wear and repeat. Not "wash" and "repeat." Just "repeat."

Even though my mother's lousy housekeeping had driven him crazy, dad wasn't much better. Oh, his place *looked* better. And he thought it *was* better. True, there were no clothes strewn about, no toys left out, no overflowing trash, but in the entire four years that I lived with my dad; the place was *never* cleaned, *never* vacuumed. The yellow linoleum floors resembled shaggy mohair brown carpet. When I walked around without shoes, tufts of floor dirt, mixed with Slugger's shedding hair, stuck to my soles making my feet look like they belonged to Sasquatch. It might have bothered me, but I associated gleaming linoleum floors with Villa Cabrini, so a dull finish was fine by me. The once white sinks were gray and greasy; you could write your name in them with a sharp object. The silverware always had remnants from a past meal stuck on them. We didn't even have dish soap; we rinsed a dish with water and a sponge and we used the same one for years. I didn't know until I was an adult that they don't make black sponges.

I started fifth grade and absolutely loved it. I was still so thrilled to be in a cheery classroom with a wonderful, warm, supportive teacher, Mr. Burns, encouraging me to do my best. Is it any wonder I got straight "A's"? I loved school so much I couldn't wait to get there. Cissy and I were again in the same class and we both did well. At school, I actually started to feel that I had something to offer. I was expressing myself creatively in so many ways; I wrote plays that Cissy and I performed for the neighborhood. I wrote my own theme song for the Dodgers when they moved to L.A. in 1958. I wrote a forty page book about a gangster named "Boom Boom Schwartz" and his gun-toting moll, "Mitzi." I designed my own paper dolls. I collected lizards. I listened to music. I read voraciously. I really thrived there. If ever an elementary school teacher doubted if he or she made a difference in the lives of their young students, let me tell you that Mr. Burns, just by being a wonderful fifth grade teacher, kindled a flame of hope and creativity that got me through a very difficult time and helped me fall in love with learning.

Part of the reason I was so productive was that when my dad was on a "down" I'd have to spend a lot of time being quiet and that was perfect for my reading, my writing, and my artwork. Even when Daddy was in the middle of an especially bad "down" stretch and I couldn't be in the house at all, I could still be creative and reflective in my little "safe place" outside the apartment, sitting against the wall. Slugger would keep me company. After finishing my homework, I could amuse myself for hours staring into the clouds and watching the magical shapes, transforming the images that I saw into my own personal creations. It often seemed like a more inviting, delicious and pillowy world up there in the clouds, and wouldn't it be wonderful to just disappear and go there.

When Daddy was on one of his "ups" he was very encouraging and supportive of my artistic endeavors. Surprisingly, my mother was also good in this area. Even though she wasn't particularly interested in what was going on in my life, she was consistently supportive of the artist in me. I heard her say many times that I was quite talented and creative.

One birthday I surprised my dad with a five foot high, anatomically correct nude drawing of Betsy Palmer, an actress that he had a crush on at the time, complete with pubic hair and perky breasts. He complimented me on my work of art but said we wouldn't be able to hang it up. I was crushed. Didn't he have a veritable museum of pin-up masterpieces prominently hung on every wall? Didn't he honor the female form as if it were a gift from the gods? I had no idea why his ten year old daughter couldn't get him what he obviously wanted for his birthday. Especially when I had knocked it out of the ballpark in terms of workmanship. Trust me, Betsy Palmer's breasts never looked better! Dad said he was truly touched by my gift, but said it was "different" than when he hung the pictures on the wall. He promised that I would understand some day, and he was right.

We still drove around looking for my mother at least once a week. A few times we even followed her as she drove away from her apartment, but either we'd lose her or she'd lose us. I was glad because I didn't know what my dad would do if we ever found her with someone else. I really ached for my father on those nights. I could feel the pain that stabbed at his heart. I couldn't imagine what it was like to love someone so much, especially my mother. But I hoped that someday someone would love me that much. I never thought of it as stalking. I never once thought my father had a problem or was suffering from an obsession. I just knew she was in his every thought.

Which is not to say that he didn't occasionally date someone else; he seemed to be quite capable of compartmentalizing. There was his heart which belonged to Eve, and then there was his very active libido which could be "lent" to any number of women who were charmed by his good looks, his quick wit and his gentle spirit. During my fifth grade year he even dated one of the mothers of a student in my class. The girl, Cindy, and I became friends. We had a lot in common; her parents were divorced and she was a bit overweight, too. We would talk about how, if my father married her mother, we would be sisters, or at least half-sisters. It was a fun thought, but it didn't last. My father's liaisons never lasted more than a few months, and then he was back on the case to win my mother back.

In his good moods, we did some fun things together. We went to Dodger baseball games; we visited Corriganville, a now defunct ranch in the Simi Valley where they used to film old westerns, and sometimes Dad would take me onto the sets of different TV shows that were popular back then, like "Peter Gunn," "Wyatt Earp," "Maverick," and "Lassie." What a shock to learn that Lassie was actually played by more than one dog and that they were all males! But even more than the actual filming, I loved watching the ballet of the crew at work; the carpenters, the prop guys, the make-up artists, the wardrobe people, the grips and electricians all doing their part to put on a show. It was magical to me and whenever I watched TV at home, I tried to imagine all those different crew members doing their part to make it all happen.

Some nights my dad, Slugger and I would go to the drive-in movies. We'd wear our Dodger caps and pack about eight bologna sandwiches and a thermos of pink lemonade for the three of us. Slugger would sit in the middle of the front seat and my dad would put his arm around him. I think Slugger really did think he was a human member of the family. Why wouldn't he? Sometimes I would share a sandwich with Slugger; he'd take a bite then I'd take a bite. It never occurred to me that it was gross or unsanitary. And it sure didn't bother my father; he just didn't trust Slugger to be a fair sharer.

One night at the drive-in, as the intermission started, my dad went to the snack bar to get some candy for us all. While he was gone the song "All the Way" started to play over the drive-in speakers and I began to panic. All I could think of was how sad my poor father would be when he heard that song. I'd seen him fall apart after only a few notes of the melody. I knew he would need me to comfort him, so I got Slugger out of the Cadillac and we hurried past the parked cars to the snack bar. At the same time, my dad had heard the song while he was in line buying candy. He got out of line and rushed back to the car as fast as he could, knowing that I would be worried about him. Meanwhile, I had reached the snack bar but I couldn't find him anywhere. Slugger and I dashed back to the car searching frantically along other aisles of cars, tears streaming down my face while "All the Way" blared out of all the car speakers. My dad wandered through the maze of cars, weaving in and out, calling my name. Back and forth we went as the song continued to play. Finally, I spotted him and at the same time he saw me. Time seemed to stand still and then I ran into his arms, both of us crying. We must have hugged for five minutes. I never felt so important to anybody in my whole life. What a wonderful thing to feel needed like that.

I still went to my mother's place on some weekends but I didn't like going there, and I'm quite sure the feeling was mutual. Even though my dad's behavior was erratic, at least he was home most of the time. My mother was almost never there. And maybe dad only had junk food in the house, but at least there was food. My mom's cupboards consisted of powdered eggs, powdered milk, and peanut butter. That was about it, unless you counted the dozens of half finished containers of Chinese take-out strewn about the apartment. For a woman who spent her twenties in the company of some of the richest and most successful people in Hollywood, she had absolutely no sense when it came to money. She was always broke. She had a job, but whatever she was doing with her paycheck, she wasn't paying bills with it. Besides being late with the rent every month and not having food in the house, there were many times when she hadn't made a car payment and had to park her car around the block to keep it from being repossessed. Then, somehow, things would magically be okay for a while. When this happened I would get my hopes up that she had somehow mended her ways and that we could relax a little. But then she'd be right back in check-bouncing mode and the creditors would be calling again. Reflecting on it now, I'm sure her boyfriend of the minute was temporarily bailing her out of a jam. And when he left, so did the extra money.

Most of the time, when I spent a weekend with mom and Chris, mom would go out Friday night on a date and that's the last we would see of her until sometime Sunday afternoon. She was still a beautiful woman so dates were never a problem. But two young children were. Babysitters cost money and that was out of the question, so we would be left to fend for ourselves; after all, we were ten and eleven, what was the big deal? I never told my father that mom didn't come home. I knew it would set him to wondering where the hell she was and with whom! And no good could ever come of that.

From the time Chris moved in with mom, she got herself ready for school every morning and came home to an empty house every afternoon. Chris wasn't afraid to be alone and she was quickly becoming very savvy about getting what she needed. Just in the short time that I had been living at dad's and she lived with mom, Chris had developed a brittle exterior. Even though I was the older sister, she was way ahead of me in a lot of ways. She had become an expert liar and a pretty good thief. When mom forgot to leave money (which was always) Chris knew how to panhandle enough change to buy us a couple of tacos at the nearby stand. I didn't even know what the word "panhandle" meant. Things had switched and I was more of the learner and Chris was becoming the teacher. She was the one who instructed me in how to look cool when holding and smoking a cigarette.

Roller skating was a popular pastime in those days and I was the one who taught Chris to skate. One day when we were skating together I fell and hurt my arm. It was badly bruised and swollen, it looked like a big eggplant and it hurt like hell. When mom got home I told her how badly it hurt, but she didn't care much for bel-lyachers and she certainly didn't "kiss it and make it better." It also didn't *get* better! When I got back to dad's he took me to a doctor. Sure enough, my arm was broken in two places and they immedi-ately put my arm into a cast. I couldn't wait to tell Chris so she'd tell mom and then she'd feel bad.

Mom didn't feel bad.

Over the next year Chris toughened up even more. Gone were the wistful looks of a young girl looking for love in all the right places, but not finding it. I could see that she was starting to give up on making any connection with dad, and her relationship with mom was one battle after another. So who could blame her if she set out to make a new family from the other latchkey kids who hung out in the local park? It's not as if mom was keeping tabs on her.

Chris was only ten, but she had the "street smarts" of some-one much older. If this were a movie about Dickensian London in the nineteenth century, Chris would be cast as one of the lov-able street orphans who scrape together a life until being discov-ered by the kindly old, rich couple who take her under their wing and introduce her to a wonderful life of love and nurturing. Well, Chris was living out the first part. She knew every trick in the book for getting what she needed to survive on the streets. The "What's Wrong With This Picture" element of all this was the fact that the "streets" in question were in the San Fernando Valley, a relatively upscale "bedroom community" of Los Angeles, not an economi-cally deprived inner city ghetto where kids didn't always have the parental guidance, or even the parents, to watch over them and keep them out of the kind of trouble Chris was running into.

Her fights with mom were becoming shouting matches and I was shocked. I'd never talked back to either of my parents. It scared me to death when either of them was angry with me, and my mother had always been such a force of nature that she could silence anyone, young and old alike, with a few well-chosen words and one of her viper-tongued threats. And now here was my ten year old sister going toe to toe with her.

All of this was new and very strange to me. My relationship with my mother was really quite simple; she scared the hell out of me and I did exactly what I was told. I thought anything less was suicide. But Chris had turned some kind of corner and now all she had to do was walk into the room and I could feel the tension between these two warriors.

My sister started doing things like making long distance calls to complete strangers and talking for hours. How much of this was anger and how much was a sad attempt to reach out to someone, anyone who would listen to her talk for more than thirty seconds, is anybody's guess. Some of the phone bills were in the hundreds of dollars --- and that's back in the 1960s. Mom thought she solved the problem by getting a lock on the phone. We had dial phones back then and you could buy a contraption – it was the size of a lemon --- that locked the dial in place so you couldn't call out. My sister figured out a way around it; she would tap the buttons that gave a dial tone ten times in a row which would cause an operator to come on the line and ask if you needed help making a call. Chris could then give the operator the number and she could make the call --- to Hawaii! Very smart, but my mom was smarter – or so she thought. Mom unscrewed the bottom part of the handle where the speaker was housed and took it to work with her. That didn't stop Chris, she just marched right up the street to the liquor store and stole the same part from the pay-phone, screwed it into mom's phone, and she was right back in business.

Chris may have been smart but mom was smarter, and when she got her next phone bill and figured out what was happening she just started locking the door to the apartment when she left for work. That way, Chris (and I) couldn't get into the apartment at all until she came home. And sometimes mom didn't come home at all. I remember the first night Chris and I were locked out. What would we do? Chris just shrugged and took me with her to the park where she panhandled some change so we could buy something to eat. Then we made our way back to the apartment and Chris led me around back to the carport where she tore up some cardboard boxes and laid them out on the concrete floor. I remember getting the strange feeling that this was not the first time she had done this. "I don't want to sleep here," I whined. "You got a better idea?" said Chris, nothing but cool confidence in her young voice. "But I'm scared; it's dark and cold out here," I whined again. But after a minute or two I laid down beside my sister. She showed me how to curl up my jacket and use it as a pillow, and then she broke the overhead light bulb so it wouldn't keep us awake. As I tried to relax, it was my little sister who lovingly stroked my hair until I could fall asleep that night.

CHAPTER 11

———— ᧞ ————

AGES TEN AND eleven are not usually years in which we reach a crossroads. Ten and eleven should be childhood years, safe years, years made up of content, not context. But when I look back on these years, Chris and I were indeed at a crossroads and I can see how and why we began to take different paths. For all the pain, and all the broken promises, and all the neglect that Chris and I had experienced in our short lives, as long as my spirit remained unbroken -- damaged certainly, tested for sure, but not broken -- then I could still find the humor in our situation. A case in point; my sister, who rarely found anything funny about our situation, had gone to great lengths to teach me how to shoplift. On the days when mom left no money, and panhandling wasn't cutting it, then it was steal or starve. One time we went to the little neighborhood market near us where she told me I had to steal some food too, or she wouldn't share hers with me. She directed me to walk in and wander around the store until I saw her enter. She would then ask the clerk a question to distract him, and that's when I should make my move, grab something and shove it in my pants. "But don't walk right out after that," she said, "it looks suspicious." She said that I should walk up and down the aisles for a while and then pay for a pack of gum and casually saunter out. Chris would swipe something while I was paying and we'd meet up around the block. I had never shoplifted anything and I was incredibly nervous walking the aisles of the market. I couldn't make up my mind and then I saw Chris walk in while I was in the freezer section. I looked around frantically and grabbed a half gallon of ice cream in a rectangle carton, forced it into the front of my pants, pulled my jacket shut and buttoned it. Then, as instructed, I started to stroll around and look innocent as Chris asked the cashier a question to distract him. Everything was working according to plan except that the cold of the ice cream was turning my stomach numb and making me shiver. Whatever question Chris had asked the cashier, his answer was taking longer than I expected and I could feel the ice cream box collapse and a chunk of ice cream started to melt and make its way down my leg. By the time I "casually" sauntered up to the counter I was so nervous that I forgot I was supposed to buy something. After a long moment of silent panic I finally grabbed a pack of chewing gum and placed a quarter on the counter. As the cashier made change, the melting ice cream began to tickle and I started to shift from one foot to the other. "Do you need to use the rest room, young lady?" the cashier asked helpfully. "No, thank you" came my strained reply. And, with that, I grabbed the change and waddled out of the store. I kept a slow pace for the next block where Chris and I were supposed to meet. By now the cardboard container had flattened and the ice cream was running all over my feet, leaving Chocolate Mint footprints in my wake. When Chris caught up with me she was not amused; this was our dinner after all. But I started laughing and just couldn't stop. I had seen enough episodes of I Love Lucy to know that this is the stuff of comedy. Chris couldn't believe that, of all the things that I could have swiped from the market, I picked a gallon of frozen ice cream to shove down my pants! And how were we supposed to eat this ice cream, melted or not, when we didn't have any utensils? Well, thank God she had lifted some decent salami and cheese. At least *somebody* knew how to act the proper thief. The two of us ended up laughing until we cried. When I look back on that moment, I think about what might have been if both of us had just run away together that afternoon and kept each other laughing for the next ten years.

One Friday night when mom didn't come home it was pouring rain. There was no way I wanted to sleep in the carport. Chris begged me not to, but I called Dad anyway and he came and got us and took us to his place. As predicted, he was furious that we were left alone but even more upset and obsessed about the whereabouts of Eve. It was the first time Chris had ever stayed at dad's place and, because it was still raining the next day, we had to stay inside. One room was crowded for two people, but for three --- and for that third person to be my sister, I thought my father would jump out of his skin. Everything Chris did annoyed him. It was so tense I almost wished we'd stayed in the carport. I made a mental note to bring along some playing cards and books the next time I visited Mom's and put them up in the storage locker in case we were stuck there again.

The next day my mother showed up at dad's accompanied by a policeman. She claimed that my father had kidnapped us. My father told the officer that she had left us alone and outside in the rain. She denied it and asked us to tell the policeman if that was true. Chris took the lead and said it wasn't true. Remember, Chris had to live with this woman. There was no upside to pissing her off. I agreed with Chris that we hadn't been left alone even though I knew my dad would be mad at me. The policeman just chalked it up to a divorced couple using the kids in an argument and chose not to make a big deal out of it and went on his way. Chris left with mom and I stayed with dad. I know she caught hell for that one --- and so did I.

─̶

Soon it was summer again; the time when dad needed some time alone. I begged and pleaded to stay with him but it got me nowhere. When I arrived at mom's I found out that Chris had been sent to live in Texas with my mother's sister, Margaret, and her family. My mother had never had a nice word to say about Margaret, she'd only complained about what a bitch she was, and then she sends my sister off to live with her. I don't know why I was surprised;

she'd done the same thing when she'd sent Chris and me to Villa Cabrini.

Mom hadn't talked to her sister since our visit to Texas a few years before. But Chris had become a real rebel and mom couldn't handle her anymore. So it was just me at mom's apartment. I tried to stay out of her way and not complain about all the time that she spent away, but it was hard. I was used to my dad being around. At least she didn't lock me out when she went to work; I guess her run-in with the police put her on some notice and I 'know she trusted me more than Chris. One night as she was getting ready to go out on a date and leave me alone again I couldn't help myself and I started to cry.

"Please don't go, Mommy," I begged.

"*Pleeeease* don't go, Mommy," she mocked me in a whiny voice. If I didn't know before, I certainly got the message that night. Crying and complaining will get you absolutely nowhere. There *is* no soft spot in this woman that might weaken at the sight of her eleven year old daughter tearfully pleading with her to stay in for one night.

A few days after that, she announced a new summer plan for me. This time she didn't promise horses or a pool. This time it was six weeks in Hesperia, California, a dry, desert town that made Blythe seem like a sparkling oasis. There was nothing to do and another completely strange family to do it with. It was yet another blisteringly hot place with temperatures over 110 in the shade – and good luck finding any shade. And there was no relief from the bone numbing boredom. There was no farm, no cows, no swimming hole. Just gray houses with gravel roofs scattered randomly over stretches of bare rocks and desert. The only good news was that the family had a daughter. Her name was Lydia and she was a few years older than me, but she was nice enough. We played cards and pick-up sticks, we watched TV. I watched lots of Jack Benny and George Burns, but even they couldn't fix an incredibly lonely summer. Lydia had lots of other friends and so most of the time I was alone. Once again, I filled my summer with reading and drawing. And, of course, my old fallback: I cried a lot.

_⌒6_

When I got back to dad's there were still a few weeks before school started. To stay out of his way I spent the rest of the summer at the North Hollywood public pool. Every day, Cissy and I would ride our bikes and be there when it opened and leave when it closed. We'd swim so hard our lungs would ache just to breathe. After the relentless heat of my summer in Hesperia, the cool water was an elixir for my body as well as my soul. That pool became my friend. No bad moods to worry about, no broken promises. Every day it was there, welcoming me. To this day I can feel a sense of calm and contentment whenever I'm able to spend time in a pool.

The side benefit to my activities schedule that summer was that I actually looked and felt clean all the time for the first time in my life. Dad knew a good deal when he saw one and he never once asked me to bathe or shower the rest of the summer.

Where was Chris? I knew she was at our Aunt Margaret's, but I didn't know much else. There were no calls, no letters. No matter that we weren't even teenagers yet, we had some war stories and I missed her. Or at least that was part of the truth; the other part was that I enjoyed the relative peace and quiet that prevailed when she was away. Even back then I felt guilty for the way I felt. But it was true. I had learned how to "work" my family system, while Chris had chosen to "buck" that system. And those choices had taken us in different directions. Had we been together we might have taught each other things, shared our thoughts and strategies. But nobody ever said a word about bringing her home so we could live together.

Soon I was back in school and starting sixth grade. Chris didn't come back from Texas after the summer ended; she stayed and went to school in Houston. Margaret told mom that she and her husband, Doug, were making progress with Chris, shaping her up and teaching her some manners. Margaret thought that sending Chris back right then would ruin all their hard work. Much to no one's surprise, Eve didn't put up a fight.

But Chris hated it there. She later described Margaret and Doug as tough, humorless tyrants, and their kids, Terry and Donnie, as absolutely terrified of them. Neither Chris nor I had ever been disciplined or punished before. That would imply hands-on, adult parenting and that particular influence had not entered our lives as yet. Margaret had a lot of rules to follow but not a lot of love. Chris was used to the lack of love part, but the rules part was new to her and she didn't take to it. The harder they pushed, the harder Chris pushed back. And Chris was used to pushing back against the indomitable Eve Whitney, so she was an Olympian. The result of all this head-butting, of course, was that Chris continued to grow harder and tougher and more and more cynical.

My world was significantly more pleasant. I had made lots of friends at school and at the pool, and I still had Cissy as my very best friend. We would walk to school together, eat lunch together, and a few days a week we'd stop at Bob's Big Boy in North Hollywood on our way home and get a "Big Boy" burger and onion rings. No wonder we were filling out. Once we got home we'd call each other from across the street and talk for an hour and then I might end up going over to her house, doing my homework, and playing until she had to eat dinner.

I was in sixth grade now and one of our first classroom assignments was to share family vacation stories. Lots of kids had entertaining adventures to recount; summer camp, Disneyland, New York, a few had even gone to Europe. I told about my stay in Hesperia, but when my epic was greeted with bland stares, I quickly added a pool and horses and (I'm pretty sure) a lost tribe of Indians who lived nearby and took me in as one of their own for several weeks. Eleven years old and I was already padding my resume.

I remember that when I got to Dad's that day I asked him how come we never took a real vacation. He was happy to share his thinking on the subject. "Go up to anyone you see on the street and ask them where they're from," he said confidently. "I bet you dollars to donuts that they're all, every single one of them, from somewhere else." Very satisfied with himself, he continued. "Now, what does that tell you?"

"I don't know," I replied.

"It tells you that everyone is coming *here,* to Los Angeles. So you see, there really is no reason to go anywhere else!"

Darned if that didn't make sense -- until I was an adult anyway.

But other than having to make up exciting vacation stories, school was going very well. I wrote an essay that made the local papers. And the best thing of all was that I had the most wonderful teacher. His name was Mr. Sherins, and if Mr. Burns, my fifth grade teacher, had been great, Mr. Sherins was super-great. He was an older man but full of enthusiasm for kids and learning. When I did well in school it made me feel absolutely terrific. And on those occasions that I was actually picked out of the class as exceptional, well, I was over the moon. These were moments that gave me a glimmer of confidence that I might actually excel at something, be somebody and fit in somewhere in a world that seemed so different than the one I lived in most days. So it was a wonderful moment when Mr. Sherins decided to include me among a dozen or so of his best students who would be participating in a special program. The idea was to learn at our own speed with no grade restrictions. We could do college level work if we were capable. He wanted us to go as far as we were able to go scholastically. We had to be at school at 8:00 in the morning. That gave us an hour before school officially started. Mr. Sherins made it so fun that none of us could wait to get there. With his encouragement and guidance we followed the stock market, discussed politics, explored the arts. Nothing was discouraged. It was very exciting. I graduated sixth grade with straight "A's".

At home, my dad's moods were still extreme but I was handling it pretty well, by which I mean I was perfecting the art of super-vigilance. I learned to recognize the subtle signs of an impending mood swing and then I would act in a way that might lengthen his good periods and shorten the bad ones. I would encourage him to spend time at the driving range; hitting golf balls always seemed to calm him. And I would try different ways to get him to write, but I was less successful in that endeavor.

If it was the first day of a crash for my dad, then I was pretty safe staying in the house and simply being quiet. I could watch TV with the volume way down, and turn on a light to do my homework. But if the bear was close to coming out of hibernation, then Daddy could be hypersensitive to noise and light. On those days it was easier to stay outside. One day after school I had to use the bath-room really badly. As I approached the house I could see that the blinds were still down. I opened the door and could make out my dad stirring on the couch. He lifted his head and started swearing and screamed for me to "shut the goddamn door!" I quickly closed the door and ran across the street to Cissy's house, but no one was home. I dashed back to dad's in a panic. I didn't know what to do; I had to pee so badly. I ran to the back of the yard, pulled down my pants and tinkled right where Slugger would go. Then I sat against the wall and waited until it was dark to go inside.

One day I was getting dressed when my dad announced, "You're not going to school today, you're smart enough." He handed me my Dodgers cap and we were off to the home team's season opener. This happened a lot with dad. Actually, neither of my parents were that interested in how I did at school. My mother had about as much respect for school as she had for anything else, which is to say none. And my father always thought his talents had blossomed *in spite of* school, not because of it. But for me, school was a place of nurturing, a place where I felt special.

That day at the Dodgers game was fantastic. Just the two of us, my dad and me, loving the crowd, loving the Dodger Dogs and carrying on a running commentary on the relative attributes of the "stacked" women in the crowd. On those days I think I was more like a son to my dad, but I had no complaints. And it didn't hurt that I really did love baseball. I played in the street with the neighborhood kids and I was pretty good. "Casey at the Bat" the kids called me and even the boys were impressed that I could hit the ball "real solid."

CHAPTER 12

MY FATHER WAS a remarkably talented and creative man. Before things started to fall apart, he wrote more than three hundred songs, most of them published and recorded. He authored over a hundred scripts for television shows. And all this happened by the time he was forty. He had published his first prose at twelve, sold his first script for radio when he was fourteen. Now it was thirty-five years later and he had arrived at a place that has sent legions of notable writers to the edge. He had hit a horrible dry spell. True, the business had changed and performers like Spike Jones and Abbot & Costello were out of favor, but many writers had made the difficult transition to the "new Hollywood." My father wasn't one of them. And the domino effect was disastrous; he couldn't find work, Eve lost patience, Eddie grew depressed and took drugs, Eve left. Eddie became despondent and took more drugs.

Making matters worse, dad's obsession with my mother consumed most of his thoughts and energy. He used up a fair amount of inventiveness coming up with new and bizarre ways to get into her apartment and snoop around while she was at work. But even in this, my father had a singular style all his own. More than once he broke into her place and stole, of all things, her diaphragm, a popular birth control device back then. On several occasions he even nailed it to her front door. Diaphragms were only available with a prescription so my mother had to keep going back to the pharmacy to order a new one. After about the fourth or fifth time she had refilled the prescription, the weary pharmacist, thinking she wasn't all that bright, took her aside and told her, "You know, Miss Whitney, these *are* re-usable."

After that my mother got a restraining order on my dad. Of course, it didn't stop him. He just got more creative and more devious. But, much to his puzzlement and chagrin, my mother always, always, *always* knew when he'd been there.

Tired of getting caught at his unauthorized sleuthing, Daddy finally came up with what he thought was a foolproof plan: he went into Eve's place as usual, but now he was armed with a Polaroid camera. That way he could take numerous photographs of the mess just exactly the way it was. He even photographed her cluttered drawers before he went through them. Sometimes he'd find something revealing: a name, a phone number, an address, some clue to my mother's private life that he could follow up on later. Before leaving, he consulted all the photos and put everything back just as it looked in the pictures, getting it perfect in its particular disarray. Didn't matter. She still knew he'd been there. Every. Single. Time. And she would be furious. He could not for the life of him figure out how the hell she knew. It bugged him for years. When I was much older and I knew that the idea of Eddie snooping around her house was no longer a threat, I asked my mother how she'd always known. And she told me her secret: "Simple," she said, with her best imitation of a sly smile, "The son of a bitch always left the toilet seat up."

Feeling like he could no longer risk breaking into Eve's place, Daddy enlisted me in a new treachery. My job was to sneak my mom's mail out of the apartment and give it to him. He would then steam it open, read through it, and reseal it, whereupon I would smuggle it back the next time I was there. I hated doing it but there was no saying "no" to him. Not for me, anyway.

Now that he had a loyal accomplice, he put me to work on even more diabolical skullduggery. He was an early fan of surveillance equipment and, even though we didn't have much money, he had somehow been able to get his hands on a small (for the times) tape recorder. Per his detailed instructions, I was to hide the recorder behind a chair in the living room. It was near the telephone and his plan was to learn something by listening to her side of whatever conversations she might have. It was incredibly nerve racking for me. I had seen my mother's violent outbursts and I wanted no part of them raining down on me. My old companion, the "air-conditioning hum" of anxiety that kept me unwelcome company while I was at Villa Cabrini, was working overtime. I had to be able to anticipate when my mother was going to make a call or receive one, and then turn on the recorder without her noticing. If I missed a window of opportunity to turn the recorder on or off at the appropriate time, the tape could run out. If I was too conspicuous, I'd be caught and god knows what fresh hell would befall me then. After a call I had to sneak back in and turn off the machine without looking suspicious. And this went on every day, three or four times a day, while I was at my mother's apartment.

One day when I opened the front door I was greeted by my mother standing in the living room holding the tape recorder. I was petrified. I literally couldn't catch my breath as I waited to see her first move.

"I know what you've been doing," she said.

I shook with fear. I knew I was going to get hit, I just didn't know where or how hard.

But my mother did something that she has rarely done in all the years of our lives. She surprised me. Instead of blasting me to Kingdom Come, she said the following words in a calm, clear voice; "I'm not blaming you. This isn't your fault. Your father has absolutely no business asking you to do his dirty work. Just see that it stops." And she walked out of the room.

I was so relieved that I almost passed out. How could it be that I wasn't in trouble? How could that possibly be? Whatever the explanation, I had received a Governor's reprieve and I told my dad that the jig was up. I had been caught and we couldn't spy on her anymore. In a way I was glad. I wasn't sure how much more anxiety I could bear before cracking.

He didn't ask me to hide the tape recorder anymore, but he still grilled me after every weekend visit with mom. Did my mother have a boyfriend over? Did he stay? What was his name? What did he do? And on and on and on. I quickly learned that it was easier to lie and tell him that it was just mom and me. I don't think he believed me.

CHAPTER 13

⸺ ❧ ⸺

WE STILL DROVE around on some nights, Daddy and I, looking for my mother. We'd always start at her place and see if her car was there. Then we would hit Ventura Boulevard, cruising in and out of restaurant parking lots; the Pump Room, Tail o' the Cock, Monty's Steak House, different motels. Just what exactly an eleven year old girl was supposed to think as she searched for her mother at various motels along Ventura Boulevard I'm not exactly sure. Usually we'd end up parked by a house and my dad would just sit there, sometimes he'd take notes. We'd wait, often for hours. One night we parked down the street from an ultra-modern glass house on stilts with a swimming pool up on Coldwater Canyon that over-looked the city. I knew the house. Chris and I had been there one night with Mom. It belonged to a boyfriend of hers named Nathan. He was the only boyfriend we'd ever met that we liked or who was even the least bit nice to us. Nathan was easy to like, he knew all the words to the Lewis Carroll Jabberwocky poem, and he took the time to recite it for us; "Twas brillig, and the slithy toves did gyre and gimble in the wabe..." It's a fond memory to this day.

It had been the middle of winter when Chris and I were at Nathan's house and, by California standards, it was freezing. It was probably about 45 degrees outside and it was nighttime, but Chris and I still wanted to go swimming in his pool. We didn't have bathing suits but Mom said it was okay. Nathan loaned us a couple of his T-shirts and we jumped right in. We turned blue and our teeth were chattering so hard I thought they'd crack -- but we were thrilled and we didn't get out of that water for hours.

But sitting out front of the house with Dad, his eyes peeled for Eve, I decided not to tell him that I knew the house; instead I crawled in the back and tried to go to sleep.

I was awakened later by the sound of my dad pounding on the steering wheel, enraged. I sat up to see that the garage door was now open and my mother's car was parked there. The car was running and Nathan was leaning into the driver's side and kissing her. She backed out of the driveway, blew him a kiss and started down the canyon. My dad couldn't stop cursing and promising to kill the goddamn whore if it was the last thing he did.

But he didn't kill her. He just cried all the way home. And then he went into a deep depression that lasted for days.

I've mentioned that my father's obsession with my mother never stopped him from looking, appreciating, flirting, and occasionally going out with other women. After a while I began to actively encourage this because I wanted him to move on with his life and be happy again. Maybe a girlfriend or wife would keep him from falling into his "down" periods. When we were out in the world I would even point out a pretty girl for him to enjoy. We had lots of silly double talk between us to disguise the stunning inappropriateness of our discussions. For instance, our code for an attractive girl became, "Well, helloooooo, Krelden." That meant one of us had spotted a real looker. If she ignored him, he would look at me and say, "I guess that's not her name."

When my dad was cleaned up and feeling good, he would have wicked fun charming the ladies and he was spectacularly good at it. He consistently got away with stuff that would have fallen flat with anyone else. Way before there were real car phones, my dad had an old phone receiver with a length of spiral cord that he kept in his convertible Caddie. When he would see a pretty girl driving, we would pull up next to her at a stoplight and he would hold the phone out to her. "It's for you," he would call out. Usually she laughed and smiled. If she didn't have a sense of humor, she might look confused and ask, "Who is it?" When that happened, we'd know that she didn't get the joke, no matter how pretty she was. But, more often than not, Daddy would charm a smile out of the woman. And then, of course, a couple of weeks later, I might have to hear, in appallingly "not-suitable-for-children" detail, how appreciative the lucky lady had been.

But the truth was, we were kidding ourselves with all this "grazing"; there was only one woman in the world for my dad, and that was Eve. Even back then I was never sure how my mother had ever become the be-all woman of his dreams, there were sure plenty of things that he didn't like about her: She was a slob, a bitch, a procrastinator, a lousy cook, a liar, she didn't pay bills and she never, *ever* apologized, to anyone, for anything. But she had two qualities that overshadowed all of that; she made him laugh, and she was always his biggest fan. No matter how furious she was with him, how disgusted, how outraged by his near psychotic behavior, Eve always thought Eddie was the most talented writer in the world. No matter how many times she protested that Eddie meant nothing to her, she couldn't disguise the fact that she knew every word of every lyric of every song he had ever written. And story lines from scripts he had forgotten years ago, Eve would remember like she had seen them just yesterday. Somehow, in spite of all the pain, and all the disappointment, she "got" him, and Eddie knew it. I remember one of the most romantic things my father ever said about my mother was: "She was the only woman I ever wanted to kiss with my eyes open."

Over the years I had met many of my mother's boyfriends. She seemed to trust me not to tell my dad about any of them -- and I didn't. Most of them weren't around long and that was fine with me. I guess they must have known that they couldn't get to Eve through me because few of them ever bothered trying to win me over. They were just another voice on the other side of the bedroom wall.

And then she met Joe, an ex-football player and a big galoot of a guy. He was maybe six foot two and solid. Joe owned a restaurant/

bar where my mother used to spend a lot of her time. He was one
of those guys whose only way of relating to kids was to tease them
mercilessly. And, of course, he thought he was being hilariously
funny. P.S., he wasn't funny. Joe, according to my mother, was a
keeper. Of all the guys that had to stick around, why this one?
People didn't talk about "energies" back then, but this guy had
a bad energy. If I had been a secure kid with no fear of deadly
reprisals I would have said something. I would have at least let my
mother know that I didn't like him. And if my mother had given
a damn about how I felt about anything, she might have seen my
discomfort and taken that into account when she decided to make
Joe a "keeper."

That didn't happen.

—6

As the holidays drew near that year, my dad and I put up a little
Christmas tree in a corner of the room. As always, Dad made a
Jewish star out of aluminum foil for the top. Mom hadn't done
much in the way of holidays when we were all together. Now with
Chris in Texas and me with Dad, she didn't do anything.

I got up my nerve one day and approached my mother, "I don't
want any presents for Christmas," I said, "All I want is for you and
Daddy to take me to dinner – together." One night. One dinner.
A tough one even for Eve to refuse. I thought my dad would be
ecstatic but the news sent him into a panic. He hadn't seen her
up close in almost four years. The drugs had made him overweight and mushy and, in his opinion, not prepared for a viewing.
Luckily he moved past fear and into excitement pretty quickly. He
cut way back on candy and dropped a few pounds over the next
few weeks.

For our big Christmas Eve dinner, I wore the party dress from
Saks that mom's long discarded boyfriend, Doc, had bought. It was
about two sizes too small but it would have to do. Unfortunately

the shoes no longer fit and I had to pair the beautiful dress with scratched up saddle shoes.

"You look gorgeous," he said. "Just like me."

"Except for the mustache," I replied.

"When did you shave?" my dad joked.

I hadn't seen my dad this spruced up in a very long time. He looked so handsome; he was even wearing a sport jacket and tie. Why couldn't mom fall back in love with him? Was that so much to ask? I certainly wasn't the first kid from a broken home with fantasies of putting things back together. But I might have been the only one who actually believed I could do it with one Christmas dinner.

It was December but Daddy insisted on keeping the top down on the Cadillac. I told him I was freezing.

"But, sweetie, we look better with the top down," he replied.

Who could argue with that?

My mother had picked The Pump Room on Ventura Boulevard for our Christmas dinner. I had been there a few times when my parents were together and it was still a wonderfully warm and cozy restaurant, especially during the holiday season when it was decorated for Christmas. I remember that the staff was in the spirit, wearing red Santa Claus hats and welcoming smiles. My dad and I got there first and our booth was waiting.

"You really think she'll come?" Dad asked.

"She's got to. I didn't ask for anything else," I said. The waiter came for our order. "A scotch and a Shirley Temple," Dad said, and then added: "She'll have the same." I don't think the waiter got the joke. Or maybe he did.

Then my mother entered or, rather, she made an entrance. All eyes were on her as she crossed the room to our table. She was breathtakingly beautiful. I was filled with awe and pride. My father stood as she approached. "Eve," he said sincerely, "you take my breath away."

Eve leveled a stare at him, "Promises, promises," she said with a raised eyebrow as she sat down.

I was so overjoyed I couldn't contain myself. "I can't believe we're really all here together; the three of us, just like a family," I gushed.

"Don't push it, kid. It's just dinner," said my mother. The waiter arrived and set down our drinks and looked to Eve for her order.

"Gin and Tonic tall. Three limes. Get it right," she said.

"Yes, Miss Whitney." The nervous waiter rushed off,

My dad was almost at a loss for words. "Eve, it seems like so long since I've seen you," he said.

"I guess you're not counting the other night when you were parked outside my apartment for three hours," she said as she let Eddie light her cigarette. "Or when you followed me over Coldwater last week."

"I meant 'legally' I haven't seen you in a while," he said. Getting nervous, I picked up the menu and started to read the specials. "Look, Mom, they have your favorite, Beef Wellington." But she was annoyed with my dad already.

"And I suppose it wasn't you who put that charming bumper sticker on my car that says "Mt. Whitney -- Everybody Does!" My dad was about to protest but changed his mind. It was too good to not take credit for. "Come on, Honey, you gotta admit; that was a good one."

Eve held a hard look to Eddie for a long, tense moment and then, thank God, she smiled. "Actually... it was one of your best." I let out a sigh of relief.

It didn't last long. I happened to look towards the bar and sitting there, watching us, was my mother's hateful boyfriend, Joe. I must've had a horrified expression on my face because my mother turned to see what I was looking at. My dad was the last one to see him and his mood darkened immediately.

"What the hell is your boyfriend doing here?" he snapped at her.

"I guess you're not the only one who follows me," she said. "I'll take care of it.

"No, I'll take care of it!" Dad said. And then he stood up from the table. I screamed, "Daddy, No!" But he ignored me, pushed the table away and rushed towards the bar. For me, everything went into slow motion from that point on. My dad reached Joe at the bar. Joe stood and was about a foot taller and several biceps wider than my dad. But Daddy took a swing anyway. It was his last. Joe began to pummel my father. My mother tried to break it up but couldn't. I ran into the middle of the fight trying to protect my dad and was almost knocked to the floor. No one noticed. I got back to my feet, numb and overwhelmed, and then I walked, slowly, through the restaurant and out the front door onto Ventura Boulevard. It was drizzling and there was a group of Christmas carolers just passing by the restaurant. "Merry Christmas," a few of them offered, smiling brightly.

The night of my dreams had become my worst nightmare. As I stood there, stunned, it began to finally sink in that my mom and dad were never going to get back together. Ever. What a disaster this night was. What a childish, foolish thing I had done in hoping I could single-handedly put my family back together again over an order of Beef Wellington. I stepped off the curb and walked to the middle of the street. I laid down and closed my eyes. I wasn't consciously thinking "suicide." I wasn't consciously thinking anything. I was just overcome with sorrow, and grief, and hopelessness. Not to mention that I had just blown the one and only gift on my Christmas list.

I should've asked for a Barbie Doll.

I don't know how long I lay in the middle of Ventura Boulevard. It could've been two seconds; it could've been two minutes. Time was non-existent. What I do know is that I was scooped off the rain soaked street by a lovely blonde angel. She had seen what had happened in the restaurant. She helped me up and led me back to the safety of the sidewalk.

"This is a disgrace!" said the angel. "Your parents should be ashamed for what they've put you through; you're coming home with me." And just like that I was in a car with a complete stranger on Christmas Eve. Her name, she told me, was Lee Mays. A measure of how out of it I was, I asked her if she was related to the famous baseball player, Willie Mays. She smiled and then told me that she was a big fan of Willie Mays, but that, no, she wasn't related. The fact that Willie was black and she was white was not within my zone of reasoning at that particular moment. Miss Mays was very pretty, in her thirties, a stewardess. She shared an apartment nearby with three other "stews" and when she explained to her roommates what had happened to poor me, on Christmas Eve no less, the girls were incensed. They fussed over me and fed me. One of the girls did my hair, another put make-up on me. It was one of the most fun nights I'd ever had. Lee said it was okay with her and the girls if I stayed with them overnight but I had to call my parents and let them know that I was okay.

What I did next was insanely stupid, even back then in what was certainly a safer and more innocent time in America. I only *pretended* to call my father. I was so enjoying the attention, so enjoying the "parenting" I was getting from these four angels that I couldn't bear to let it end. I also hoped that mom and dad would be so worried about *their* daughter that maybe it would bring them close again. In my own pathetic way, I was trying to snatch victory out of the jaws of defeat. Maybe my "family Christmas dinner" idea didn't work out so well, but what if my subsequent disappearance did the trick? So I told Lee that it was okay with my parents if I stayed. In the morning I placed a real call to my dad who was, to say the least, furious with me. Later I found out that each of them thought I'd gone home with the other.

I gave him the address and soon he was there to get me. He looked awful, Joe had really pummeled him. He had two black eyes, a swollen cheek and a fat lip. Miss Mays, my new best friend, was still upset with my father for allowing me to end up in the middle of Ventura Boulevard, but Miss Mays was a very pretty girl and the power of my father's charm was such that the meeting soon turned into a "meet-cute." Dad's anger about my stunt evaporated like a bottle of Jean Nate and soon he and Miss Mays were dating. I suppose I should have seen the inconsistency in a man who just got the hell beat out of him because of his jealousy over one woman (my mother), now asking a different woman (Miss Mays) out on a date. But this was par for the course for my father.

Miss Mays lasted about a month. She actually *liked* my father and where's the angst in that?

⟋

CHAPTER 14

———— ✧ ————

THE SUMMER AFTER sixth grade was the first one that my dad didn't send me to my mother's. I was so thrilled that I repaid the favor by going to the public pool almost every day and staying there until it closed so that I wouldn't be around to get on his nerves. It turned out to be a fun, blessedly uneventful summer. I had no way of knowing that it was also the proverbial calm before the storm.

Come September Cissy and I were starting junior high school. Girls in their early teens almost always have a tough time of it, but junior high hit me like a ton of bricks. In addition to all the usual psychological changes that go along with this age (or perhaps *because* of them) I suddenly became super aware of the fact that I had no real family. My father was a guessing game; I still looked to see if the blinds were up or down as I approached his place. My mother was more AWOL than ever. And my sister had grown farther and farther apart from me. Whatever was happening in my heart, I needed a safe place to share it and realized, maybe for the first time, that I didn't have one. And if that weren't enough, I was going through an incredibly awkward time physically; All my father's "Maxwell Specials," not to mention a steady diet of Butter Brickle and m&m's had made me quite chubby. Of course "chubby" is not a word used by teen-aged girls, or boys for that matter. The word is "fat" and that's what I felt. And I had certainly learned well what "fat" meant in this world. My father had never missed a chance, when cursing my mother, to wish her fat "so nobody would love her!" So far, so incredibly insecure. My clothes, what few I had, were all wrong. I hadn't seen my mother in months so her "boyfriend du jour" couldn't try to buy my allegiance with a party dress from Saks, so I was stuck with whatever I had from a year and a half ago. Everything about me was wrong. I felt ugly. I felt poor. Instead of my beloved, caring teacher, Mr. Sherins, now I had six teachers who had too many kids to make any one of us feel special.

I could sense that my dad had no patience for all my insecurity. To make matters worse my body was maturing and I had no idea what to do about it. I didn't have anyone to talk to about personal things like getting a bra, or shaving my legs. I still had no room of my own, no privacy.

For the first time in my life I wasn't doing well in school. Even at Villa Cabrini I had done well scholastically. Now, I didn't do well at anything. I especially hated P.E., gym class. I looked like a blimp in my shorts and shirt and the other girls weren't shy about letting me know just how "different" I was. My wardrobe, or lack thereof, meant that I had to wear the same outfits over and over and over again, and the kids made fun of me. I should've been able to tell my dad some of the things that were going on but he had grown less and less patient with me as I grew older. He was still so invested in his own misery that I didn't dare complain. And even this long after Villa Cabrini, I still had the fear of being sent away if I made waves of any kind.

One of the classes that I did like was music. If I couldn't put my fears and anxieties into words, maybe I could put them into music. Everyone had to pick an instrument to learn and my first choice was the accordion. I brought it home and my father quickly urged me to choose something else, *anything* else. It seems he had very strong views when it came to the accordion and women.

"Any girl who would play the accordion," he said, "would own her own bowling ball and spit on the sidewalk."

I didn't understand what that meant and, in fact, I still don't, but I returned the accordion immediately and picked a violin instead. Strike two. The violin is a beautiful instrument and, when mastered, can produce some of the most celestial sounds ever heard.

But listening to someone *learn* to play it is not anyone's idea of a good time. Even Itzak Perlman has said as much. And, to be fair to my dad, we lived in one small room so I had nowhere to practice. I tried the bathroom, outside, in the garage. He could still hear me loud and screechingly clear. After about a month my father said to me, "I love music, I *really* love music, and I'd like to keep it that way. What will it cost me for you to stop playing that goddamn instrument of torture?" We settled on thirty-five dollars and I took a "D" in the class.

One day after school, Cissy and I were walking up our street, heading home, when her mother stopped me before I reached my house. She said that my dad wasn't feeling well and that I'd be staying at their house for a few nights. That was odd since it was a school night but I didn't protest. I wanted to go check on him first but Mrs. Raufman was adamant about me not disturbing him. I assumed this meant that Daddy was deeply into a "down" stretch and that life would be easier at the Raufman's. At least I knew I'd be eating well for the next few days; easy on the Butter Brickle, heavy on the pot roast. Cissy and I did our homework together and took turns taking baths. More than one bath or shower in any given month was a brand new experience for me and I loved it! Plus, I got to wear Cissy's clothes to school the next few days. All in all, it felt like a Club Med vacation to me. By the weekend Mrs. Raufman said I could go back across the street to see my father.

I walked in to find Daddy sobbing. Nothing new there; I figured the tears were over my mother as usual, but he said he was crying because Slugger had run away. He was inconsolable but I did my best to reassure him. Slugger had run away dozens of times, and he had always returned. One day he'd even shown up at my school, which was over a mile away. Everyone was so envious that my dog was there waiting for me. It was so "Lassie." Dad wasn't hearing anything I said. After curling up in a ball for two more days he finally told me the truth. Slugger hadn't run away; he was dead. I felt like I'd been kicked in the stomach; I couldn't believe it. Daddy said that Slugger must have tried to jump over the chain link fence but his collar had caught on one of the links and he had somehow hung himself. That's how Daddy had found him. Now it was my turn to sob uncontrollably. My true friend, my confidant, my buddy, my brother, was gone, and in such a horrible way. I would never be able to walk out the door and look at that fence without seeing where it happened. To make matters worse my father's drug paranoia, combined with his obsessive love/hate relationship with my mother, caused him to put a horrible spin on the whole tragic event.

"You realize that your mother killed Slugger," he told me. "This is all her fault." I was dumbfounded. I was certainly no defender of my mother's honor, but how on earth could she be responsible for Slugger accidentally hanging himself, on *our* fence? "If she hadn't left me, I wouldn't have moved here," he explained without a hint of irony. "And if I hadn't had to move here, Slugger wouldn't be dead." To a twelve year old, it had a certain logic to it. And, given the choice between admitting that my father was crazy, and having one more thing for which to blame my absentee mother, I welcomed his tortured logic and held my mother accountable for years.

⁓𝒮

Somehow, I made it through the seventh grade and it was summer again. My dad was still having breakdowns, sometimes over my mom, sometimes over Slugger, sometimes over God knows what. Whatever fantasies I had about "curing" my father of his horrible moods by being the bestest, cutest, funniest little girl in the world were beginning to fray a little around the edges. In addition, I was going through my own drama; my body was still maturing and it scared the hell out of me. I got my period and I was completely freaked out. I was too frightened and embarrassed to tell my father. I hadn't seen or spoken to my mother in quite a while.

I was too mortified to go to our local market and buy sanitary napkins so I just wadded up a bunch of toilet paper and stuffed them in my underwear. I figured that maybe I could talk to Mrs. Raufman across the street about it. But before I got up my courage to do that, something else happened.

I had gone to the library with Cissy and come home with an armload of new books. When I walked in, all my belongings were in boxes, sitting at the front door.

"I'm sorry," my dad said. "You can't stay here anymore. You're getting too old. You need your own room. You need a mother." Did he think that sending me back to mine would help? It didn't matter. That was that. My dad put my things in the car and drove me to my mother's. I cried the whole way. I kept asking what I did wrong and promised I'd change if he'd give me another chance. He said it wasn't my fault and that it was just time for me to go.

My father had obviously talked to my mother because when I got to her place she was expecting me. My sister was there, too; she had been back from Texas for a week. Margaret had told my mom she couldn't handle Chris anymore so she'd been kicked out, too. It had been over a year and a half since we'd last seen each other. I wanted to rush into her arms and take some comfort in that bond. I wanted her to rush into *my* arms so that I would feel needed, like I had felt needed by my father until a few short hours ago. But we were like strangers. I almost didn't recognize her, she had dyed her blond hair black and she was wearing heavy, black eye make-up. She was a few months shy of twelve and I was about to turn thirteen but Chris looked several years older. She had already staked out her territory in mom's small apartment. She let me know that I would be sharing *her* room and not the other way around.

The world, which hadn't exactly been an orderly piece of work in the first place, was now officially upside down.

᠊ᡒ

105

Mom's apartment was as much of a shit hole as ever. Predictably, she didn't even stay home my first night back. But things were different now, especially with Chris. As soon as mom left the house, Chris got dressed to leave. I tried to exert some authority. "Where the hell do you think you're going?" I demanded. "Out," she said. I was shocked by the certainty in her voice. Whatever had happened in Texas, Chris now had a steely-eyed resolve that was totally new to me, and not a little intimidating. I gave it one more shot. "You're eleven years old; you can't just go out at night by yourself," I told her, my own voice shaking with nerves. She came nose to nose with me. "Try and stop me," she said. And that was that.

Until that moment, I hadn't realized that she had actually gotten bigger than me; in size, in strength, in raw energy. I didn't succeed in stopping her and she went out for the rest of the night. I tried to straighten up the apartment but I was too overwhelmed, by the job as well as the situation. I had awakened that morning in my dad's place and I would be going to bed that same night in my mother's apartment. Everything was different and I had had absolutely no warning. But what I did extremely well was to make the best of a situation and that's what I tried desperately to do now. I wanted to feel grateful that, after almost four years at Dad's, I finally had a real bed and a real bedroom. But all I *really* wanted was to go back to the totally unpredictable, on again-off again, sometimes tender, sometimes terrifying affections of my father. That's how welcome I felt at my mother's apartment.

We were out of school for the summer and I was scared to death that mom was going to come up with one of her plans to send us to some new stranger's house in yet another godforsaken hellhole, but that didn't happen. She felt we were plenty old enough to take care of ourselves, meaning we were old enough to stay the hell out of her hair. Chris was pretty bad at doing that, so she and mom battled hourly. The result being that mom resorted to her old habit of locking us out of the apartment.

Mom was still working as a bookkeeper and left the apartment by eight in the morning (on those nights she had bothered to sleep at home). If Chris and I were up and dressed, she would drop us off at North Hollywood Park for the day. The first few times we went to the park, I went directly to the public pool and swam all day. It's how I had spent the previous summer, staying out my other parent's hair, and I thought Chris would love it as well. But Chris was way too cool for the pool. Instead she made a bee line for the park that bordered the pool and spent her days with a rough bunch of kids who hung out there. The pool had a chain link fence around it so I could see what was going on in the park. There was Chris, drinking beer and smoking with a group of teenaged kids ranging in age from about fifteen to nineteen years old. She was eleven. I felt envious watching my kid sister interact so confidently with the older kids. The way she held herself. So tough. So fearless.

And just like that I traded in the pool for a pack of Marlboros.

I asked Chris if I could hang with her and her friends and she said it would be okay. She had told them that she was fourteen and now she explained that I was her fifteen year old sister. Always good to start off with a lie.

I was very shy at first. The size of the group varied but usually there were about ten kids, most of them boys, and some of them as old as eighteen and nineteen. A few of them had tattoos, rode motorcycles and wore leather jackets, others were just average teenagers, there were a few girls who hung out and I could see where Chris had gotten her new look. All the kids smoked and drank, so I did too. Sloe Gin and Coke was the drink of choice and I had my first one there at the park. I liked the way it made me feel all warm and fuzzy inside. We'd just sit or lay on the grass under a big tree, smoking one cigarette after another and shooting the breeze. Now I was on the outside of the fence looking at the kids in the pool and it made me feel very strange. The pool was safe. Nothing bad had happened and it had served its purpose of keeping me out of my father's way. Now I was hanging with a crowd, my sister included, who were much more sophisticated than I was. I don't think I could have put a name to it at the time, but, looking back, I think some part of me realized that my childhood was coming to an end.

CHAPTER 15

———— ⟋ ————

CHRIS SCARED ME. She had turned into a bit of a wild child, game for anything. She would hitchhike, get in a car with a complete stranger, ask people she didn't know for money. If I was nervous about taking a few steps away from my childhood, Chris was ready to rock 'n roll and it showed in her every move.

On more than one occasion, Chris got caught stealing money and jewelry from mom. This was always good for a knockdown, drag out fight. Mom would slap her around and threaten all sorts of punishment which Chris would laugh off because she knew damn well that mom would never be around long enough to enforce it.

Some nights when my mother didn't come home, Chris would invite guys to the apartment. I was totally clueless and didn't know that by the time Chris was eleven she was experimenting with drugs and having sex. My mother knew. After threatening Chris a few times with no results, my mother simply called the authorities and had her arrested for being incorrigible. The police took her to Juvenile Hall and booked her.

⟋

After that it was just me again at the apartment with Mom. The good news was that she didn't lock me out and I could be reasonably sure of sleeping in my own bed at night. The bad news was that the apartment was so filthy that it became unbearably depressing to be there alone, at least during the day. I kept trying to straighten the place up a bit, but it was like sweeping the beach; it was endless and I never seemed to make a dent. Besides, I didn't know how to clean. After about a week I got up the nerve to go to the park on my own and hang out with Chris' gang. It felt good to have some human contact but I still wasn't brave enough to leave the apartment at night, even though I was hungry and there was rarely anything to eat there. However "good" (compared to Chris, certainly) my behavior was, I was beginning to feel anger towards my mother. I had heard some of the arguments screamed at her by Chris, and some of them made a lot of sense. I was beginning to realize that maybe, just maybe, my mother's inability to show me any love had more to do with her than me. It was a brand new concept and it didn't quite fit yet, but it fueled a resentment that was growing inside. And I was angry with my father, too. How could he have abandoned me? Why didn't *he* give *me* another chance! When my mother was home I began to take on Chris' role and argue with her. She couldn't have cared less. She wiped the floor with me. I was Marcia Brady getting in the ring with Mike Tyson. But at least I tried.

And, of course, like any truly impossible parent, my mother would throw me a curve every once in a while. One day, to my pleasant surprise, she came home with a carload of groceries. Thrilled to see food less than a month old, I rushed down to help her bring them up.

We each carried up a bag of food and then we went down for another load, but when we got downstairs – the car was *gone.* I thought someone had stolen it but mom knew right away what had happened. The car had been repossessed. She had been parking down the street again and had planned to move it out of sight after she got the groceries upstairs, but this time they'd been waiting for her. She learned two lessons that day: don't buy a lot of food at one time! *And,* bring up the expensive stuff first. Mind you, she had a real job and a decent, if not robust salary. I know for a fact that she didn't gamble and had no interest in drugs, so the money wasn't going there; god knows where it did go.

None of this slowed my mother down one bit. She somehow had a new car in a matter of days and was right back on her old schedule. I continued going to the park during the day and, for better or worse, I was starting to fit in with Chris' crowd. They welcomed me. They were glad to see me when I showed up.

There was one very nice, but very shy, young guy in the group. His name was Don and he was handsome in a quiet way. I probably saw him about five times before he said a word. He was eighteen and had just graduated from North Hollywood High. After summer he planned to go to college. Somehow I knew, even at thirteen, that he was a decent person and wouldn't hurt me. I began to look forward to seeing him at the park, so I guess it qualified as a crush. Don had a car, a 1957 Ford, and he would drive me home at the end of the day (so I guess he had a little crush on me as well.) He was so shy that it put me at ease. Even though he was older, I felt like I was more the aggressor around him. I had watched my sister invite boys to the apartment, so I did the same. I told him the place was a mess because we'd just moved in, but I doubt he cared much about the decor. It was exciting and a little scary to be breaking one of mom's rules; Nobody in the apartment without her knowledge!

Since he wasn't much of a talker, we moved onto kissing fairly soon. I don't remember for sure, but I probably made the first move. My impressions of sex were so different than most girls my age. I had grown up with it as a part of my everyday life. My father had never made an attempt to shield me from his lascivious exploits, and my mother brought plenty of men home for a weekend of lust, so I never got that memo that most kids get that sex is something special and mysterious, something that should be well considered before doing.

It was a pretty sure bet that if my mom didn't come right home from work that she would be out very late or not come home at all. And so, one day, I asked Don if he would lay with me in my bed. We "made out" for a while, but mostly I just wanted to be held. Neither Don nor I had any idea of what we were doing, but none of that mattered. Somebody nice liked me. Somebody nice wanted to spend time with me. What was not to like? I started talking about how great it would be if we could just run off and live together somewhere. I had no idea where the words were coming from. I had never made a formal plan in my head to run away. I don't think I ever thought of it as an option, not at thirteen. Don probably thought I was joking and decided to humor me. Boys will frequently do that when they find themselves lying on a bed with a girl who likes kissing them. I'm sure he thought I would let it go eventually. But I didn't. The idea just burrowed deeper and deeper into my mind. I wanted out of my situation so badly. Soon it was all I talked about. It took a while for Don to realize I was serious, but I kept pressing him, demanding a deadline for his decision, and I threatened to break up with him if he didn't come through. It was, of course, an insane idea. I was only thirteen years old and where the hell were we going to run away? Anywhere other than *here* was a good enough answer for me.

For a normal eighteen year old boy, Don had been remarkably respectful; he never pressured me or pushed me into sex. I was the one who insisted we go "all the way." Whether it was simple hunger for contact and pleasure, or a tactic to convince him that there would be rewards should he sign on to my "runaway" plan, I don't know. I know it wasn't love.

We were both virgins and the experience was an awkward one at best. In an ideal world making love should be something that two people have grown into, getting to know one another, feeling their attraction develop into something wonderful and sensuous and exciting. In an ideal world there would have been months of exploring each other's bodies; kissing, and then touching, learning all the things that feel good to both of you. But in an ideal world this story wouldn't be about a thirteen year old girl so desperately unhappy that she was willing to do anything to escape the barren landscape that was her home and family.

When Don and I finally "did it," it wasn't rough, but it wasn't tender. I'm sure Don felt awkward; who *doesn't* their first time? I wanted so much for this act to be the elixir that would take all my pain away. Such a big deal had been made of it all my life; by my father, and my mother, and my sister, that I hoped against hope that it really was everything they said it was. But when it finally happened I cried. I cried because I felt nothing. I think this is pretty common among girls (and boys) who engage in sex very early and for all the wrong reasons. They're looking for something that they won't find, and they're disappointed when they discover their mistake.

My mother had never uttered a word to me about the actual particulars of sex. No mention of condoms or contraceptives, and I'm quite sure that "abstinence" never occurred to her, ever, about anything. All I knew was that both my parents talked about sex as if it were the answer to any and all problems. I remember once, when I was nine or ten years old and my mother was dating a particularly monosyllabic idiot, I asked her why she liked someone so remarkably uninteresting. "He's not here for the conversation, kiddo," she said.

I was disappointed with my physical experiment with Don, but not discouraged about my plan to escape. Sex may not have been the answer, but getting far away from Eve still sounded like a good idea to me. Rare is the eighteen year old boy who isn't thrilled to have a girlfriend who is willing to satisfy his sexual needs and Don began to change his mind about running away with me. He promised he'd think about it.

It had been two months since Chris had been sent away to Juvenile Hall and now she was returning home. When she walked in the front door, I couldn't believe this was my little sister. She looked incredibly hard and mean, even dangerous. She had packed on about forty or fifty pounds. She had shaved her eyebrows, penciled in dark, unnatural ones above where her eyebrows used to be and she was sporting tattoos on all her fingers; one hand spelled out L-O-V-E, the other said H-A-T-E. She had more tattoos on her wrists and feet. She had spent her twelfth birthday in Juvenile Hall and there wasn't a trace of innocence left in her face. Any hope I had of Chris coming back with a new attitude, maybe a new-found desire to play by the rules, was gone. I was devastated by the sight of her, and furious with my mother. What was she thinking?! Didn't she *know* this would happen? Of course, the truth was that my mother didn't give it a thought. She just wanted Chris out of her house. Whatever residual effect the experience of two months of living with truly hardened delinquents, they never entered her head. And if I was angry, Chris seemed angrier. *Much* angrier. Now the lines were drawn, and not just on her eyebrows. Now it was all out war between Chris and my mom. Every day was a battle and neither one of them was going to give an inch.

I told Don that I couldn't take it for much longer. He finally agreed to a plan; we would wait until school started next week and then we'd take off. I was prepared way ahead of time. My clothes were already packed in a bag in the closet. Also in the bag was a note I'd written ahead of time to leave my mother telling her that I had run away and that she shouldn't worry. Here I was leaving home because I was so angry with my family, but I was still so invested in being a good girl that I wrote a reassuring note to my mother.

On the chosen day, I left the apartment, pretending to go to school. Don picked me up around the corner and we planned to wait in the car until we saw my mother leave for work. Then I would retrieve my clothes and we'd be on our way. We waited and watched but my mother didn't leave. Finally we saw my sister walk down the stairs of the apartment building. She was wearing a blue jacket of mine; a jacket that had been packed and in the closet in my get-away bag! That meant that Chris had also found the note that I was going to leave for my mother and *that's* why mom wasn't leaving for work; she was waiting for me to come back and get my things. *Shit!* That meant that I couldn't go back and get anything. If we were going to do this, we would have to just leave, and leave now.

CHAPTER 16

WE JUST STARTED driving. Don had a suitcase full of clothes, a full tank of gas, and two hundred dollars. I had the clothes on my back. I didn't even have a toothbrush, not that I used one with regularity anyway. Don said that he had left his parents a note as well. He didn't say where we were going since we had no idea ourselves. There never was any kind of plan other than getting out of Los Angeles. As we took off I looked back one last time at my mother's apartment. I felt a mix of fear and excitement as we drove off. Whatever the future held now, it had to be better than the life I was leaving.

Several times while we were driving I crawled in the backseat and let the movement of the car rock me gently to sleep. It brought back memories of the nights that dad and I would go searching for my mom. As we headed out of town I ached with sadness.

It didn't take long before a little reality intruded on our runaway adventure. We got hungry. It was 1962 and McDonald's was a pretty new phenomenon. As we were making our way out of California and heading to Nevada, we stopped to try one. The burgers were fifteen cents. We each got two burgers plus fries and a coke. And that ended up being what we ate every single day. Compared to my usual steady menu of candy and ice cream, burgers and fries were practically health food.

Once in Nevada, we pulled over so Don could get some sleep. He slept in the front seat and I slept in the back. Nobody said a word about sex. The reality of what we were doing was beginning to set in and it rendered both of us very quiet. The next day we were back on the road early. Like the old joke, we didn't know where we were going, but we were making great time. We stopped to get me a toothbrush and we picked up some playing cards, too. Later, when we stopped for burgers, we played a few games of gin. Not exactly a wild ride to debauchery.

It started raining before we were out of Nevada and continued all through Utah. We didn't do anything but drive, eat, look for bathrooms, and sleep. And if we thought that we'd become easy conversationalists once we had a few hundred miles under our belts, we were wrong. I taught Don how to play "Ghost." It's a word game where one person says a letter and the other person adds to it. The object of the game is to not let a word end on you. If it does then you're a quarter of a ghost. Whoever ends up being a whole ghost loses the game. We played off and on as we drove endlessly in the pouring rain. We couldn't even see the landscape. Eventually we entered Colorado. It was still pouring but I could see that it was very green.

Don decided to treat us to a good night's sleep in a real bed. We stopped at a motel and he checked us in. He didn't want them to see how young I was so I stayed in the car while he got the room and I met him there. Don took a long, hot shower. "It's all yours," he said when he came out. How ridiculous that I hadn't even con-sidered a shower for myself, I was just going to crawl in the bed with several hundred miles' worth of road grime in my hair and skin. Other than a dunk in the public pool or a good scrubbing from my "Gummy," I never really thought about baths or show-ers. Neither my mother nor my father were that concerned about cleanliness, so now, when Don offered me a turn in the shower I nodded nervously and stepped in. It's tough to screw up a shower but I managed to wash my chin length hair with the bar of soap that was in the bathtub. I didn't have a fresh change of underwear but I could have at least washed the ones I was wearing; I just didn't think of it. The sad fact is that I showered so seldom that when I did wash and towel dried myself, it was normal to see little, dark pieces of skin and dirt that looked like brown rice rolling off my body.

When I finished showering I got into bed with Don. We lay there silently for what seemed like an eternity. And then, without a word, we had something approximating sex. Afterwards, we rolled over and went to sleep without uttering a word. In the morning Don gave me one of his shirts and a pair of his jeans to wear. With my wet, shortish hair just combed, I looked like a young boy. I supposed that was good in case the police were looking for us.

I wondered if my mom was upset or even worried. Once again, my mind wandered to all those television moms I watched on lonely afternoons. If "Bud," or "Dennis," or "The Beaver" were gone for over an hour, their mothers would be climbing the walls. But, try as I might, I couldn't imagine Eve worried. And *forget* about her feeling guilty. I don't think I'd ever seen her express either of those emotions. There are theories that posit that, in families, certain emotions, if not acknowledged by the adults, are taken on by the children. I don't remember a day of my life that I didn't feel guilt. I felt guilty about my father, that somehow it was my fault he fell into his terrible depressions, and it was certainly my fault that I hadn't heard from him in months and months. I was guilty about Chris. Maybe if I had stood up for her, she would still be the sweet sister I remember having when I was a child. I even found a way to feel guilty about my mother. Somehow it was my needs, my inability to do things exactly as she wanted them done that were the reason for all the strife in our house. For a kid my age, I had an incredible capacity for guilt. And now I was feeling guilty about running away. I knew that part of the reason for doing it was my not so secret hope that it might get their attention, especially my father's. Part of me wanted him to worry and to feel so sorry for sending me to my mother's that he would "make it up to me" by taking me back. That was the plan, anyway.

The days droned on, driving, driving and more driving; across Nevada, Utah, Colorado, and most of it in the rain. I'd never seen so much rain in my life!

There were long stretches of absolute silence. There were no CD's back then, radios were strictly AM, and the only AM stations coming through were Bible Thumping preachers telling us we were surely going to burn in the everlasting fires of hell; Like we didn't know that already!

And then we were in Kansas. It had finally stopped raining and we could see the lush farmland, and the trees and the cows of Kansas. "We're not in Los Angeles anymore, Toto," I said, but neither Don nor I were much in the mood for jokes. We were still stopping only to eat, gas up, use the bathroom and get back on the road. As we drove through Kansas and entered Missouri, it started to dawn on both of us that we would soon run out of money. And then what? I had no idea. My brilliant plan had only gotten us out of town and fifteen hundred miles into the middle of nowhere. What came after our bankroll of two hundred dollars ran out was a mystery. Would we get jobs? Who would hire a thirteen year old girl? It had been almost two weeks and we realized that we would probably get caught, and then we'd be in big trouble. Every time we saw a cop car we both held our breath until it went by us.

We stopped to eat in Kansas City, Missouri. We picked at our food and we were both quiet a long time. Finally Don spoke up.

"What do you think about going home?" Don asked me.

"Yeah, I guess so," I said. It all seemed so ridiculous now. The heavens hadn't opened up and furnished me with an answer to all my troubles. It was over, this was the end of the line, and we both knew it.

The thought of going back to life with my mother filled me with dread, but we turned the car around and started back the way we came. We didn't even pull over to rest. We just drove through Missouri and back into Kansas. And if things were quiet in the car as we were heading East, they were pin-drop silent heading West.

Early on the second morning we were driving through a small town in Kansas called Beloit. We passed a patrol car and we saw the cops notice us. They turned on the siren and pulled us over. Don and I hadn't bothered to get any story straight until that very moment. As two sheriffs approached, I whispered to Don that since I didn't have any I.D, he shouldn't give them my real name or age.

The officers told us to get out of the car. One took Don and led him to the rear of the car and the other took me to the front. They asked me for my name and birth date. I thought quickly and told them I was Francine Bower, age eighteen.

"When were you born, Miss Bower?" asked the officer.

"Eighteen years ago," I said. "I just told you." From what I could see Don wasn't doing much better. His officer put him in the back of the squad car. My cop led me around the other side and I got in next to Don. The officer who had questioned me was angry. He told us that he knew we were runaways and that we were going to be in big trouble unless we told the truth. He knew Don was eighteen and was sure that I was underage. He threatened Don with charges of kidnapping and statutory rape. We tried to stay calm but we were scared shitless. As we drove to the station, we passed a building and the officer told me that it was a home for wayward girls and that it had been there since the late 1800's. He said that's where I would be going if I didn't tell the truth, and fast. I didn't say a word.

I have no idea where I suddenly got all this bravura. My dealings with the police were limited to the time my mother had called them on my father. But then again, I had spent time with my sister, and maybe some of her nervy attitude had rubbed off. I decided to treat everything that was happening as an adventure and that gave me the strength to stick to my story, no matter how many times it changed!

The cops took us to what, from the outside, looked to be someone's house. Inside it had been converted to a jail with three or four cells. A sheriff and his wife ran the small facility and Don and I were quickly put into neighboring cells. They were completely closed with thick walls and a big, solid door. There were no windows. There was a small bed, a toilet and a sink. In the middle of the door, a small area opened up that was the size of a shoe box that allowed food to be slid in and out.

Once I was actually locked up inside, I realized how much trouble we were in. The only good news in all this was that the sheriff and his wife were actually very nice to us; much gentler than my mother, so I was in the ironic position of "enjoying" some of the most gracious hospitality I had ever experienced --- in a jail! The sheriff's wife did the cooking for the inmates and the food was pretty darn good, a lot better than the fast food fare we'd been eating on the road. This sweet woman also brought me comic books and talked to me through the food opening in the door. I don't know how much of this kind attention was a tactic to get me to tell the truth, but even if it was, it sure felt nice. She even brought cigarettes and let me and Don smoke a few.

I was looking forward to sleeping on a real mattress, even if there weren't sheets or a pillow to go with it. Unfortunately there was a bare light bulb hanging from the ceiling and it was always on, glaring down on me, making it very hard to go to sleep. But I guess the point wasn't to make your stay so cozy and comfy that you'd want to make plans to come back on your next trip through town.

It took the authorities a long time to check out each name I'd given them; this was long before computers and we weren't in a big city with state-of-the-art equipment. By this time I would have gladly given them my real name but I was afraid that I'd end up in that school for wayward girls that the officer had pointed out on the way into Beloit. So, when they found out that I had given them a fake name, I just gave them a new one: Stephanie Grassey. I hoped this would at least buy me some time. Time for what, I'm not sure. They knew who Don was from his driver's license; it would surely only be a matter of hours before they found out who I was.

While they were busy tracking down information on the latest name I'd given, Don and I passed the time playing Ghost. We couldn't see each other, but if each of us laid on the floor in front of our cell door, there was about an inch of air and we could talk back and forth that way. After a day of playing Ghost, we heard a deep, southern voice call out from another cell. "Hey, I wanna play," he called out. "I bin listenin' and I think maybe I can play with y'all." We gladly accepted a new player and a good thing, too. The sheriff told us later that the man was in for armed robbery and that he was "one, mean sumbitch." If I'd known that at the time, I might've let him win a lot more games. When Don and I wanted to talk without the other prisoner listening in, we found that if each of us stood on our sinks and leaned towards the corner of the room where a water pipe ran through, we could hear each other through the gap around the pipe.

On our third day there, Don's father arrived. The police had contacted him and he had flown to Beloit. His plan was to drive back in Don's car.

The next time the sheriff's wife brought food to me, she asked me to tell her the truth about who I was. She said if they could verify who I was that maybe I could drive back home with Don and his father. She promised that I wouldn't be put in the school for wayward girls. I gave the sheriff my real name and gave him my mother's phone number. He went to check it out. I remember how much I enjoyed what I assumed would be my last meal in jail. I knew damn well that I wouldn't be eating this well for quite some time.

Later that day, when the sheriff showed up, he was very angry with me. He said that there was no answer at the phone number I'd given and no one had reported anyone with the name of Casey Maxwell missing. I couldn't believe it. More than two weeks had gone by and my mother hadn't even reported me missing! I gave them my dad's phone number but again there was no answer. Don's father was ready to take him home. He couldn't take me with them if I wasn't positively identified. I had never met Don's father so he couldn't legally identify me. Don swore that I was who I said I was, but Don had lost credibility and I never had any to begin with. The sheriff's wife tried my mother's phone number one last time and thankfully she answered. I talked to her and asked her to convince them that I was who I said I was. They couldn't understand how a mother could let her daughter go missing for two weeks and not report it. There was talk of not letting me go with Don's father, but finally they relented and I said good-bye to Beloit forever.

CHAPTER 17

⸺ ᕼ ⸺

THESE WEREN'T EXACTLY ideal circumstances in which to meet Don's father. I really looked like hell by then and I'm sure his father was wondering why his son, the one who was on his way to USC, had chosen to run off with a mess like me. His name was also Don and he was actually a very nice man. Quiet, but nice, like his son. We drove in near silence, Don Jr. rode shotgun, and I rode by myself in the backseat. It was a long drive and the silence was excruciating. All of this was my idea and I knew it. I certainly didn't set out to hurt Don, but I knew by now that I hadn't done him any good. And what had I accomplished? Here we were, heading back to Los Angeles where I would step right back into the life I had left. Only now there were several people angry with me. Somewhere in the middle of Utah, the car engine blew up and it was determined that Don's car would have to be towed back to California. We ended up taking a Greyhound bus the rest of the way home.

On the long ride home, Don Sr. didn't ask any questions about our "trip" and we didn't offer any information. The truth is we didn't have any stories to tell. We hadn't stopped to see any of the sights, or taken in any local culture, or enjoyed any of the country's beauty. We had just been "on the run." I remember sitting on the bus, looking out as we passed through miles and miles of empty desert, and smiling as I thought of what my father had said about traveling out of L.A.:

"Everyone's coming *to* California, so why go anywhere else?"

ᕼ

Don's father brought me to my mother's door and knocked. My mother opened it and invited us in as if nothing out of the ordinary had happened. She seemed not the least bit embarrassed about the "early epicenter" décor of the apartment. She cleared a spot on a couch and did her best to make light of the situation. She told Don's dad a story about the time she sent my sister out to buy a pack of cigarettes and how she didn't come back for six days. Her response was supposed to be the punch line: "What happened? Did you forget my brand?" My mom laughed. Don Sr. didn't. He said he'd better be getting Don home to his worried mother and they left.

It felt strange being back. I didn't know how I was supposed to act. My mother asked me a few questions about the trip. Nothing about why I felt the need to run away from home. Nothing about whether there was anything on my mind. No, she just seemed impressed that we'd gotten so far. When I mentioned that we'd driven through her home state of Colorado, she asked, "Did you get to Denver?" I told her it had been raining the whole time that we'd been driving through and that we didn't see anything. She seemed disappointed about that. It was a strange conversation, both of us talking about everything except what we *should* have been talking about.

One reason I never said anything *real* to my mother was that I knew only too well the response I would get. And that response would only be salt in the wound. Better to let us both skate along the surface of our relationship and thereby avoid any "severe tire damage" that might make things worse.

I wanted to call my dad, to hear his voice, but I was afraid of his reaction. "Is Daddy very mad at me?" I asked.

"I didn't tell him you were gone," she said. I was crushed. Part of my incentive to run away was to make my father feel guilty; now I find out that my mother never even told him. And that was the end of it --no lecture, no punishment. Nothing. The next day was a school day at a new junior high and my only instructions were to get a good night's sleep.

I awoke about two in the morning when my sister came into the bedroom and unceremoniously flipped on the light. She had a mangy looking dog with her that she called "Roach." I wasn't surprised that she'd use a drug reference to name her dog; she had been "using" for quite some time and calling out "Roach" on a regular basis was just one more way she could annoy my mother. When she walked into the room she was pretty stoned but it was still good to see her.

Chris told me about some of the girls she'd gotten to know in Juvenile Hall. Most of them had come from broken homes with uneducated parents who didn't have a clue how to take care of them. But Chris had come, as had I, from a home in which our father was a brilliant, clever, creative man who was once at the top of a very challenging profession. And our mother was just as bright, just as clever as he was. What was their excuse? They *knew* better. They just *chose* to treat us the way they did.

We stayed up and talked for hours, catching up and comparing notes on our lives. Only instead of normal twelve and thirteen year old sister talk, I told her about my time in a Beloit, Kansas jail and she told me about being beaten up and gang raped at Juvenile Hall. And here comes the sad part; it was the closest we'd felt to each other in years.

—❦—

I was transferred to Madison Junior High in North Hollywood for eighth grade because it was closer to my mom's place. I had already missed the first three weeks due to my "trip" and had a lot of catching up to do. I had no choice but to try and make things work at my mom's; there was nowhere else to go. I didn't talk to Don for a least a month. I figured he must be very glad to be back in his own clean house with a mom and dad who cared about him. I tried to buckle down and concentrate on my school work.

My sister was enrolled at Madison too, but it was more of a technicality. She wasn't in the least bit interested in school. She didn't go very often and my mother quickly gave up trying to force her. For that matter, mom had pretty much given up enforcing *any* rules with Chris.

I tried to call my dad several times since I'd been back but there was never any answer. I missed him and just wanted to hear his voice. I felt like he'd forgotten all about me and I wanted desperately to apologize. I had no idea for what, but I must have done *something* to make this man completely desert me. But there was never an answer when I called his number.

For the first time I actually looked forward to being alone in mom's apartment. If my mother or Chris or, worse, both of them at the same time, were home, all they did was scream at each other. My mother called Chris the same names my father had called her: a whore and a slut. Chris would just yell back, flip her off and slam out. But when Chris was out looking for trouble, and mom was doing the same, then the apartment was mine and I could relax in the quiet that allowed my mind to wander to a more pleasant future.

One way I nurtured myself was to invent a fantasy life in my diary. While most diaries make note of what actually happened on a given day, nothing that I wrote in that little book was true. You could call it my first stab at writing fiction. I wrote about all the calls and visits I had with my dad. I wrote that I was pretty and popular and talked about all the boys who liked me, and all the school dances I was invited to. I wrote about my dog, Slugger, as if he hadn't died. I was writing about the life I wished I had. Although I didn't write about my parents getting back together anymore; that was beyond the beyond, even for my fantasy diary.

Sometimes it was hard to tell what was more unbelievable; my diary or what was actually going on in my house. One night my mother got a call that my sister had been arrested. I went with her to pick Chris up and when we checked in at the police station, the officer said that Chris and another underage girl had been picked up at the park for curfew. The police were willing to release Chris to a parent and about ten minutes later a skinny girl with ratty, bleached blond hair, accompanied by an officer, came walking out of the holding area. The skinny girl was walking with my sister's dog, Roach, on a leash. "Hi, Mom," she said trying to sell it. My mother pointed to Roach, *"That* dog I know!" she told the officer. Then, pointing to the bleached blonde, she said "But *that* one, I've never seen before!" I guess Chris thought the switch was a good idea that would get them both out of jail. They almost held Chris in Juvenile Hall for an added offense.

The next few months passed uneventfully. Mom went about her business, whatever that was. Chris went about *her* business, whatever *that* was. And I sought refuge in my schoolwork, pouring myself into my classes and making up for lost time.

And then I got the flu.

But as you already know, it wasn't the flu. I was pregnant. And, as you also already know, my mother gave me three choices: give up the baby for adoption, get an abortion, or get married. No discussion, no insights about what one path might mean versus another. And so, on my own at thirteen, about to make one of the most important decisions of my life, looking at a chance to escape the madness that was my childhood, I blindly, desperately, chose to get married.

The author's mother, Eve Whitney.

The author's father, Eddie Maxwell Cherkose.

This 1944 George Hurrell photograph of Eve Whitney appeared in Esquire Magazine and was also made into a popular jigsaw puzzle.

Another George Hurrell photograph of Eve Whitney.

**The author's mother, grandmother, and father
at the Coconut Grove in the 1940s.**

**Frankie Little, Spike Jones, and Junior "Locks"
Martin, part of Spike Jones and his City Slickers.**
Photo courtesy of Jordan R. Young.

**Sheet music from the song Eddie Maxwell
wrote with Desi Arnaz.**

**Eve Whitney and Eddie Maxwell Cherkose
at the Hollywood Canteen in the 1940s.**

Eve and Eddie with their boxers.

Casey with her very own "Lucy" doll.

**Desi, Lucy, Little Lucie, Casey, Desi Jr.,
and Eddie watching TV. This picture appeared in
a fan magazine called TV MIRROR in 1953.**

Casey and Chris, ages 3 and 2.

Chris and Casey in matching outfits

**Casey and Chris, another year,
another matching outfit.**

Casey and the first Slugger.

The author with her "brother," Slugger #2.

The author as a brand new 14 year old mommy.

The author at age 22.

CHAPTER 18

—————————— ✑ ——————————

AFTER MEETING WITH Don's parents wherein my mother "convinced" them that Don had no choice, they agreed to let us get married. Within a week, on a late Friday afternoon, Don and I were in my mother's 1958 Ford convertible heading down to Mexico. My mother drove like a maniac but I don't think that was the reason that I was so nauseous. We had to pull over twice so I could throw up. How much was morning sickness and how much was the realization that nothing would ever be the same in my life, I had no idea. I just knew that I was plenty sick all the way to Mexico. Nobody said much on the drive. As we neared San Diego we hit a solid wall of fog. I'm sure I didn't know words like "metaphor" or "ironic," but I remember thinking how "perfect" it was that I was lost in a thick fog that made it impossible to see what was in front of me. We were in the fast lane but had now come to a complete standstill. We could barely see another car around us. We inched along the freeway at a snail's pace for more than an hour. It was scary as hell but at least it took our minds off what was really going on. Miraculously we made it to the border just as the fog lifted.

It must have been about seven o'clock in the evening when we entered Mexico. None of us knew what to expect but it was still a shock when dozens of people, including young children, rushed our car from every direction, all of them armed with souvenirs to sell; brightly colored statues, piñatas, busts of Jesus, pottery. We drove over the bridge and entered the town of Tijuana. Even though the town itself was rundown, the energy was lively and spirited and very colorful, like a full-time street carnival. I had no idea that Tijuana had quite a reputation as a party town. I also didn't know that it was where you went when you were doing something outside the law. There were rows and rows of bars and clubs, as well as small, open stalls lining the streets. Everybody was selling something: souvenirs, leather bags, drugs, sex.

We hadn't made any arrangements so my mother drove around looking for a motel. After circling the city she decided that we would definitely not be staying in town. And that's saying something from a woman who lived in a pigsty.

The road was bumpy and pot-holed and we bounced around for a couple more hours. Don and I fell asleep. I awoke just as we were pulling into a motel parking lot. It was pretty dilapidated but I don't think we had much choice. I was nauseous, scared, and that low hum of anxiety that was my constant companion was revving at incredibly high rpm's.

My mother got us a single room with two beds. As expected, it wasn't exactly sparkling but we were all bone tired and it would have to do. At least the sheets looked fresh. Eve, still dressed, got into one of the beds.

"Try to get some sleep," she said to Don and me.

I guessed that meant I was sleeping in the same bed with Don. That was strange all on its own, but to have my mother in the next bed, well, that was one for the books. We got into bed with our clothes on, too. I barely slept that night, partly because I was trying very hard not to touch body parts with Don and partly because I felt like there were things crawling all over me.

In the morning mom and I left Don sleeping and went to town in search of a judge who would marry us. We got directions from the very nice woman with no teeth at the desk, and then we drove to the courthouse. I waited in the car while my mom went inside to talk to someone. After about twenty minutes she returned with the news that the judge could do it today at four o'clock. Less than six hours away.

"You're going to need a dress," my mother said.

I didn't have much in the way of clothes, just a few skirts and blouses that I rotated for school and that's what I had brought, a pleated skirt and plain blouse. I would never have asked for a new dress; I'd already caused enough problems. But it was good to know that I would be wearing something special to get married in. Neither of us spoke Spanish; it never occurred to my mother that we were, after all, in Mexico where the language happened to *be* Spanish. It just pissed her off that no one spoke English. We found a little dress shop in town and went inside. My mother spoke loudly to the young salesgirl even adding a little Spanish accent to her words as if that qualified as speaking the language. The salesgirl didn't understand what we were saying so I hummed the bridal march and mimed walking down the aisle. The sweet-faced girl nodded enthusiastically and hurried off. She returned with an armful of dresses. Some were frilly, some were gaudy; none were flattering. Part of the reason is that I was a chunky girl with lumps and bumps, and secondly, the dresses were too mature for me. It came down to the only dress that fit. It was a bright, brassy gold satin number with huge, puffy sleeves, a too tight bodice and a full skirt. I thought it was beautiful. Up until that moment, the most important event in my life had been my graduation from elementary school the year before, and I had worn the party dress from Saks Fifth Avenue for that occasion. I couldn't have guessed that I'd be wearing a bridal gown *before* I'd need a prom dress. Mom surprised me by springing for a pair of matching gold, satin pumps to go with the dress.

We were famished by then. We picked up some tacos from a little stand and took them back to the motel. Don was awake and sitting on the bed when we came in. He hadn't eaten or left the room. He seemed pretty shell-shocked and the news that we'd be getting married later that day did nothing to alter that. He ate his tacos in silence. Afterward, he took his suitcase and went into the bathroom to shower for the happy event. Once he was out of the room my mom rolled her eyes at me.

"Couldn't you find one who talks?" she said. "The kid has no pulse. The entire family doesn't have one interesting personality between them. Couldn't even come up with a new name for the kid. Don senior, Don junior. No imagination." I didn't know it at the time, but this speech was a perfect litmus test for what my mother considered important in life. To be interesting, to be memorable was everything. Don was a decent, honest kid who, up until the time I lured him away from his life, had honored his responsibilities and was on his way to making a contribution to the world. My mother, on the other hand, was a complete narcissist whose only ethic in life was to never, *ever* be boring. The fact that Don didn't have a quick wit or a spicy come-back put him in the "reject" category forever.

I didn't defend him. I didn't know how. I knew that he was extremely quiet, and I also knew that my mother would have just laughed if I had reminded her of how nice he was. Besides, up until that moment I really hadn't given much thought to who I was actually marrying. Even though we had spent two weeks driving halfway across the country, we didn't really know each other at all. Running away together, having an adventure is certainly not the same thing as falling in love and getting married. Women much more mature than I was have trouble enough understanding everything that's going on at such a time. And then there was the fact that I was pregnant as well. I didn't know much about such things, but I knew that in six months I would be having a baby. There were many moments when the whole thing felt like a dream, or a nightmare, depending on the day. But I was wide awake and now it looked like we were really going to do this. My mind wandered to questions that no kid should have to ask herself; where would I live? Would we all live together? My parents had been divorced half of my life so I didn't really have a picture of what married life was supposed to look like. I had finished the seventh grade exactly three months ago and the truth was that I knew nothing about anything.

Don came out of the bathroom dressed in a sport jacket and tie. His crew cut was slicked with pomade. He actually looked very handsome. Next it was my turn to clean up. I showered and washed my hair. Ever since my sister had come out of Juvenile Hall she had been wearing her hair big and puffy; that was the look – early Priscilla Presley style. Chris had shown me how to do that, how to backcomb my hair to make it really big. But I had to do something simpler with my hair. I wouldn't be able to achieve a proper "boffo" bouffant because I lacked the teasing comb and full can of hairspray that it would take for my hair to reach the proper mass and rigidity. What on earth were we thinking back then?

I saw Don's toothbrush on the sink and realized that among the many things I hadn't brought was a toothbrush. My mom and I hadn't really packed so much as thrown a few things in a paper bag and headed off into the sunset. Don, on the other hand, had brought an organized little valise with compartments for everything: his toothbrush and toothpaste, his soap and acne medicine, a razor and blades, a styptic pencil, Band-Aids, shampoo, fingernail clippers, a nail file, pomade for his flat top, a comb, a little mirror, aspirin, and mouthwash.. He had a change of clean clothes, fresh underwear and socks. If ever there was a "tip-off" that Don and I might not be perfectly matched for a lifetime of marital bliss, it was the way he packed for this trip versus the way I did.

I hesitated briefly, and then I put some toothpaste on his toothbrush and brushed my teeth.

I called out to my mom to bring me the dress and shoes. She helped me into the gown and zipped me up. I slipped on the matching gold heels. There wasn't a full length mirror in the motel room so I had to be satisfied with what I could see in the foggy bathroom mirror. Then I removed the towel from my hair and water immediately began to drip down my dress, spotting it. My mother threw a dry towel around my shoulders and stood behind me, both of us looking at me in the mirror. Neither of us said anything. She didn't have to. I felt ridiculous. Whoever said all brides were beautiful on their wedding day had never seen me.

"You'll be fine," she said. Was that reassurance in her voice? And, if so, where did it come from? And was there more inside her? This was always the problem with my mother. Every once in a blue moon she would show some small sign of humanity that would give me hope that I could make a connection with her if I just worked at it a little harder. This was one of those moments. I let it hang in the air for the full four seconds that it lasted. And then it was over. She lit two cigarettes, gave me one, and then she left me to finish getting ready. I combed out my wet hair and put it in a ponytail. It would have to do. My mother returned with an eyebrow pencil and rimmed my eyes in black. It at least had the desired effect of adding a couple of years to my baby face.

I exited the bathroom and tentatively approached Don for approval. Don said I looked very nice. Then he asked my mom if he could step outside for some air.

"You didn't ask if you could knock up my daughter, but suddenly you need my permission to take a walk?" Missing the point, poor, shy Don sat back down on the bed. My mother just shrugged. She didn't make much of an effort for my big day. She skipped the shower and just wore the same slacks and blouse she'd worn the day before.

After another excruciating twenty minutes of silence, it was finally time to go to the courthouse. It was more of an office actually. A clerk who spoke a little English asked my mother for proof of our ages. Don handed over his driver's license. Then the clerk asked for my driver's license or my birth certificate. They needed proof that I was at *least* fourteen, the youngest age you could marry in Mexico, even with parental consent.

Whoops! Clearly my mother hadn't done all her homework, but that didn't slow her down. Without skipping a beat, she just lied and swore that I was fourteen and that she hadn't known she should bring my birth certificate. Then she slipped the clerk a twenty dollar bill. Five minutes later we were standing in front of a judge.

Even though the ceremony was in English, it was *very* difficult to understand the judge's accent and we all had a hard time knowing what was happening. The only saving grace was that it was all over in less than five minutes. I became Mrs. Donald Kratz. I hadn't had time to think about it -- no long, lazy hours spent daydreaming, scribbling my married name on my school notebook --- no pajama parties with my high school girlfriends, swapping notes about our "perfect guy." So it was a bit of a shock to suddenly realize that I would now be known as Casey Kratz. They say that the letter "k" is funny and I probably would have loved the name Casey Kratz if it belonged to the hapless new bride in a sit-com I was watching.

I immediately felt overcome with nausea as it began to sink in that my life would never, *ever* be the same again.

CHAPTER 19

—— ᗑ ——

WHEN WE GOT back from Mexico, my mother took us directly to Don's house. I guess it had been decided that we would be staying with his parents. I was already scared and terribly ashamed of myself; the idea of living under the deeply disappointed eyes of Don's parents filled me with a brand new helping of dread.

Don's bedroom could have been a twelve year old boy's room. There were twin beds with blue and red plaid bedspreads, sports banners and posters lining the walls, baseball trophies, a globe, a set of encyclopedias. Don gave me the guest twin bed.

My head was spinning as I floated through this bizarre scene. Everything was strange, including the fact that I was now living in a house I didn't know, with people who were understandably furious with me. Don's mother, Elsie, made a leg of lamb for dinner that first night. I hated it. I had never had *anything* that I didn't like before -- meats, vegetables -- I loved it all. But I didn't like this. To me it tasted like mint coated sawdust. I ate it anyway, every last gamey bite. No one said a word during dinner. Silent tears ran down Elsie's face as we ate in silence.

It was agreed that I would continue to go to school. I had been kicked out of Madison Jr. High because I'd run away. Now I would be going to Fulton Junior High. I would have to get up at five a.m. to catch two buses to get there. Don would go to work at the job his father had gotten him at a printing factory.

It was very strange to go to school and realize I was going home to my "husband." It was beyond bizarre. I would get home before Don and do my homework at his bedroom desk. I tried to stay out of Elsie's way because it was evident that she despised me. If we walked into a room at the same time we'd both go five feet out of our way to avoid being in the same path. Don and I were not having sex at his parents' home and that was fine by me. The more time we spent together the more I realized that we couldn't be more different. And yet, here we were, husband and wife, with a "little one" on the way. Absolutely nothing made sense in my little life and I swear it was all I could do to put one foot in front of the other as I took off for school each day.

At night, when Don and I were in our respective beds, we could hear the raised voices of Don's parents. We could hear enough to know that Elsie was having a hard time with me being there. I had ruined everyone's life; Don's, his parents', and my own. Such was the lullaby that rocked me to sleep each night.

A few weeks later I came home from school to find that, once again, my belongings were packed in a bag. I would be moving again. I didn't know where I was going but I was not sad about leaving this time.

My mother picked me up and I assumed that she was taking me to her apartment. As horrible as that sounded, at least it was a hell on earth with which I was familiar. But instead she took me to her cousin, Jane's house. Jane had divorced George Selleck and was now living on her own, working as a secretary, supporting her three boys, John, sixteen, and Doug and Gregg, three and four. I was happy about staying with Jane. First of all, I *knew* her. She loved my sister and me, and I loved my cousins. Jane had a young girl from Mexico who lived with her, cleaned house and helped out with the boys. My job would be to help her out. She spoke very little English but we got along just fine and she quickly became a much needed girlfriend. The health risks of smoking while pregnant weren't widely known back then and we would sneak out every once in a while for a cigarette.

I continued going to the same school as if nothing had happened. My pregnancy was beginning to show, but because I was

149

chubby anyway, no one really noticed – yet. I knew that it was only a matter of time before my secret wasn't a secret anymore, but I had gotten very good at living in denial. I would deal with that day when it came. I suppose that it was fitting that I felt the baby kick for the very first time while I was in my introductory biology class.

The more my pregnancy started to show, the more Jane's anger showed. I don't think she was actually angry at *me* so much as at my mother and father. She had always wanted girls and had felt close to Chris and me from the time we were babies. She had seen the damage my parents had done to Chris and now she blamed them for my situation. Unfortunately neither of them was around to deal with her anger; but I was. And if she'd had a drink or two she would share her sadness and disappointment with me. "I knew Chris was a lost cause a long time ago," she would say. "But I had hope for you, you always showed such promise. And now your life is over, it's ruined."

One more person I had disappointed.

One night Jane walked into the bathroom as I was preparing to take a shower. She took one look at my pregnant body and she burst into tears.

As I entered my sixth month of pregnancy, I stopped dressing for P.E. class. I didn't want anyone else to have to see my stomach or my stretch marks. But one day my mother got a call from the school requesting that she come in for a consultation. I hadn't seen my mother in weeks. And she didn't look happy to see me now. On the way to the principal's office she accused me of "opening my big mouth about the baby."

"I didn't tell anyone," I said, and I wasn't lying. Why on earth would I tell such a thing? But even though I wore big, baggy tops that hung down below my waist, I don't think I was fooling anyone. The principal asked my mother outright if I was pregnant and demanded that she tell the truth. My mother looked her right in the eye and lied. "Absolutely not," she said, completely offended. The principal, another in a long line of those intimidated by the mighty Eve, chose to believe her and let me stay. The next few weeks were torture at school. I was used to the kids making fun of me, but now even the teachers snickered and talked behind my back. I begged my mother to let me quit. Finally, mercifully, even *she* had to concede that I now looked unmistakably pregnant and agreed to let me leave. But quitting eighth grade wasn't quite as easy as either of us thought. It turns out that you can't just stop going to school at thirteen even if your mother says you can, *even* if that mother is Eve Whitney. The School District let us know that I would be enrolled in a program designed for handicapped children. Equipment would be installed at home that would enable me to get my lessons over a "two-way radio" type system. As weird as it sounds, I loved the idea. No more teasing by the other students, and I wouldn't have to overhear a whispered "disgusting" from a teacher as I made my way down the hall. Headphones sounded just fine to me.

About this time Jane reached her limit. She had her hands full with her own children and having me there was just too much, especially when my mother was perfectly capable, if unwilling, to take care of her own daughter during this difficult time. They had a terrible screaming match where Jane told Eve what a lousy mother she was. I know it came out of love for me and concern for my situation, but the result was that I was on the road once again. My mother did *not* like being criticized by anybody, so she grabbed my things and hauled me out of there.

We went back to her apartment. Chris had been gone over a week, God knows where. My mother didn't say a word to me, other than to tell me to "Quit it!" when I tried to clean up the disaster that was her kitchen sink. A while later Joe, the thug who had beat the crap out of my father two years ago, the man I couldn't stand, showed up. I didn't know until then that she was still seeing him. I also didn't know until then that he was a married man, but now I clearly saw his wedding ring. As I lay in bed that night, I could hear my mom and Joe's muffled voices. As with Don's parents, I couldn't make out exactly what they were saying but it didn't sound good. I didn't bother to unpack my bag.

Sure enough, the very next day my mom had a new plan for me. She said that, if I was going to keep this baby with Don, the time had come for Don and me to get our own place. I guess that one full night of providing shelter for her pregnant daughter was her quota of mothering for the year. So off we went looking for an apartment. She found a little one-bedroom duplex on Klump Street in North Hollywood. It was fifty dollars a month. Words and letters, and the harmonies they sometimes contain, have always been of particular interest to me. When I lived with my dad, we would play word games, putting together strings of like-sounding syllables that made up a harmonious line. It's one of the things he did so well in his songs, and I was thrilled he thought I was good at it as well. So I couldn't help but notice that now, with this move, I would henceforth be, not just Casey Kratz, but Casey Kratz on Klump. Let it hang there for a moment. The brittle sound of the "K's," the wonderful proximity of Klump to Dump and, let's face it, Kratz sounds like a skin disease of a genital nature. Casey Kratz on Klump. It said it all in four little words.

My mother paid the first and last month's rent. Don's parents donated a second- hand bed, a couch, and a small refrigerator. We were living together by the end of the week.

I thought it would be strange to live on my own but it wasn't that much different than being at my mom's. I tried to keep the place fairly neat, but I still hadn't learned the basics of housekeeping, so I wasn't very good at it. I had no idea about when it was time to wash sheets or even how to use a washing machine. Don was no help; his mother had done everything for him. We went to the market to buy some food, but all we did was stock up on TV dinners and canned soup. People openly stared at us, obviously shocked at the sight of such a young girl six months pregnant. If I happened to be smiling or enjoying a moment, their disapproving looks were instant reminders that I didn't deserve that moment. When I look at photographs of myself from that time, I can see the light beginning to disappear from my eyes, replaced by a sterner, more protected look. Throughout my childhood, I had always been able to "medicate" myself with humor. But it was harder and harder to find something funny in all this.

And there was still the matter of school. The electronic equipment was installed on Klump. I would wear a headset that hooked me up to a teacher and other "handicapped" students who were in the hospital or at home, and we would "go to school" for five hours a day, with a morning break and a lunch period. It was hard to concentrate without a real teacher in the room and my mind wandered constantly. It didn't help that the baby was kicking up a storm. But after two months I finished my semester of eighth grade with passing marks.

I never thought I'd miss the "headset school" but without that five hour diversion I had nothing to do all day. I had no friends, no one to talk to. My mother rarely visited, I still had no idea where my father was and, as far as I knew, my little sister was out robbing banks. I either watched our little black and white TV, or slept or ate until Don came home from work. And then we just ate some more and watched TV. One day I consumed an entire chocolate cream pie before Don came home. Even for someone raised in a house where Butter Brickle was a primary food group, this was too much. "Depression" was another word that I'm quite sure I wasn't familiar with, but I'm just as sure that this is what I was experiencing. Everyone had abandoned me and the one woman I actually liked and respected, my aunt Jane, had thrown her hands up and told me flat out that my life was over. And if Jane said it was over, then who was I to think anything different. These were the worst of times, and the worst of times.

Don, of course, expected real meals when he came home. His mother had always cooked for him and he was tired of canned soup and TV dinners. I didn't know how to cook anything but egg salad, which I had learned to make at Jane's house, but egg salad isn't anybody's favorite as a steady diet. Don must've told his mother that I needed help in that department because she came over one day with a leg of lamb and showed me how to cook it. Ugh! And ugh again! The dreaded leg of lamb. I had never let on how much I hated it when she cooked it before, and now I was paying the price. I listened "attentively" as she went through the steps of the recipe, silently wondering why she had forgotten to mention sawdust in the list of ingredients. The next day I went back to making egg salad again.

When my mother did come to visit she would usually bring something to eat and stay for an hour or so. I really enjoyed those visits and missed her when she was gone. But mostly I missed my dad. I missed him achingly. By now I hadn't seen or talked to my father in well over a year. Did he forget me? What other possible explanation could there be? My mother had hinted that he had been ill and that he was getting treatment, but she never told me for what. I had always had a vivid imagination and, of course, it ran wild with terrible possibilities. He was dead and they just weren't telling me. He was on death row and I was going to hear about his execution on the radio one dark and lonely night. He had run away to Europe with Gina Lollobrigida and had never given me another thought.

I finally got a call on May twenty-third, my fourteenth birthday. Our birthdays were two days apart so it would be hard for my father to forget mine, although he had managed to forget it the year before. It was instantly wonderful to hear his voice. He sounded clear and strong, and I wanted to see him more than anything in the world. He told me he had hurt his back and had surgery on a slipped disc. He had been in the hospital for a few months but now he was home and feeling better. He said that he loved me and missed me and that we'd see each as soon as he could drive again. I offered to come to see him right that second but he said it would be better to wait. He didn't say it but I got the feeling that he couldn't handle seeing me pregnant. That was a pretty low point for me. I needed him so much, needed his arms around me, needed him to reassure me that he loved me no matter what. There was a long, uncomfortable silence before we stammered through our good-byes. I hung up the phone feeling worse than I did before.

The baby was due in five weeks. Don's mother was appalled that I hadn't been to a doctor since my pregnancy had been confirmed months before. She found an Ob-Gyn and Don and I went to the appointment. Sitting in that waiting room was one of the more uncomfortable experiences of my life. There was a pregnant mother accompanied by a girl about my age. The mother looked at me and openly shook her head in disgust. Then she put her arm around her daughter protectively. These are the kinds of scenes you see in bad movies and you think to yourself; people don't really act like that, do they? They do.

The doctor wasn't much better. It felt awful to be judged so blatantly and harshly. It showed even in the rough way he handled me. I so wished someone would say something, or do something that would reassure me that things were going to turn out okay, but all I got was raised eyebrows and pursed expressions. There was not an iota of joy in any part of this, for me or anyone around me. The good news was that I was healthy and all seemed well physically. The doctor told us to come back in two weeks, but I already knew I wouldn't be coming back.

Living together in our dumpy duplex on Klump, Don and I barely spoke anymore. We weren't angry with each other; we just had nothing to say. Neither of us had any interest in sex. To make matters worse, Don had begun to gamble. He would stop off at a bar on his way home from work with some guys from the printing factory. He was too young to drink but apparently he wasn't too young to bet his entire paycheck away on a few games of darts. We were already living from paycheck to paycheck and now he was gambling that away.

My mother bought us a crib and some baby clothes. There would be no baby shower or party for this event; it wasn't something anyone wanted to celebrate. As my due date drew nearer I really started to feel the panic swell up into my throat; my breathing became short and I could, once again, feel that low hum of anxiety buzzing in my brain, keeping me up at nights and filling my days with sheer terror. My God, I was really going to have a baby. How did this happen? Obviously I knew, physically, how it happened. But how could my life have possibly turned out this bad?

What did I know about raising a baby? No one had even *raised me*! So where on earth would I have learned any of the tools or techniques necessary to raise my own child? Don and I tried our best to do normal things; we set up the baby's crib in our room. We put the baby's little clothes in drawers and tried to feel excited, but we were both scared to death. Neither of us had the heart to say it, but we both knew that, if I hadn't gotten pregnant, we would have broken up long ago; A madcap cross-country adventure in our resume and a wild story to tell.

It was the last day of June when I felt the first pain. Don called the doctor we'd seen a few weeks earlier. His service said he was on vacation but they had a referral doctor for us. He said to call him again when the pains were closer together. My labor was irregular; some pains were twenty minutes apart, some over an hour or more. I never needed my mother more than at this moment and, thankfully, she came through. She stayed with me the whole time. It went on like that for eighteen hours. When the pains were fifteen minutes apart we went to the hospital. Mom held my hand and told me to relax. I cried, I moaned, I screamed. I did not relax. When it got really bad I begged her to let me change my mind about the whole baby thing and go home with her where I promised I'd be a good little girl for the rest of my life. The pain, both physical as well as emotional, was unbearable at times. This really was happening!

I'd been in labor about twenty-six hours when things started to move quickly. The on-call doctor arrived and he turned out to be even worse than the original doctor. He cursed at my mother and then turned his venom on me: "You're a disgrace," he said. Those were the first words out of his mouth. He looked like something out of a "B" horror movie; a stern expression chiseled onto his face and black eye patch over one eye. He looked more like an angry pirate than a caring doctor, but there was nothing we could do about it, the baby was coming right now!

My little girl was born on July first at ten in the morning. She was tiny; just six pounds, one ounce. I named her Melanie after my childhood friend, Melanie Rose, the daughter of my father's army buddy from Ft. Roach, composer David Rose.

As soon as she was cleaned up, I got to hold her. I felt terror. I had never held a baby before, ever. I'd never even babysat a baby or a toddler and now I had my own living, breathing human infant. I tried briefly to breastfeed Melanie but the doctor didn't think it was a good idea. The nurses showed me how to feed Melanie, change her and burp her. I hoped I'd remember all of it when I got home. Over the next three days that I stayed in the hospital, my mind was a swirl of mixed emotions. Even though I don't think I had ever experienced a "maternal instinct" from my mother, I was hoping that I could feel a bond with this tiny creature curled up in my arms. I wish I could say that the happiness and the love I felt for Melanie superseded everything else that was going on, but the truth is that there was also fear and anxiety as I wondered what my future held.

Finally, it was time to go home with my husband and baby. My mother offered to stay with us the first week. I was thrilled and relieved. I had never seen her like this, attentive and helpful. She would sleep on the couch and assist me with the night feedings. Aunt Jane had gotten us a diaper service for the first six months and that really helped. I was okay with wet diapers, but every time I changed a "messy" diaper I promptly threw up. My mother said that I'd get used to it eventually, but I never did. That week was the most time I'd ever spent with my mother. It was amazing to watch her with Melanie; she was so confident and natural. Who knew she liked babies? Maybe she just didn't like her own. Years later it was pointed out to me that my mother was introduced to my daughter after she had given up on living the high life. She had grown tired of dating and any hopes of continuing her career in acting or modeling had long since disappeared. So maybe the key was that Melanie came along at a time when an infant with no agenda of her own might actually be just the thing for my mother. Whatever the reasons, be they benevolent or narcissistic, I was just glad to have her help.

The first meal my mom made for us was egg salad. I thought Don would choke, but he didn't say a word, he just ate it slowly. Between my mother and me, we had a cooking resume that consisted of a dynamite egg salad sandwich and various combinations of sweets and ice cream. All in all, Melanie ate better than we did, thanks to Gerber and Beech-Nut.

It was a good thing my mother *was* there because I didn't always hear Melanie cry at night. I guess that part of "mother's instinct" has a minimum age requirement. The first week went by so quickly and then my mother was gone. She disappeared back into her own world and I only heard from her occasionally. With Don at work and out most nights, it was just me and Melanie, all day long and well into the night.

Some days were better than others. Basically, if Melanie cried, I fed her. If she continued to cry, I changed her diaper. If she kept crying after that -- then I cried too. Many times the two of us would just fall asleep from the exhaustion of crying. I thought I had experienced the depths of loneliness in those weeks and months after finding out I was pregnant, but all that was nothing compared to the deep pit of wrenching loneliness I felt now. I had absolutely no one to talk to and I was so afraid of Melanie, afraid to hold her, afraid to be in charge, afraid I would make some horrible mistake that would do her irreparable harm. I think she could feel that I didn't know what I was doing and that seemed to make her even fussier. There were many times when she was crying that I would hold her and rock her, but she would just keep wailing. Maybe she was waiting to feel that calm and confidence that mothers are supposed to convey to their children, but I couldn't give her something I didn't have. And then someone *else* would hold her and she'd stop; just like that. It was devastating. And, making it worse was the fact that I was so unbelievably tired all the time.

I let the place go. It wasn't as bad as my mom's apartment, but it was pretty bad. Don's mother even came over and gave the place a real cleaning. Then she did the same for Melanie, albeit begrudgingly. Between the two, I'd say she got more joy from scouring the oven than she did from bathing her new grandchild. I never would have thought that *my* mother would be the more nurturing in such a comparison.

A few months went by and I began to feel like I could hold my baby without breaking her. I was still too nervous to pull off pure enjoyment.

One day when Don was at work, my sister came by with a tough looking guy and his even tougher looking girlfriend; the guy looked like he was at least sixteen and he was driving a car, so he was definitely older than Chris or I. Chris had just turned thirteen but she looked every bit as old and tough as her friends. She had even more tattoos and she gave off an aura that was more than a little bit intimidating. But she still liked me and she would come by to visit me and Melanie. Usually she was high on something and this day was no different. My sister and the girl giggled lamely while the guy just stared at the TV that wasn't even turned on. And here's the sad part; I didn't care. I didn't care if they were stoned out of their minds, I didn't care if they couldn't form a complete sentence and would forget being here fifteen minutes after they left, I didn't even care if they ate whatever food was in the fridge. I was just happy for the company.

CHAPTER 20

—— ⌒ ——

MELANIE WAS THREE months old when I got a call from my dad. Whatever anger I had in my heart about his going AWOL disappeared as I listened to the warm tone in his voice. He sounded really good and suddenly that's all that mattered. Better yet, he said he wanted to see me and meet Don and the baby. I was thrilled. He told me where he was living and I said we'd come that weekend. The fact that he had a new address made me feel very disconnected; to hear that my father had moved somewhere else without me knowing about it only heightened my sense of not being a part of his life.

When we got to his new place that Saturday, I was in for a surprise. It was a very nice two-story building with about thirty apartments on each floor, all facing a beautiful pool in the middle of the complex. Several people were swimming and sunning themselves, others were sitting together chatting. It seemed like a nice, friendly environment. My dad's apartment was on the ground floor near the pool. He opened the door and we hugged for a long time. I introduced him to Don and his new granddaughter. He held Melanie and charmed Don. My dad looked remarkably healthy and fit. He was even clean shaven except for his mustache. His apartment was small, a studio, but it was bright and cheery. Melanie started to fuss and Don offered to walk around outside with her. That gave me and my dad some time to catch up alone. He had more good news: he had landed a full time writing gig. He and a friend named Eddie Brandt, one of the writers with whom my dad had worked with on "The Spike Jones Show," had gotten offers from Bob Clampett to be staff writers on the "Beany and Cecil" cartoon show. The money was good and that's why he had been able to move to a better place. He also said that he had started dating a little. Not that he had gotten over Eve, he made this very clear, but he was over "the hoping." I was very happy for my dad, although it was strange to see him so damn healthy and, well… normal. When did *that* happen and why did it happen when I wasn't around? I had known him in his "up" moods, his "down" moods, his "angry" moods and his warm tender "loving" moods. But I had never seen him "normal." How long had he been like this? And why, if he was so stunningly normal, couldn't he have gotten in touch with me sooner?

A terrible thought was forming in my mind and setting the wet cement of my still young heart: I must not be someone who was loveable full time, not even by my parents. That thought stayed with me for most of my life. If someone loved me, then they could stop loving me in an instant and for no reason. But I didn't want to ruin this moment, not for anything. So whatever questions I had, I shoved to the back of my mind and just bathed in the warmth that was my daddy.

He told me about his back surgery and how he had been under the weather for a long time and hadn't been up to company until now. It had been almost two years since I had heard one word from my father, years filled with confusion and turmoil, life changing mistakes and bone crushing loneliness that might have disappeared, if only for a few minutes, had I been able to just see him even once in that time. But a few words about a back injury was all I was going to get. I wanted to hear him say he missed me as much as I missed him; more! But my father, for all his brilliance at putting emotions into words on paper, was never comfortable looking inward when there was pain to be faced.

And what about Chris? He hadn't seen or spoken to her in even longer. He didn't even ask.

So our visit was a bit awkward, but I wrote it off to how much time had gone by. I was now a fourteen year old wife and mother. Even I had to admit that was reason enough for a father to act a little strange.

I was very quiet on the drive home. Don asked me what the matter was. I lied and said "nothing" because it was just too hard to articulate, even to myself, the admixture of feelings swirling inside of me. And it seemed so ungracious to finally get what I had wanted for so long and still have conflicted feelings about the meeting and my dad's new life. I was happy that he was feeling better and that he had a new job and a spiffy new place -- but what if he had all of that because I was no longer holding him back? That's the tape that kept playing in my head. All of his pain and suffering ended, or so it seemed to me, when he sent me away. He was in pain when I left him and he was much, *much* happier now. And the only thing that was different was the fact that he had had no contact with me for almost two years. I may have been a wife and mother, but I still had a child's distorted sense of her own importance. I had been such a vital part of my father's life when I lived with him that I couldn't wrap my mind around the possibility that this dramatic improvement was a result of factors having nothing to do with me. And so I blamed myself for the misery he had felt when he lived with me. I didn't tell Don any of this; I didn't think he'd understand. It all just sounded like sour grapes, as if I were jealous of my dad's new life. And, to tell the truth, I probably was. He seemed happy, and I was anything but. Years later I found out that, in addition to the slipped disc surgery, my father had suffered a complete mental breakdown and had been hospitalized for over six months. While undergoing treatment in the mental ward, he had been forced to kick a ten year drug habit of fifty to sixty amphetamines per day. So it is perhaps understandable that a proud man might want to hide that sad chapter from his daughter.

―♭

I wasn't the only one on Klump Ave. who was unhappy. One day Don was working on his car outside our apartment. I could see through the kitchen window that he was having trouble making the driver door stay closed. He tried again and again, but with no results. He was getting angry as he repeatedly slammed the door. I went back to washing dishes when the next thing I knew he threw open the front door, walked up to me, his face full of frustration and rage; he drew back his fist and he punched me square in the face. I went down immediately. Don turned on his heel and left. He got in his car and tore out of the driveway. I laid there for several minutes, more shocked than hurt, as some strange new reality dawned on me. I don't know exactly what happened or where I got the nerve, but I stood up and calmly began to gather some clothes for Melanie and myself into a bag. I didn't know where I was going but I didn't want to be here anymore.

I didn't really have a lot of choices, no friends I could call. So I called my mother and asked if she'd come get me. To think that I had run away, gotten pregnant, gotten married – *all* to get away from my mother – only to end up going back to her, it was to laugh.

Don showed up at my mother's later that day. He apologized over and over. He was not a violent person, he said, just a frustrated one. He begged for my forgiveness and then he used the magic words; "Can't you give me another chance?" It was a sentence that I had heard as long as I could remember. My mother hadn't given my dad a second chance and that was all he'd ever wanted, all he ever talked about, cried about. I remember, as a child, telling myself that I would always give someone another chance. I would never put anyone through the agony my mother put my father through. When I thought of how different my life would have been "if only" my mother could have found it in her heart to give dad another chance. Hell, as far as I knew, even my dog Slugger would still be alive if she had shown a little mercy.

So I gave Don a second chance – for him, for my dad, for Slugger. Over the next few decades, I gave a lot of people a second chance, many of whom didn't deserve it.

Don never hit me again. It was true what he had said; he wasn't a bad person, just a frustrated one. But both of us were really still children, totally unprepared for a real relationship and, even if we had been ready, we were completely wrong for each other. Our relationship was officially over a few months later.

CHAPTER 21

———— ⌐ ————

MELANIE AND I moved in with my mother and sister. Nothing had changed except now I was a fourteen and a half year old divorcee with a six month old baby. I would've been in the ninth grade this year but there was no way they would let me attend junior high and the decision was made for me to not continue with the home schooling program. I was a full-time mother.

My sister showed up to eat and sleep occasionally but most of the time she stayed somewhere else. School was pretty much a thing of the past for Chris. For a while truant officers would show up at our apartment, but they eventually stopped coming because they could see that my mother didn't care whether my little sister went to school or not.

My life was so overloaded that I couldn't even dream about helping Chris. And even if I had tried, it was too late. She had found a new life in a world full of tough-as-nails drop outs, and new friends who loved her for who she was and never had a judgmental word to say about her. She was in trouble for something at least once a week: shoplifting, drugs, curfew, being under the influence. She began to spend more and more time in "juvenile hall" and that suited my mother just fine. "At least I know where the hell she is," my mother would say, and that would be the end of it.

The apartment was still a wreck. I tried to keep the bedroom I shared with Chris a little bit neater, but with all the stuff that was crammed into the bedroom it never looked clean. My mother went to work, as usual, and didn't come home much, as usual. I was alone in the apartment with Melanie all the time. Sometimes, just to stave off boredom and depression, I would change her outfits over and over again just like I was playing with a doll.

On my fifteenth birthday I was at home with Melanie when my sister came by looking for some money to get something to eat. I asked if I could bring Melanie and join her and her friends. They all hung out at a bowling alley. Chris told everyone it was my birthday and they cheered and sang to me. It was exhilarating to be out in the world, joking and laughing and feeling carefree for the first time in a very long time.

And I met a boy there.

Jeff was seventeen and seemed like a nice guy. He talked to me for the longest time, and then he asked for my number. When he called and asked if he could take me to the movies, my mother agreed to baby sit.

How strange it was to be on a date. I was a divorcee and a mother, but I had never been on a real date. It was wonderful. Halfway through the movie Jeff leaned over and gently kissed me on the lips. It was, in a manner of speaking, the first real tender moment I had ever experienced. Yes, I had obviously had sex with Don. But this was different. This had sensuality about it. This moved slowly and gently and sent chills up and down my spine. I remember thinking, "This is really nice." Whether Jeff really did like me, or perhaps just thought he had a "sure thing" with a girl who clearly wasn't a virgin, I don't know. I just know that kissing Jeff was really nice.

My mother and I still hadn't had anything close to a mother/daughter "talk" about sex. Not a word. And now I was dating a new boy, and I had little or no more knowledge than I did a year ago.

Well, it's hard to ask a guy to go slow once a girl's had a baby, especially if nobody has told her how to make that difficult speech. And I was a fifteen year old girl who had spent every day for the last six months in her apartment with only her baby for company. I was so starved for attention and affection that it wasn't too surprising that one night when Jeff came over and we had sex.

Just once.

And then he stopped calling me.

I felt like such a fool. I was crushed. I was humiliated. I was mortified. Even after all I'd been through, I was still this incredibly naive woman/child who really had no idea how the real world worked.

_6

Just when I was reconciled to the fact that I would never see an ounce of maternal instinct coming from the heart of my mother, a strange thing happened. She started coming home from work instead of going out on the town, and she started spending time with Melanie. Stranger still was the fact that she seemed to be enjoying herself. She was patient and almost affectionate with her granddaughter, qualities she had spent my entire life openly mocking. The fact was that she and Melanie were actually bonding, and whatever feelings of envy I might have had were superseded by the fact that my baby was getting some extra love.

On Melanie's first birthday, I wanted to have a little party at the park for her. I had a legitimate reason to want my father there; after all, Melanie was _his_ grandchild, too. Mom reluctantly agreed to call a truce and share air space with "the fucking stalker" as she affectionately called him. Don and his parents came. My sister and a few of her "hoodlum" friends were there as well. There were a few moments of tension as I watched to see if World War Three was going to break out. But Mom and Dad both seemed to enjoy playing with Melanie. Maybe my dad was feigning interest in Melanie to woo my mother but I don't think so. Melanie was his first grandchild and I think she had quite an effect on him. How strange that my baby Melanie, born under bizarre circumstances to say the least, should be the cause of my parents being civil to each other for the first time in years. My dad hadn't seen Chris in ages and he bristled when he saw that she had put on a lot of weight and had so many tattoos. Chris, however, when she saw her father, ran up to greet him with tears in her eyes and a big, loving hug. This man who had turned his back on her when she was a child, blamed her for every piece of bad luck in his life, denied her even the most basic gifts that a father should provide; this man was still the man that brought tears to her eyes. For one brief moment I could see a child's love in her face as she hoped against hope that this one time he might be happy to see her.

He wasn't. He just didn't have it in him. Whatever happened to my father all those years ago that made him deaf to her needs, it was still very much intact. And the stone cold truth was that Chris, at this point, truly had become an incorrigible, drugged-out juvenile delinquent, so his feelings about her almost seemed justified. The most loving, generous father in the world would have had a hard time getting close to Chris now. She had become the proverbial self-fulfilling prophecy. I look back now at that day in the park and I wish I had had the courage to just stop everything and set my father straight. After all, none of Chris' bad choices had really caused him any problems. He was never around to deal with any of it, so why did he get to react so badly? To say nothing of the fact that anybody could see that his rejection of her had been the key ingredient in Chris' problems from the very beginning. Who knows, maybe it wasn't too late back then for me to have made a difference. Maybe a big, dramatic speech might have changed everything. I'll never know, because I wasn't that courageous. I was much too concerned with my own little life and how I was going to get through the days and nights of it without breaking down.

As she was about to leave, Chris overheard Daddy talking about his new apartment and she asked if she could visit him sometime. He didn't say no, but he told her that now wasn't a good time. But when Chris asked him why, he had no answer. And when she asked if next week might be better, he still had no answer. Even though Chris looked hard and tough, I could see the hurt little girl in her piercing blue eyes. And I can still see it today.

~

My periods had never been regular so it took me a while to realize that I hadn't gotten one in some time. I had only been getting my period for a year before I got pregnant, and I still hadn't been given any instruction on how the hell my body worked; so, stupid as it sounds, when I realized I had missed several periods it didn't occur to me that I might be pregnant again. I had gotten straight "A's" in grammar school, so I couldn't blame a pathetically low I.Q. No, this was a heady mix of ignorance and denial. As soon as I forced myself to look at the facts I was horrified. I didn't say a word to anyone hoping that I might be wrong. After all, I reasoned with myself, I didn't have morning sickness as I did before. But deep down, I knew. And if I had a low opinion of myself before, well, I just moved into the Olympics of Self Hatred. What a stupid, stupid, useless girl I was! How could I have been such an idiot?! My first thought was that I should just kill myself. Or, I could tell my mother and *she* could kill me! I don't know how close I was to hurting myself. I *do* know that I couldn't imagine ever getting over the shame and humiliation of what I had done. And I know that it was my daughter who gave me the strength to do the right thing and face this moment, no matter what may come of it.

I picked a night and waited for my mother to come home from one of her dates with Joe. She didn't get in until very late and she wasn't in the mood for a mother/daughter chat. But I found enough nerve to sit her down and tell her that I thought I was pregnant. Again.

"It happens," she said, as if I had told her that I had dented the bumper on her car. "Don't beat yourself up." And then she added "But I'll take care of it this time. I know a doctor."

"An abortion?" I asked. "I don't want an abortion."

"I didn't *ask* you. I'm not taking care of you and two kids. You hear me? I've had thirteen of these. They're no big deal," she said. And then she went to bed.

Thirteen abortions? It was mind boggling. This was completely new information to me and I had absolutely no idea how to handle it. I knew what the word meant, but I had never grappled with any of the moral and ethical considerations contained in the word. And now my mother had tossed off the fact that she had had thirteen of them with no more concern than a trip to the market. She had also made it clear… in no uncertain terms, that she wasn't interested in a discussion. She was only interested in getting this "problem taken care of." I was so consumed with shame and self-loathing that I said nothing. I felt that I had lost my right to a vote in this, or any other matter concerning my life. And, to be honest, as horrified as I was by my mother's casual tone, I was also relieved that, whatever her reasons, she wasn't furious with me.

Abortions were illegal at that time, but that didn't slow down my mother one bit. She knew a doctor who would do the procedure. It turned out to be an office fairly close by in Sherman Oaks; he asked us to meet him there at eight o'clock at night. Everything was clean and professional. I felt as safe as I could feel considering the situation.

And then the doctor examined me. I was much further along than he'd been led to believe and he didn't want to go through with it. My mother didn't hesitate. She threatened to expose him if he didn't do the procedure and, weighing his options and seeing the look on my mother's face, he finally agreed. He gave me something to put me out and he performed the abortion.

I remember my mother and the doctor helping to put me into my mother's car. There were thick towels soaked with blood between my legs. I passed out. The next thing I remember was waking up in my bed at my mother's apartment. I was in and out of consciousness for the next few days. I was still losing blood and every time I tried to get up, I would pass out again. My mother tried to get in touch with the doctor but he wouldn't take her calls. After several days I started hemorrhaging a frightening amount of blood. What a strange sensation to feel the floor rushing up to crash into my face and then: total blackness. My mother had to rush me to the emergency hospital where I came very close to dying. Because of the circumstances and the bruises on my face from fainting, there were a lot of questions from the hospital. I don't know what my mother told them but somehow, when I was better, she was allowed to take me home. With medication and rest I slowly got stronger.

Physically I improved but mentally I was suffering. Wherever my mind might wander, it always returned to the same thought; I was a waste of space on the planet. I had this sweet baby who didn't ask to have me for a mother. She deserved to have a good mother and I felt completely ill-equipped to handle the job. I sunk into a very bad depression and I stayed there for many months. The days went by, I went through the motions, I tried to put on a happy face, but I was very lost.

CHAPTER 22

⁐

I MET CHARLIE Clair towards the end of that year. I was fifteen and a half. I wonder how many mothers still counted their age in half years. My sister, now fourteen, had recently stolen some of my mother's jewelry and disappeared. Chris had run away countless times, but this time she had taken some of mom's good stuff, so it warranted a manhunt for her. We got in the car one night and hit all of Chris' known haunts, asking people if they'd seen her. We ended up at a donut shop in North Hollywood where a group of teenagers were gathered. I got out and asked the kids if they knew my sister. No one recognized her description but one boy, Charlie, took my number and said he'd call me if he saw her. Well, he called, but not because he had seen my sister. We talked on the phone a few times; I told him about my situation, mainly that I had a one and a half year old baby girl. I assumed that would scare him off, but it didn't. For some reason he didn't think I was the absolute scum of the earth so it felt particularly good to talk to him. He thought I was smart, and funny and pretty, all the things I was sure I wasn't. And he *must* know what he's talking about; after all, he was nineteen years old, and handsome, and confident. After a few phone calls that made me feel a whole lot better about myself, we went out on a few dates. Some nights we hung out at the donut shop and I got to know some of the kids there. I made my first real friend since Cissy. Her name was Gail, she was also fifteen and her boyfriend was a friend of Charlie's, so we all went out together. It was the closest thing to a normal teenage life I had ever had.

I think Gail and I bonded because her home life was nearly as messed up as mine. She had a strict Catholic father who couldn't make up his mind about his sexuality, a mother who had the morals of an alley cat, and siblings whose ideas about family loyalty came from Mata Hari. How Gail got up in the morning was a mystery to me, but she did and I was glad she did. We both had the same "re-set" of joy. How much of that joy was real and how much was manufactured I don't know, but it was something we had in common from the very beginning.

I felt very accepted by her, and acceptance was the one thing I was desperate for. And, next to acceptance, fun was the other item in short supply in my life.

Charlie was cute and funny and he liked my daughter. After a few dates I even shared my shameful secret about the abortion and he didn't hate me. He came from a nice, normal, middle class family; he had two normal sisters and he had a normal mom and dad. They lived in a nice, normal home in the valley. It was like a drug to me, all this normalcy that Charlie brought into my life.

I'm sure his parents weren't thrilled that he was dating a young girl with a baby but they were always nice and polite and included me in many family meals. If I didn't know better, I'd say that they liked me. Whatever it was, I was really starting to feel hopeful about my life.

And then Charlie told me that he loved me.

Other than my father, no one had ever told me that they loved me. Not my mother, my sister, not even my beloved grandmother had said those words. It changed everything. Charlie said me he loved me and wanted to spend his life with me. And within a few months we started having sex.

If you think it was easy typing those words, you're wrong. And if you're someone who has always learned from your mistakes, and learned quickly, then you will no doubt be shocked by my behavior. But if you look back over your life and find that there are one or two incidents that make you wince with shame and deep regret, then, by all means, keep reading.

That's what happened. Charlie said he loved me and we started having sex.

Let me begin by saying that I blame only one person in this episode; myself. While it is true that I had *still* not heard word one about the why's and wherefores of contraception, and it is true that my mother had given me the distinct impression that if I *were* to ever accidentally get pregnant again it wouldn't be a problem to resolve things, and it's true that Charlie, at nineteen, might have thought to take charge in the safe-sex department when sleeping with a fifteen year old, I *still* take full responsibility for my actions. I wasn't an idiot and I could have figured some of these things out for myself. But I was needy, and lonely, and when you don't know how to differentiate between *feelings* like those, and *thoughts* such as "do NOT have sex again because you can get pregnant and you do NOT want to get pregnant," then you are susceptible to making incredibly stupid mistakes.

I told him as soon as I suspected that I was pregnant. He didn't know what to do but we agreed that we weren't prepared for a baby. Or I should say *another* baby. Could there *be* a more despicable girl than me on the face of the earth? More stupid? More worthless? My answer was a categorical "no."

Encouraged by her "que sera sera" attitude the last time we had this conversation, I went to my mother, who, once again, was unfazed by my revelation. She told me to get five hundred dollars from Charlie and she would make the arrangements.

I was a hopeless mess. Even my sister hadn't messed up this badly. She may have been a rebel and a drug addict and a con artist, but she wasn't this monumentally stupid!

Abortion was still illegal in 1964 and my mother wasn't able to find a doctor in town who would perform the procedure. Maybe her name had gotten around after she had threatened the last doctor when he tried to change his mind. She made a few calls and finally got the number of a willing doctor in Tijuana. I'm sure that Charlie was upset by the news but he did little to reassure me.

In fact he opted not to go with me, which should have told me something about the content of his character right then and there. But, needless to say, I wasn't exactly in a position to be criticizing anyone else's character, so when my mother offered to take me, I gratefully accepted.

The drive to Mexico looked much different this time without the fog, but it wasn't any more pleasant. Any hopes I had for a good life as a decent person were pretty much dashed. It was final, the verdict was in; I was a bad person. It was really that simple. Some people were bank robbers, some were doctors or lawyers, I was a bad person. I had now proven this point on several occasions and I saw no reason for this description to ever change. It's a strange thought when you've spent your whole life thinking that maybe, under the right circumstances, you might actually be a good person, to now realize for certain, that you're not.

It was a long drive.

When we got to Tijuana that night, my mother went to a phone booth and made a call. We were instructed to drive to another phone booth and wait for a call there. There was a huge crackdown on illegal abortions going on in Tijuana and her "contact" wanted to make sure that this wasn't a trap. After several dry runs revealed that we weren't being followed, my mother was instructed to go to the Jai Lai stadium, then park, and someone would meet us. A few minutes later an old sedan pulled up. We got in and the man drove to the main street and parked behind a building. On the main drag all the store fronts were lit and open for business on the street level, but almost all of the second stories were dark. Any light on a second story was a red flag to the police that something illegal was going on. We followed the man through the back of a pottery store and up the stairs to a dark apartment. It smelled like bad food rotting. The man led us to a tiny bedroom where another man who he introduced as "el doctor" was waiting. When my eyes adjusted I got a look at him. He didn't look like a doctor; that was for sure. He was unshaven and wore khaki pants and a dark shirt.

A dim green night light was the only illumination in the room. There was a twin bed with plastic on it; the doctor told me in broken English to lie down and then he filled a syringe and gave me a shot. My last thought before going out was, if I almost died under sanitary conditions in Sherman Oaks, California, then I would surely die now, tonight, in this dark, dirty room in Mexico. The strange thing is that it seemed only right to me. I deserved this.

$$\sim_6$$

The next thing I remember is being awakened and led down the stairs. My mother held one arm and the driver held the other. I felt groggy but mostly I felt surprised. I couldn't believe I was still alive.

I was still living at my mother's apartment with Melanie and I spent the next day or two in and out of bed, taking care of Mel as well as myself. Physically, I felt normal fairly quickly. But mentally, emotionally, I felt like I was at a precipice of some kind, my life hanging in the balance. I had committed one screw up after another and there was no reason to think that pattern was going to change. And if that was the case, then why continue? Was I suicidal? Not in the sense that I was eyeing razor blades or hoarding tranquillizers. But there are many ways to give up on yourself and not all of them involve actually ending your life. The temptation was to just let it all go; turn off my mind and my heart, abandon whatever hope I had left, and let life just happen. I watched my sister do it and, right now, it didn't seem like such a bad idea.

Cheerful thoughts like those hung in the air for several days. But two things happened that made me think I still had a little more gas left in the tank. The first thing was the look in the eyes of my baby girl. I may have been scared to death of all the responsibilities associated with raising that tiny creature, but I realized that I loved her, and I got the distinct feeling she loved me, or at least needed me, which put her light years ahead of my parents in the emotionally-connected department. The second thought that kept ringing in my ears was that there must be a reason I got another chance to live. I was so sure that I was going to die on that dirty little bed in Tijuana, so sure that death was my punishment for all my stupid mistakes that I couldn't help but look at this second chance as a huge gift from God or the Universe. Wherever it came from, I felt a responsibility to make the most of it.

CHAPTER 23

─────── ✏ ───────

I MADE THE decision to go back to school. It was sheer force of will and I can't say I had much confidence in my ability to pull it off, but I knew that if I was going to salvage something of my life, then graduating high school would be a pretty good start. It would not be as easy as just enrolling at North Hollywood High and showing up like a normal sixteen year old. I was a "special case" and, frankly, the principal made it pretty clear that she didn't want me there at all. I remember our first meeting and how I recognized the mix of disgust and judgment in her voice. It was a tone I knew very well by then.

Luckily, a very kind counselor took over my case. She was gentle with me and not only did she bend over backwards to make it all happen, she also bent some rules to get me into the classes I needed. I had missed ninth grade completely so I was lacking some necessary credits. My hope was to start the tenth grade as if I hadn't missed a year of school. The counselor arranged for me to take several tests to determine my grade level. With her encouragement, I tested very well. She also took into consideration my interest in drawing and art and put together a curriculum that complemented those areas. I was determined to do well and make her proud of me. I knew the statistics on teen-age mothers who try to go back and finish school and they weren't good; 90% of mothers under age sixteen will never finish high school. I wanted very much to be part of the 10% who made it.

The next hurdle was child care. My mother offered to quit her job and watch Melanie if I could get financial aid. I went through the demeaning ordeal of applying for Welfare and was accepted.

Between the state assistance and the sixty dollars a month that Don gave me for Melanie, we were able to get by. I was still seeing Charlie but I was doing things differently. I would no longer be a victim of my hormones; I did what I should have done long before. I went to a doctor and got on birth control.

Going back to school proved to be much more than just a scholastic challenge. Many of the kids I'd known in grammar school were now in the tenth grade at North Hollywood High and I was in the same classes with a lot of them. Word spread quickly about me. Everywhere I went people pointed and whispered about the unmarried girl with the two year old baby. Once again it felt like I was trapped in a badly done teen flick where I was the butt of everyone's joke. Do people really point and whisper behind your back? Yes, as a matter of fact, they do.

The first day that I saw Cissy, my childhood best friend, I had a surge of hope that I had found someone who knew me and would see past all the gossip. We hadn't seen each other since I'd left my father's house when I was twelve. Barely four years had passed. It felt like a lifetime. She was a normal sixteen year old and a very successful high school student. She was a member or the president of just about every club in school. Physically, she hadn't changed that much. I, on the other hand, had been through a lot and it showed. I didn't look like other girls my age, I didn't have that innocence. And I still didn't have the right clothes. I was never going to be a cheerleader or a homecoming queen, I would never be able to date the captain of the football team, never go to a school dance. All this I knew, but I hoped that I could rekindle my childhood friendship with Cissy. It didn't happen. She was cordial, and I was cordial, but it was painfully awkward for both of us. Our lives had turned out so differently and we had absolutely nothing in common anymore. It was sad but I didn't have much time to feel sorry for myself. I had a daughter, a boyfriend, and a lot of homework.

Going back to school, focusing on the work and ignoring all the chatter and static wasn't easy. Many was the time that I just wanted to

179

throw my hands up and call it quits, but I didn't. After all my screw-ups, I was succeeding where everybody told me I couldn't. I did well in all my classes and, after a while, I actually *wanted* to be there.

And then a wonderful thing happened. My friend, Gail, got into a fist-fight with another girl and she got suspended from her high school. How was this a good thing? Because they sent her to North Hollywood to finish the semester. I was ecstatic. We were happy outcasts together and we bonded more than ever. Oh, how I looked forward to seeing Gail at school every day; it was such a relief to have someone to eat lunch with and laugh with, someone to walk those halls with and feel protected. And it didn't hurt that she came with a reputation for kicking ass! That friendship was the only thing that made me feel like a normal girl.

Meanwhile, life at home was anything but normal. One after-noon I came home from school and my mother and Melanie were gone. I took advantage of the quiet and lay down to take a nap. Sometime later I felt Charlie lay down on the bed and curl up behind me. I must've napped for a long time because now it was dark outside. I felt him pull me close to him and I smelled alcohol on his breath. Then I felt his hand roughly pull my bra up and paw at my breasts. I turned to ask him what the hell was going on when I realized that it wasn't Charlie. It was my mother's pig of a boyfriend, Joe. And he was drunk. I tried to jump over him to make a dash for the door, but he grabbed my arm and kept me from moving. He relaxed a minute then and I kicked him in the shins, rolled off the bed and ran out the door into the courtyard of the complex. I hid around a corner, trying to catch my breath. My heart was pounding and images of the beating Joe gave to my father were racing through my mind. I waited, trying to stay perfectly still. Finally I leaned out and saw Joe stumble out the door and head toward the garage. I ran back into the apartment, locked the door and bolted it. I didn't know what to do. I didn't want to call the police because I thought my mother would be furious with me. Besides, I thought that when she found out what had happened, she would do a lot more harm to him than the police would.

I was wrong.

When I told my mother what had happened, I expected her to lose her mind with rage, but instead she shrugged. "So he had too much to drink and touched your breast." Then she added, matter of factly. "Don't make a big deal out of it; it's not like you're a virgin."

The concept of "self esteem" has gotten quite a work-out over the last few decades and the term has lost some of its meaning. But there *is* such a thing and it's a very nice thing to have if you're trying to figure out who the hell you are in the world. Theoretically it gives you a starting point of "I'm worth something," and then you go from there. Well, it's very hard to feel very much self-esteem when your own mother dismisses a violation like that. Was I worth a moment's outrage from my famously outrageous mother? Apparently not. She not only dismissed my anger but managed to imply that my past mistakes had robbed me of the right to be angry in the future as well.

And that was the end of it.

I was too ashamed to tell Charlie what happened but I did ask him to stay over more often. He was still living at home with his parents but had the freedom to come and go as he pleased. Because he came from a traditional family with a mother who cooked and cleaned, and a father who worked, he was used to a house in which at least *some* of the things that were supposed to be in the cabinets and closets actually *were* in the cabinets and closets. When he saw what went on in my mother's apartment, Charlie pitched in and showed me *how* to clean. Not just the apartment but also myself. He made suggestions about ways to improve my personal hygiene habits, and far from being insulted, I was grateful.

Not only was it impossible to keep my mother's apartment clean for any length of time --- it made her furious that we touched her stuff. Even if we emptied the overflowing ashtrays, or scraped the layer of grease that floated atop the dishes in her sink. She *liked* it that way, and we could go fuck ourselves if we thought we were going to change it, or her. We decided that as soon as we had enough money, we would rent our own place.

Charlie loved teaching me the proper way to do things. Later I would see that this could turn controlling, but right now I just appreciated the attention and the help. And just as I didn't see the controlling aspect of his helpful nature, I also mistook his jealousy for love. In my life I had never known a man who loved a woman more than my father loved my mother. And I had never known a man more jealous than my father. So perhaps it was understandable that I would see the two qualities as one and the same. This unfortunate bit of blurred vision was to cause me untold amounts of grief throughout my life, but at the moment I was blissfully ignorant.

—⟲—

It was 1965 and the draft was in full swing. Charlie decided to enlist in the Marine Reserves. While he was away, I started my junior year of high school and continued to do well, getting excellent grades. I was extremely grateful that State Aid had been available, enabling me to go to school, and I felt I had used it the way it had been intended. But now I was ready to work. I wanted to be able to keep paying my mother to watch Melanie. I got an after-school job at the snack bar at Universal Studios, and then I got a second job working at the snack bar at Pickwick Pool and Skating Rink in nearby Burbank. I was so busy running from one thing to another that I dropped twenty pounds in a just a few months. I wish it were nothing more than burning some extra calories, but there was more to it than that. My mother saw that I was overwhelmed and so she did what any good mother would do; she introduced me to diet pills. She said they'd give me the energy to get all my work done and still have some left over for when I got home. Granted, it was a different time back then and the dangers associated with amphetamines were still somewhat unknown, but I'm guessing that there weren't too many other sixteen year old girls in high school who were getting "uppers" from their moms.

Report cards came in and I did well. It felt great to be doing well in at least one area of my life. Some of my discipline was because I genuinely loved school; I always had. But to be totally honest, my responsibilities as a young mother were so incredibly difficult and frightening, that some of what passed for studiousness was actually an escape from my duties at home. At school, if I got a question or an assignment, I knew I could figure it out if I studied hard enough, but at home there were questions that had no answer. There's no "right answer" for all the needs of a two year old child. It's a trial and error situation and I had made so many errors in my life that I still didn't trust myself. And so I poured my energy into that stellar report card.

The bookwork I could handle, but emotionally there were still a lot of obstacles at school to overcome. The snide comments and disgusted looks of the kids were awful, but what I got from some of the teachers was worse. I had a science teacher that year, let's call him Mr. Gregory, who took a real disliking to me. My co-dependent nature had already started to blossom so I just worked that much harder, and was that much more eager in his class; as if I could win him over if he saw how diligent I was. For a science report on molecules, I went all out and spent every spare minute working on my project. I even brought it to both my jobs in case I had a free second to devote to it. Then I'd go home and work on it some more. I was very proud of this report. Not only was it detailed and well researched, I'd added beautiful, well designed charts and graphs to illustrate it. After turning it in I waited anxiously for my grade. A week later the teacher was handing back the graded assignments and mine wasn't among them. After class I waited to talk to him. He knew why I was there and, as I shyly made my way up to his desk, he took my report out of a drawer and ripped it up right in front of me. And then he put all the pieces into his brief-case and closed it. He said that I disgusted him and that as far as he was concerned I never turned in the assignment. With a smirk on his face he told me that I would be getting a "D" in his class. "It'll be my word against yours," he said. "And who do you think they'll believe?" I was too shocked to even cry. I had experienced a lot of judgment and disappointment from people, but never any-thing like this. He went on to say that I didn't belong in any class with wholesome kids, that there were places for girls like me. And I believed him.

I didn't even go to work that day. I called in sick, went home and straight to my room to cry. Even though I said I didn't want to talk about it, my mother wouldn't let it rest. I finally pulled myself together and told her what had happened. Much to my surprise, she was furious. She was beyond furious, she was incensed. I'd never seen my mother with so much anger mustered because of something that had happened to me. This was the same woman who reacted with a dismissive shrug when I told her that her abu-sive boyfriend had tried to molest me.

I convinced my mother that I was already the laughing stock of the school and that it wouldn't do me any good if she retaliated by "breaking the fucking kneecaps" of my science teacher. It took a while but she reluctantly promised that she wouldn't do anything.

I should've known better.

The next day, while I was in my science class, my mother entered. "Are you Mr. Gregory?" she asked sweetly. He said he was. "Could I see you in the hall for a moment?" she asked, smiling. The teacher excused himself and walked out with my mother. Within seconds everyone could hear my mother screaming a viscous string of threats. All the kids, except me, rushed to the door to see what was happening. My mother called him every name under the sun and threatened to break off both of his arms and beat him over the head with them if he didn't fess up to what he'd done. Then I heard the principal and another teacher trying to calm my mother down. Some of it's a blur; I was anxious, thrilled and embarrassed, all at the same time. What I remember clearly, however, is being in the principal's office a few minutes later. I don't know what further threats of bodily harm my mother whispered in the teacher's ear, but he actually admitted that I turned in the report and that, yes, it was an "A" report and that, yes, and he had destroyed it on purpose and had intended to say that I never turned it in. It didn't matter how hard I worked, he still felt that I didn't belong and needed to be taught a lesson. I wish I could say that he got fired. He didn't. I wish I could say that I got to change classes. I didn't. But for the rest of the year I didn't put out much effort and he steered well clear of me. I got a "C" in the class and that was just fine by me. But I did switch schools at the end of the semester. When Gail transferred back to Polytechnic High in Sun Valley, I went with her.

Why had my mom gotten so angry at my teacher? I didn't know then and I don't know now. Just when she did something, or a long series of somethings, that made me think that my only salvation lie in getting as far away from her as possible, she would do something that made me think she cared. She didn't have to march down to that school and read half the administration the riot act. How much of it was a caring mother coming to the defense of her daughter, and how much of it was just her idea of a good time, I'll never know. But occasionally she would throw me a curve that would give me hope that I might find a pony in there after all.

But those good feelings never lasted long. My sister showed up soon after that and she wanted, actually she insisted on, moving back in with us. Whatever drugs she was doing, they weren't curbing her appetite. She was only five foot five and she now weighed at least two hundred and fifty pounds. She was constantly stoned out of her mind, angry, and unreasonable. I didn't want her around Melanie when she was like that and I told her so. Not surprisingly, we got into a big, screaming fight. I was standing in front of the door when Chris got so angry that she went to punch me. I ducked at the last minute and her fist went through the front door. Thank

God she hadn't hit her target or I could've ended up with my nose coming out the back of my head. My mother threw a coke bottle in our direction to try and stop the fight. It hit the coffee table and shattered sending a shard of glass ricocheting off the table leg and hitting my baby toe, almost severing it. Blood was spurting everywhere. Melanie, who was now almost three, ran out the door crying that her grandmother was trying to kill her mother. Mom rushed me to the E.R. where they stitched my baby toe back in place. Chris was gone when we got back.

The day after the big commotion, I came home to find the front door missing from our apartment. The landlord had removed it, taking it completely off its hinges and exposing, for all the world to see, the pile of crap we called home. That's when I found out that my mother had not been paying the rent for the last six months. God knows what she did with our money. I had been giving her every cent of my paychecks, as well as my government assistance check, and while it wasn't anybody's idea of a fortune, it was certainly enough to keep the door on its hinges!

This act on the part of the landlord was meant to humiliate and embarrass my mother. Good luck with that, sir. It did no such thing. The "open door policy" *did* succeed, however, in completely mortifying *me*. All of the neighbors were up in arms about what "pigs" we were and I was hard-pressed to argue with them.

I was so upset with my mother that I actually raised my voice to her. "I don't have to explain myself to you!" she blasted back. And then she was gone.

I knew that my mother gave money to Chris from time to time, not out of a sense of obligation or even guilt, but to keep her away. And she bought Melanie nice things. A nicer thing would have been to pay the rent. Her immediate solution to the open gaping cavity that looked onto the living room was to take the bathroom door off its hinges and lean it against the front door opening. It wasn't big enough to cover but it was better than nothing. If I'd had anywhere else in the world to go that night, I surely would have. Somehow we got through the night but the drama wasn't over. The Marshall arrived bright and early the next morning and served my mother papers. Within minutes workmen entered the house with furniture dollies and started throwing our stuff into boxes. My mother and I grabbed what we could and we left with Melanie.

―⁂―

We went to a coffee shop on Van Nuys Blvd and tried to figure out what to do next. My mother wanted to call her dumb ass, child abuser boyfriend (not to put too fine a point on it) Joe to ask for his help, but I threatened to call the police and Mom decided to call another old boyfriend, Nathan, who kindly offered to let us stay at his house for a few days. This was excellent news. He was the sweet man with the glass house on stilts and the swimming pool; the one Chris and I had hoped against hope that mom might stay with. It had been about eight years since I'd seen him and he could barely hide his shock at learning that I had a baby. Still, he couldn't have been nicer. Melanie and I shared a room and I'm pretty sure my mother and Nathan shared a room; the wages of "first, last and a security deposit."

The next day, miraculously, my mother "somehow" had enough money to get all of our belongings back – and set us up in a new place; not a lot better than the old place, but it had a front door.

My daughter Melanie was the one person who could bring my sister and me back together once in a while. Chris was crazy about Melanie and, for someone who didn't get much love in her own life, Chris still found ways of giving love to her young niece. On those rare occasions when she wasn't high on something, she would play with Melanie for hours. She was remarkably patient with her. There were times when, unseen, I would watch them together and wonder what it would have been like to have had *that* Chris as my sister.

Not long after we moved into the apartment, Chris was arrested for possession of drugs and sentenced to six months in Juvenile Hall. My mother could barely contain her relief. Once again, Chris was out of her hair.

Each time I visited her I saw Chris fall deeper into a bizarre place that was both dark and light at the same time. The darkness came from the hardness and ugliness of the place and the lack of anything resembling compassion. And the light came from her fervent embrace of religion. For some, religion is truly a place to find the spiritual strength to become a better person, and for others it's simply an escape. The rules of this earthly world meant nothing to Chris anymore. No matter what the offense, Jesus would forgive her; Jesus would make it all right.

When Chris got out after doing her six months she was a different girl; she had dropped some weight, added some muscle, and elaborate tattoos of Jesus now adorned her arms and her chest. Also, she now buttoned every sentence with "Praise the Lord." She may have just sworn to "rip your fucking heart out of your chest and feed it to your dog"-- but she'd end with "Praise the Lord." How much of that was because my father was Jewish and she was rebelling, I'm not sure. I didn't care. But if she was using religion as a drug of sorts, then at least it got her off the old "hard" drugs for the first time since she was ten.

With the help of a sponsor Chris even enrolled in night school and talked about getting her diploma. She spent her days skating at the roller rink and it was clear from watching Chris move that this was her sport; she had found something she loved and that she was good at. In the late 1960s the Roller Derby was very popular. It was broadcast on television and the skaters could actually make some decent money. It was also a sport for which my sister had the right look and body type. The rougher and tougher you looked -- the better. The whole enterprise was very theatrical, much like wrestling, complete with feuds and nasty girl fights. Chris worked really hard and after a few months she was approached by a scout for a farm team. She moved in with a girl she trained with and it looked like Chris just might turn her life around, courtesy of the Roller Derby.

I was thrilled. Actually, I found myself envying my sister's life for the very first time. She had found her passion and she had the freedom to pursue it. I rooted for her to make this dream come true. The truth was that, until competitive skating came along, I had given up on my sister. But this looked like it might really work out. "That's some good shit, Maynard" I said to her when I saw her skating particularly well. That was a signature saying of Chris' --- No matter what the subject; a movie, a moment, a particularly good joint of "spleeph" -- if she approved, she let you know with "That's some good shit, Maynard." And it felt good to be able to say those words to her.

CHAPTER 24

───────── ❧ ─────────

CHARLIE CAME BACK from the Marines. A year and a half flew by and soon I was actually graduating High School. I'd done it! Whatever else I had so royally messed up in my life, whatever feelings I had of failure and unworthiness, I did this one thing and nobody could take it away from me. My mother and father were at the ceremony, Charlie was there and, most memorably, my daughter, Melanie, was there. Guaranteed I was the only graduate with a four year old child shouting proudly, "There's my mommy, there's my mommy!"

Charlie and I rented a tiny house of our own in North Hollywood on a street called Cleon. "Casey Clair on Cleon." That sounded a little better than Casey Kratz on Klump, right? We didn't have much money but we were happy. We got a little Boxer puppy who we named "Slugger" after my first dog. Charlie was a good dad to Melanie. So was Don, her real father. Don was always there for birthdays and holidays. Melanie was having a good life and so was I. The house was neat and organized. There was food in the fridge. We were all clean. Charlie still told me what to do and how to do it and when; but that still looked like love to me and things were good.

And then my mother showed up. She had been evicted – again. I didn't want her to stay with us but she had nowhere else to go. I wanted to say "no" but she wouldn't hear it. She was still an incredibly strong, intimidating woman and she just bulldozed her way in. Charlie was no less intimidated than I was. I don't think the term "force of nature" has ever been so aptly applied than to Eve Whitney.

She'd been there about two weeks when she got a phone call from a lawyer telling her that her old boyfriend, Nathan, had passed away and had left her $60,000.00! This was in 1969 when that was an incredible amount of money. Now she could afford to move somewhere else, except that her credit was shot. Our credit was good, so she offered to use some of her money as a down payment on a house for us if we would make the payments and, of course, let her live there, too. My gut screamed "NO!!!" but Charlie's and my weakness, as well as blind materialism, said "okay."

We bought a nice, three bedroom ranch style house in a nice part of Van Nuys with a fenced in yard and a big swimming pool. I remember taking a walk from room to room and actually thinking that the tough times were gone and that it would be smooth sailing from here on out. A house, a husband, a healthy child... wasn't that the entire ingredient list for a happy life?

There were big problems right off the bat. The obvious one was that I didn't like my mother and she wasn't all that fond of me, so the spacious rooms were filled with tension night and day. And, if that weren't enough, she was *still* a major league slob and she wasn't about to change just because she lived with us. Making matters worse was the fact that Charlie was a bit of a neat freak, so it was a constant battle to keep the house acceptable to both mom and Charlie. Most of the time, I failed.

Right after we moved in Charlie got the good news that he'd been accepted onto the Los Angeles Fire Department. It had been his dream and he was thrilled when he found out. His new schedule meant that he'd frequently be gone twenty-four hours at a time -- which was good news because it also meant that now he'd only be annoyed with me half of the time. I was sure that, if I was lovable at all, it was only in small doses.

Charlie *loved* being a fireman, he loved everything about it. Unfortunately what he loved most about it were the young women who *loved* firemen. And there were legions of them; groupies who hung around the station and made it very clear that they had a fire that desperately needed tending to. I didn't know any of this was going on at first. I had suspicions, but I didn't want to believe them. Like millions of wives (and husbands, I'm sure) since the beginning of time, I pretended not to see what was right in front of me. I wasn't surprised by his infidelities because, in my heart, I didn't expect him or anyone else to be true to me. So I looked the other way and opted for denial in order for my hard won "normal" life to go on without interruption.

A few short months after I graduated high school, it was Melanie's turn to start school. I threw myself into being Super PTA mom. Unlike my parents, I was determined to be involved in Melanie's home and school life. I signed up to be a room mother, I baked cupcakes, I volunteered to work fundraisers, I made phone calls, I drove carpools; whatever they would let me do, I did. It never occurred to me that I might be an embarrassment to my daughter. I truly thought that my exuberance and enthusiasm would thrill my child. But I was a full decade younger than most of the moms and, making matters even worse, I looked and dressed like a cross between Cher and Lady Gaga. I wore too much make-up and wore my skirts too short. I was completely clueless that this type of dress might not be appropriate. My heart was in the right place but it had to be tough on my daughter.

Another thing that was tough on Melanie was *me*; regardless of how I dressed or wore my hair. In an effort to show how much I loved and cared about her, I did something that no one ever did for me: I made rules. I disciplined her. It wasn't my intention be so strict, but I didn't know *how* to go about proper, balanced parenting. And when my rules weren't followed, I yelled at her, I grounded her, I spanked her. I did not abuse my baby, but I deeply regret the many rules and needlessly tough punishments that I handed out. I had no idea that there might be a happy medium between rules and relaxation. I thought the important thing was for me to be involved. On the positive side of that assumption, I read to her, I told her that I loved her a hundred times a day; I wanted to know everything that happened in her life. If involvement equaled love, then I loved this kid with all my heart! But I'm afraid, like many first born children, Melanie was a little like a first pancake; I made many of my beginner mistakes on her.

CHAPTER 25

———— ᓚ ————

MY SISTER WAS still skating when she met a man named Kenny Williams. She was crazy about him; he was crazy about her. Unfortunately, Kenny was not, as they say, "good for her sobriety." Soon Chris discovered that she was pregnant and her skating career came to a screeching halt; the sport was much too violent and dangerous for her condition. My mother, of course, was ready to drive her down to Mexico and have it "taken care of," but Chris' religious beliefs wouldn't allow her to even consider it; she would *have* the baby. Sadly, her Catholic leanings didn't stop her from stealing everything she and Kenny could get their hands on and doing drugs again. Throughout her pregnancy, my sister was strung out on heroin most of the time. So was Kenny. When Chris gave birth to her baby daughter, Rochelle Samantha, she was born addicted to heroin. It was touch and go, and horrible to witness; but miraculously Sammie made it through all right and was an otherwise healthy baby. Unfortunately, Chris didn't clean up her act one bit. I looked at her with a mix of anger and pity. She had come *so* close to making something of her life. Roller Derby, Astrophysics, who cares; she had her heart set on a goal and she was focused. Now her life was a drugged-up mess once again.

Charlie and I were having our own problems as well. He was hyper-critical of me, overtly and subtly. He controlled everything I did, and somehow I ended up never quite making the grade. Nothing was ever quite clean enough, or organized enough, or smart enough. And it was getting harder and harder to look the other way when it came to his cheating. But he would spin me around with stories that could only come from a pathological liar. Even about the stupidest things, he would sooner lie than tell the truth. And why not? He usually got away with it. When I did catch him in a lie he would just keep talking, and lying, and lying some more until he convinced me that I had imagined the whole thing. I had so little confidence in my own perception of reality that I deferred to others no matter what. If Charlie said the girl I saw sticking her tongue down his throat at the fire station was just a neighborhood kid in need of a friend, why couldn't I believe that? Why did I have to assume he was guilty of something wrong? I thought about leaving him but I didn't think I had the right to leave, and I was terribly afraid; afraid my life would go back to what it was before we met. On the surface my life had greatly improved and I freely gave Charlie credit. It never occurred to me that I might have been responsible for some of that positive change. No, I was convinced that Charlie deserved all the credit and that I owed him my loyalty, no matter what. And Charlie wholeheartedly agreed.

⸺ᴄ⸺

My dad had recently moved to a new apartment building. It was called the Oakwood Gardens and it was a lively, active, "mostly singles" kind of place. It was a terrific move for my dad. Everybody was crazy about him and thought he was the funniest, wittiest, most charming person they'd ever met. He was so happy and energetic at this time in his life. He played tennis every day and took long walks in the neighborhood, and he was seeing several ladies. As always, however, he was still in love with my mother, happy enough just to see her whenever he could. He seemed to have given up any illusions that they would get back together. He seemed satisfied that she didn't hate him anymore. No calls to the police, no restraining orders. Life was good.

It's interesting that even though my dad was the one who was still in love with my mother, he was the one who was dating, while my mother seemed to have stopped going out at all. Why would she stay home now, I wondered, when I would have been *very* happy for her to go out more? Once again both my parents continued to surprise. My mother's repeated generosity and moments of gracious behavior ruined my chance to simply put her into the "evil" category and leave her there. And my father was even more difficult to peg. Almost two years without a word to me and now he was back, and more charming than ever, and I couldn't bring myself to do anything but love him and treasure the moments we had again.

⎯ᴄ⎯

My dad started a weekend tradition at his apartment of serving a punch of his own devising. It was a little concoction he liked to call a "Maxwell Massacre" and it consisted of a giant bowl of equal parts Spanada (a cheap red wine), vodka, and Seven-Up. A hangover in a bowl is what *I* called it. Crowds would gather in the morning at his outside table and go through several bowls, usually well into the night.

I was about twenty-two years old at this time, very tan, which was considered an indicator of radiant health back then. More importantly, I was thin. My father was very proud of the way I looked and would beg me to come visit on the weekends so that he could "show me off." As you can imagine, I had very mixed feelings about his praise; I felt good that I was finally making him proud and that he thought I was pretty, but the other tiny voice in me was resentful and scared. Where was he when I was a chubby girl of twelve? Where was he when I got pregnant and I felt so alone and unattractive? And what if I got fat again? What if he didn't think I was pretty anymore? He certainly wasn't inviting my fat sister with the tattoos over to meet his friends. It was a confusing message and I didn't handle it well. Interestingly enough, my mother had put on weight and my dad still found her attractive. But mom was always a special case when it came to my father's heart. As shallow and superficial as my father could be when it came to women, his love for my mother ran deeper than anything I'd ever known.

At some point I felt comfortable enough in my relationship with my father to bring up the past. I talked about how different things had been when I was a child. He admitted that he had been pretty out of it on drugs most of the time back then. We had never talked about it before, but I told him how devastating it had been to come home that day and, without any warning, find all my belongings packed in boxes, and being told I couldn't live there any longer. He told me that, because I was beginning to mature, it had scared the hell out of him; he felt I needed more privacy and that I needed a mother. It was probably true that I needed *a* mother, but *my* mother!? That wasn't the right choice, that's for sure. Didn't he know that? "I didn't see you or talk to you for almost two years," I said. "I felt like I'd done something horribly wrong. I still do."

Now it was getting real. It was obvious that he felt guilty but he was very uncomfortable talking about any of this. "I'm very sorry," he said. "It kills me that I did that to you. I was sick at the time. But don't be upset with me; I hate it when you're mad at me. I promise I'll make it up to you." Then he started to cry and, true to form, I ended up comforting him. That wasn't exactly what I'd had in mind. I had hoped we would somehow be able to open up a new level of communication; two equals trying our damnedest to figure out what happened all those years ago and how it affects us now. That's what I hoped for. What I got was a sweet, hurried admission of guilt and a tearful pleading that we move on to some other topic.

I wondered if someday I would be able to summon the courage to ask my mother the same tough questions.

CHAPTER 26

————— ⟲ —————

WHILE MY FATHER was coming into his own as a grandparent, my sister was not doing well in her role as a mother. Chris ended up bringing three year old Samantha over to our house almost all the time. She and Kenny were so strung out on drugs that Chris decided it would be better to give Sammie up for adoption. I got hysterical. It pushed every button in my heart. The thought of my little niece being abandoned to strangers was more than I could take. And Samantha was such a sweet, well behaved little girl that the idea of taking care of her didn't seem as daunting as it might. I offered to adopt Sammie, and Charlie, to his credit, agreed. Chris dumped her off and we didn't see my sister for nearly six months. Sammie was doing well with us and I think Melanie, who was by now close to eight years old, enjoyed having her little cousin there. But then Chris' boyfriend, Kenny, got arrested and my sister starting coming back around a lot. She was high on drugs, she was surly, and she always wanted something, whether it was food, money, or a place to stay. We let her crash on the couch for a while but then she began to bring dangerous looking strangers back to the house. Soon money and jewelry were missing. It was upsetting to us, to say the least, and Chris' presence was upsetting for Sammie. I told my sister that we would happily keep Sammie if Chris would either get off drugs or not come around when she was high. She didn't much care for either suggestion; she wanted her cake and her drugs, too, so she took Sammie from us and placed her in a foster home. And there wasn't a thing we could do about it.

⟲

My friend, Gail, had gotten a job styling wigs at Robinson's Department Store in Panorama City. She called me one day and said that the head of the Display Department was looking for someone to dress the windows. Gail had always been very complimentary of my fashion sense; she knew that I didn't have much money to spend on clothes but she was always impressed with how I had put things together. She thought I would be very good at a job like this and had told the department manager. His name was Pepe and Gail assured him that I had done windows before.

I was scared to death. Working at a snack bar hadn't required any real skills. I hesitated for a day or two, but then I called Pepe and made the appointment for an interview. I had no idea what to expect but I thought we'd talk about the job, and then, if he thought I was right, there would be some training involved. Instead we spoke for all of two minutes and then he said, "Why don't you do the front store window and we'll see how it goes."

Something very strange was happening. It was the oddest feeling. I wasn't panicking. I was anxious, but it was only because I wanted to do a good job. It wasn't dread, and that was very new to me. In so many other areas of my life I had absolutely no confidence. So much of my life had been lived on the fly that I had never built that emotional foundation that lets a person know that they have certain skills and talents they can rely on. So loud were the voices in my head that I was too fat, or too underfoot, or too much trouble to stick around for... But there had always been one area for which I had been complimented by both my father as well as my mother. They had both been impressed over the years by my visual sense and my artistic capabilities, and that was the voice that was bringing my heartbeat back to normal.

The "audition" was very physical, it required hauling big items, climbing up ladders. There was lots of building, hammering, sawing, and assembling of things. And I loved it. I looked at my watch and, so far, I'd used up an hour and a half. I had a nice country setting for my mannequin. I ran around the store gathering items:

gaucho pants in fall colors, a tan cashmere sweater, a poncho, knee boots. Pepe showed up just in time to watch me put it all together.

And that's when I ran into trouble. I realized that I had no clue how to take a dummy apart. My naked mannequin was standing with her legs apart and there was a steel rod that ran from the floor into her rear end that kept her from falling over. But how would I get a pair of pants over her spread legs? And what do I do about that rod in her be-hind? I twisted her torso but her top half fell to the floor sending an arm flying. I quickly retrieved the parts and tried to screw them back on. "I'm sorry," I said to Pepe as it became obvious that I was messing this up badly. "These are different than the mannequins I normally work with," I offered weakly. Pepe smiled. He helped me dress the dummy and put her back together. He slit a small hole in the crotch of the pants to allow the rod to go back in place. So *that's* how it's done, I thought. I was pretty sure I'd blown the job at this point but I finished the display anyway. Then I accompanied Pepe outside the store to see how the window turned out. To my utter surprise and delight he said, "Good job," and hired me right then and there. I was walking on air after that.

After I'd been on the job for a few days, I learned that, mechanically speaking, there was only *one* kind of mannequin. So Pepe *knew* all along that I had never done this before and I got the job anyway.

The next hurdle was telling Charlie. He had been away in Oklahoma at the Marine Reserve camp. He wasn't too happy about my news, especially since I'd gotten the job while he was gone. It wasn't like me to make a decision like that without checking with him first, but I knew he would have discouraged me from even trying out for it if he'd had a say in the matter. It would be years before I understood the many ways in which controlling people exert their power in relationships. Perhaps if I knew then what I know now I might have put two and two together and figured out that a healthy relationship wouldn't be threatened by the mere act of my getting a job. But that knowledge was years away.

I couldn't wait to get to work in the morning. The positive feed-back was exhilarating. I was developing a little self-esteem and it wasn't because of Charlie. This, of course, is exactly what Charlie was afraid would happen. It was a very social atmosphere in the store and, much to my surprise and delight, I was a popular girl; it was everything that high school hadn't been, and with a twenty percent "employee discount" thrown into the mix. It was during this time that I made another life-long friend named Darlene. She worked at the store and she had a family history that rivaled mine for dysfunction. We bonded immediately. What a wonderful, strange new feeling; a dream job and two real girlfriends. And the timing couldn't have been better. It helped fill the sadness of missing Sammie. My daughter Melanie, who had been my constant companion for the last eight years, was now in third grade and doing well. I even felt pretty; or at least I should have felt pretty. I had lost weight and my body had settled into a shape that fit the styles of the day. I might have taken some pleasure in the flirta-tions that were directed my way, but I still had an incredibly hard time erasing those old tapes that told me I was fat and that I would always *be* fat, no matter what the mirror told me. I remember being at work one day, looking at a woman across the store, and wish-ing I could look like her. She had pretty, long hair to her waist, a nice face and a cute figure. It took me a second to realize it was my reflection in the mirror that I was seeing, and in that instant the image morphed and grew into an unattractive woman with a million flaws. Contained in that second was my beginner lesson in how hard it was going to be to overcome my past, no matter how well things appeared on the surface.

⟶

And if my work and home life wasn't exciting enough already, my sister would liven things up when she would occasionally "crash" at our house; always unannounced of course.

201

One morning I woke up to find my sister passed out in the living room. None of us could wake her up and she slept most of the day. I was furious because Melanie was supposed to have a friend over that day. My sister finally got up around three in the afternoon. I was prepared to give her hell but, for some reason, Chris was in an unusually upbeat mood. She was bright, and cheery, and downright funny. It was a mood I hadn't seen from her in many years and it made me nostalgic for the sister I used to have a lifetime ago. She had been so angry, for so long, that this goofy mood was a welcome change. For hours we laughed and had a good old time, and then I got very sad. I told her how much I missed her, missed the sister I had known and loved. And then, throwing a Hail Mary into the end zone, I asked her if she would check into a facility and get some help. She surprised everyone by saying she would go right now, right this very minute. There was a new rehab facility in Sylmar, California, called Olive View that I had recently learned about. We called and, miraculously, they said that they would take Chris right way. Even the drive over was joyous. Chris led Charlie and me in an impromptu version of the song "All of Me," replacing the original lyrics with "Olive View; Why not take Olive View. All of me; is ready for Olive View." It was a wonderfully unusual experience to see my sister so happy. Of course, her giddiness may have just been drugs, but I didn't care. We got there and checked her in without incident. I visited her the next day and was thrilled to see that she was still enthusiastic about the idea of getting sober and putting her life back together.

Twenty-four hours later the famous Sylmar earthquake of 1971 hit and most of Olive View collapsed. Fortunately, my sister was not in one of the buildings that went down. *Unfortunately*, Chris took the earthquake as a sign that she wasn't meant to be there and she checked herself out.

Things were going well at work. It was a fun group and I felt like really I fit in. The only one who wasn't so happy with my new life was Charlie. The job, and the confidence I was feeling, changed the dynamic in our relationship. One of the things that had drawn me to Charlie was how he took charge. Even though he was only four years older than I was, he was, for all intents and purposes, the first real parent I'd ever had. Whatever domestic skills I had, such as they were, I had learned from Charlie. How to wash dishes, how to do laundry, how to cook, how to write a check; Charlie had taught me all these things. He was the teacher, I was the willing and submissive student. It was a hierarchal relationship and Charlie liked it that way. And, for several years, so did I. It felt good to be "parented" at last. But with the job at Robinson's Department Store came a new confidence in my ability to figure things out for myself. That's what didn't go down so well at home. And because I had gotten the job while he was gone, Charlie had always viewed it as a betrayal. He was always jealous if I spent too much time away from him and, unfortunately, I had always viewed that jealousy as love. I suppose we could have talked about the issues, maybe gone to a therapist, and turned the friction into an opportunity to grow closer; I suppose. But that would have required a level of caring communication which wasn't exactly the strong suit of my marriage to Charlie. Instead, he decided that one betrayal deserved another, and he amped up his already stunning number of sexual conquests. And instead of ending the marriage, I started to have affairs of my own, and I did so with my mother's blessing. She even babysat.

Around this time, Charlie began pressuring me to have a baby. He had never before mentioned wanting a child and I was absolutely against it. Even though I adored my daughter, having another child wasn't something I *ever* wanted to do again. A shameful pregnancy, a pathetic trip to Ensenada for a marriage that should have never been, exhaustion, depression and fear of never being a decent mother, no matter how hard I tried. And now

Charlie wanted me to go through it all over again? No thanks. I think I'll just focus on making the best life I can for the daughter I already have.

I don't think for a minute that Charlie had a sudden desire to have a child of his own, even though that's what he claimed. No, it was just another way to pull me out of a working situation that seemed to be giving me the one thing that's always poison to a controlling relationship; self-confidence.

Of course, I knew none of this at the time. And, even if I *had* known, I doubt if I would have had the strength to do anything about it. Charlie told me that even though he loved being a step-father to Melanie, he really wanted the experience of having his *own* child.

So, after two years at my job, I finally agreed to his wishes and went off of birth control. I was pregnant the next month. One of the guys took over the physical part of the job for me but I finally had to give notice when I was five months along.

As my pregnancy started to show I noticed something happening that was completely unfamiliar to me: people smiled when they saw my bulging tummy. My condition actually made people happy. "When are you due?" they'd ask. It was so different from the looks of scorn and disgust I'd gotten before. And my dad still seemed to love me, even as I put on weight. He hadn't been around for my pregnancy or delivery with Melanie, but he was there for me this time. As the new baby started to move inside me, I felt beautiful and motherly. I realized that I really *wanted* this baby.

Two months later, I gave birth to my second daughter, Tiffany. Melanie was thrilled to have a baby sister and I was glad that she and Tiffany were nearly ten years apart. It seemed like too much of an age difference for them to ever experience the kind of conflict and competition that had existed between Chris and me.

Tiffany was a healthy, happy baby. Charlie seemed to love being a new dad; he pitched right in changing diapers, doing feedings, and getting up in the middle of the night. For a while, having a new baby made things *seem* better with Charlie and me, but they weren't. I found out that he had taken a girl to a hotel the very night I gave birth to Tiffany. He had even put the dinner and hotel charges right on our credit card! Firemen make great heroes; but they don't always make great husbands.

Instead of the outrage that would propel any self-respecting woman right out the door – or at least to a marriage counselor's office -- I just felt hurt and guilty. And if I ever did threaten to leave, he would utter those darkly magical words "Please give me another chance." The words were Kryptonite to me and he knew it.

CHAPTER 27

—⁓—

I STAYED HOME with Tiffany the next couple of years and really loved it. I was getting better as a housekeeper but I still wasn't much of a cook. My mother, now in her early fifties, had suddenly begun to experiment with cooking. After a lifetime of avoiding anything that even looked like a stove, she was now flipping through cook books and duplicating meals she had had at restaurants. I couldn't help but ask: "Why now? Why didn't you even try to put a decent meal on the table when Chris and I were young?" "Are you kidding me!" she said incredulously. "I was goddamn gorgeous back then; I didn't *need* to learn how to cook." Not exactly the answer I was hoping for, but it was the truth. She was stunning back then, and she never lacked for a suitor to wine and dine her, seven nights a week. It was amazing how effortlessly she had given up that life. She was now a good forty pounds heavier and didn't give a thought to her hair or makeup. She knew that she had been one of the standout beauties of Hollywood, and it didn't seem to bother her in the least that those days were gone. Most women who had a glamorous life that was built around their beauty fought like hell to hang on to it. Not Eve. That was then, and now is now. "Let's just get on with it, for chrissakes!" was her mantra and I couldn't help but admire her for that.

—⁓—

Charlie's cheating didn't stop and we separated and got back together several more times. During one of those separations,

Charlie got especially jealous and nasty and closed out our checking account, took the credit cards, and hid my car. I was literally stranded and I felt powerless. So I did what had empowered me once before. I went back to school. I enrolled at Valley College and signed up for several art and design classes.

One night in my advertising design class we had a guest speaker. He was an art director at a movie advertising agency and, after looking at my portfolio, he asked if I would be interested in coming in for an interview the next day. I remember the rush as the low hum of my everyday anxiety faded away and was replaced by the normal kind of nervousness and anxiety that we all feel when something valuable is on the line.

I showed up the next day and, after the head art director reviewed my portfolio, I was put right to work doing lay outs and paste-up for a movie ad; the film was a remake of "A Star is Born." I was so excited I forgot that I'd parked at a meter and had only put in enough money for an hour. But not even the sight of a fifty dollar parking ticket plastered on my windshield could dampen my spirits that day. Even though I was only designing newspaper ads, it made me feel like I was working in the movies. And they were paying me eight dollars an hour! Life was good.

⁓

My mother's brash manner got her a new job selling second trust deeds and she was actually pretty good at it. Through her office she was introduced to a client who was in management at a well-known drug rehab facility in Santa Monica. It was called Synanon and it occupied a building right on the beach where the very fashionable Casa del Mar Hotel stands today. Because of Synanon's location and excellent reputation, it wasn't easy to get into, you really had to *be* someone or *know* someone. My sister was in really bad shape at this time and was in desperate need of help. In fact, Chris had recently overdosed and, when they got her to the hospital, the doctors told my mother that the only vein in Chris' body that they could use for an IV was inside her vagina. All the others had collapsed from overuse.

After pulling some strings, my mother managed to get Chris into Synanon. But the facility had some very tough rules and one of them was that you couldn't smoke cigarettes. They saw smoking as another addiction and that you should kick all such substances. The irony was that Chris, a stone cold heroin addict, got through the horrible agony of detoxing from heroin in the first few weeks. But she just couldn't bring herself to give up cigarettes and she was forced to leave the program. Mom and I were furious with her. How could she possibly blow this chance just because of a cigarette habit?! But she maintained that it had been easier to kick heroin than cigarettes. It was only a matter of days before she was back on heroin as well.

Once again it was my mother who tracked down a clinic and managed to get Chris in right away. For a long time I was confused by this uncharacteristic generosity on my mother's part. It was a tremendous amount of work to get someone into a facility back then, especially when the patient didn't have any money. But mom managed to find dozens over the years and never once complained. I once asked her where this streak of caring and kindness came from; her answer was honest if not comforting. "If I can get her into a clinic, then she's not my fucking problem," she said. So much for her generous spirit.

Eve found a group house called Cri-Help where Chris promptly broke the rules by starting a relationship with her recovered addict/counselor, Tony. When they were found out, Tony was promptly fired and Chris was kicked out of the program. They ended up getting a little place together and, for a while, they actually made a go of it. They were both getting regular doses of Methadone so they were even fairly coherent. Chris took Samantha out of the foster home to live with her and Tony and the three of them lived a somewhat normal life.

It seemed like my sister was, once again, really trying to get it together and I started to include her in my life again. Over the next few years Chris had two more kids, Antoinette and Chad. We all hoped that having the responsibility of three children might nudge Chris into a frame of mind that would lead to a more productive life. But, as had happened so many times before, something occurred that put her right back into a bad place. Tony fell off the wagon; he started using and soon he was back on heroin. I wanted Chris to leave him; I wanted her to have a life away from all the things that come with drugs. Charlie and I offered to help. But within a few months she was right back where she'd been -- only now she had two more children to care for. She finally left Tony but immediately replaced him with a new druggie boyfriend named Kenny. Same old drugs, new Kenny. And then my sister had *another* child, a boy named Rick. She was, of course, overwhelmed, and so was I. There's only so much energy in each of us and I could feel myself running low.

For Chris things did not get better. She was still hooked on heroin and her kids bounced around to various foster homes, then back to Chris, and then back again to the homes.

Tony, the father of her children, died a few years later; he was found dead in the bathtub from a drug overdose.

─෧─

My life, as far as my career was concerned, was going pretty well. I had been a free-lance designer for several agencies that specialized in movie advertising and I was starting to make some pretty good money. Together with Charlie's salary we were living quite comfortably, we were even able to afford a few trappings of success; he bought a used black Porsche coupe and I bought a matching white one. We bought a small boat and our weekends were often spent on waterskiing trips. On the surface things looked pretty good. But when I look back on those years I realize that almost every one of those non-stop, "fun packed" weekends was fueled by a steady stream of alcohol. The blender was working overtime whipping up Margarita's and Pina Coladas. My life, or at least my "life-style," looked like a huge success. It was so much better than anything I could have ever hoped for when I was growing up that I just let myself be swept away by all the energy and shiny new objects. But snapshots taken during those years reveal a growing unhappiness that was showing up in my features. My eyes look hard and suspicious, my smile a forced attempt that probably convinced nobody but me. And my sense of humor that had always been my life raft during difficult times seemed to be drifting into the distance.

_6_

It was becoming a regular tradition that my father would come over at least one weekend a month. We'd barbeque and swim, and consume numerous "Maxwell Massacre's," but mostly we'd laugh. Daddy had that effect on just about everyone he ever met. Without the drugs fueling his roller coaster moods, his sweetness was free to surface and indeed he charmed everyone who came within a mile of him. For reasons that I didn't quite understand at the time, he and my mom were actually getting along very well as "friends." I think the fact that my mother had basically given up on a love life helped calm her usual frustration with him and, without a love life, my father had nothing to be jealous of. Stripped of all the broken promises of love, the two of them seemed content to enjoy what they had always enjoyed, even when they were at each other's throats; their wonderfully unique sense of totally irreverent fun. Regardless of her steady stream of put downs, no one "got" my father's sense of humor like my mother, and they both knew it. Even though their history was fraught with disappointment, betrayal, and downright abuse, it was a history nonetheless.

And, like it or not, no one "got" my mother better than my father --- actually no one "got" my mother, period, *except* my father, and she knew *that* as well. It was strange to see, actually. Having spent my entire life negotiating truces that were instantly broken by one or the other of them, dreaming day and night that one day they might come back together so we could be the family we once were, or at least I *imagined* we were, here I was witnessing the two of them chatting, laughing, sharing a story or an old song like nothing harsh or ugly had ever happened during the last twenty years.

At one point my mother shocked us all by consenting to "re-marry" my father. I was dumbfounded; I hadn't realized that they'd been getting along *that* well. My mother assured me that she wasn't getting married for love or anything that romantic. It was purely for practical reasons: "Eddie wants me to get his ASCAP royalties for songwriting, and his G.I. benefits when he's gone and he can't do that unless we're married."

"Well, Daddy must be happy," I said. "He's loved you for so long…"

"And I *like* him," was her clipped response

Now, if that's not romance, then what is?

CHAPTER 28

IN 1979, I was offered a full-time position at Warner Brothers as the Director of Advertising. I was given a small office in the old animation building on the lot. It was my first real office and I loved it. Sometimes I would catch my reflection in the window and it was always a shock to see me there. I was doing the work; I just couldn't *believe* I was doing the work. Our creative team of four would be given a feature script to read and then we would meet and throw around design and copy ideas for the posters, or "one-sheets" as they're known. We also came up with concepts for "trailers," TV, and radio spots.

Sometimes at night, after work, I would walk around the Warner Brothers lot by myself. The studio had such a rich history. So many classics had been filmed there: "Casablanca," "The Maltese Falcon," "Streetcar Named Desire," dozens of others. Both of my parents had worked at Warner Brothers at different times in their careers and I imagined them being a part of such a grand time and place. It reminded me of the beautiful publicity photographs of my mother that I used to take to school for "show and tell." It also brought back fond memories of my dad taking me to the studios when I was a kid.

My own office had a special touch of personal history; I was told that the famous writer and animator Bob Clampett, who had a major hand in creating Bugs Bunny, had occupied the very room I now worked in. If that was true then it was a real six degrees of separation between me and my father, because Bob Clampett went on to create the "Beany and Cecil" cartoon show for which my father later wrote.

I worked for a woman named Candace who took me under her wing. One day she gave me a much needed tutorial on how to be taken seriously in the corporate world. "You're a very bright, imaginative, and productive person; *I* know that, and someday you'll know that" she said. "But if your desire is to be taken seriously, you don't do yourself any favors with the big hair and short skirts; that's what people talk about, not your talent."

When I got over the initial hurt feelings and really thought about it, I could see that what she said made sense. It didn't happen overnight, but gradually I replaced the mini-skirts with longer ones and styled my hair more suitably. I was still the same person inside but I was learning to be comfortable presenting myself as a qualified, creative person. After two years, Candace was hired away by ABC as the vice-president in charge of advertising and promotion and she asked me to come work for her there.

Charlie had mixed feelings about me taking the job at ABC. He was thrilled with the additional money that would be coming in, but I could see that he was, once again, threatened by my increased independence.

When I gave notice at Warner Brothers, my friends and co-workers put together a very nice going away party for me at a nearby restaurant. We were already ordering food and drinks when Charlie arrived. From the moment he got there, Charlie started flirting with a girl that I worked with. He began to order drink after drink and I knew that meant that he was laying the groundwork for "It wasn't my fault; I was drunk out of my mind." Sure enough, a few hours into the party, Charlie was dancing and grinding away with my co-worker, who was also fairly blotto. It was humiliating, to say the least. At one point they actually stopped dancing and just stood there in the middle of the floor making out. We'd been through scenes like this before but none so blatant, and not in front of my co-workers. You don't have to be Sigmund Freud to know that Charlie was saying "fuck you and your fancy job," challenging me to do anything about it. He'd tested me before and I had always failed. No matter how hurt or angry I'd get, I would always cave. And here he was testing me in front of a room full of people who had come to honor my promotion. What I should have done, of course, was grabbed the nearest vase and broken it over his head. What I *did* do was tap him on the shoulder and whisper, "You really shouldn't be doing that here." Charlie's reply was a simple, declarative sentence, "You're right," he said.

I returned to the table thinking that I'd found a discreet way of handling things and that Charlie was right behind me. But instead he decided to play things out… he took my statement literally, that he shouldn't be doing that *there*.

He and my co-worker walked out of the restaurant --- together!

I turned to look back at my friends, hoping they'd been engrossed in their conversations and had missed what had just happened, but no such luck. Between the synchronized jaw dropping and the head shaking, it was apparent they'd seen everything, and they were beyond shocked.

Who *does* that?!? The most callous, unthinking, philandering husband will at least *try* to cover his tracks, if only not to get caught and then have to deal with the drama of it all. But Charlie was so sure of my powerlessness, so intent on stealing the spotlight and punishing me for having the nerve to succeed, that he did what he did in front of all my colleagues. I was mortified, embarrassed, ashamed and angry. But I'd been all those things before, a million times over.

I sat with all those emotions for a few minutes. And a few minutes more. And then a half hour went by. Something was different. Maybe it was all the positive reinforcement I had been getting at work, all the encouragement from my friends and colleagues that had finally given me a sense of worth. I don't know what combination came together at this exact moment, but for the first time in my life I didn't blame myself for something bad that had happened to me. There *was* no excuse for Charlie's behavior, and that "muscle" of co-dependent weakness and denial had just been blown out by the sheer magnitude of what had happened. It wasn't just the cruelty and disregard he inflicted, it was the fact that he actually seemed to enjoy the fact that I was in pain. It's one thing to be selfish and narcissistic; there's plenty of that around and there always will be. But to take pleasure in the knowledge that you were causing another person pain? That was what I finally understood at that moment. And that was what pushed me over the edge

I left the restaurant and started to drive. I had no idea where I was going. Eventually I had to go home, but for a while I just drove around the valley letting this strange new feeling wash over me. And then I did something completely out of the ordinary for me. I pulled into a Jack-in-the-Box restaurant and ordered a Chicken Supreme and an order of onion rings. Not exactly the Champagne and caviar that some would associate with a life changing moment, but, for me, it was big. Late night calories were unthinkable, and I had just ordered them dipped in batter and deep fried.

After I got my food I pulled into a space, parked, and contemplated my life. My first thought was, "Wow, I'm eating all by myself." I had always felt a deep sense of shame about eating, and eating *alone* was something I would never risk being caught doing. I sat there trying to figure out what I was feeling. I absolutely expected to break down sobbing, but it just wasn't happening. I took another bite of my gooey good sandwich and ate another onion ring. *Damn, that tastes good,* I thought as I waited for the tears to come. Finally I realized what I was feeling. It was relief.

My marriage was over. Even *I* didn't deserve the treatment that Charlie had just doled out. This is what I had been waiting for. It took something this big to pierce my armor of fear and insecurity.

I woke up my mom when I got home and told her what had happened. Whatever else Eve was, she was a tough broad who didn't take crap from anybody. Certainly she would be furious with this blatant display of disrespect to her daughter.

Wrong. Oh, she was annoyed, that's for sure. But the person she was annoyed with was me. The fact that I was stating categorically that I had *had* it and was filing for divorce struck her as a huge overreaction. Men cheat, she said. It was a fact of life, and how naïve of me to think otherwise. More importantly, if I divorced Charlie and moved out or asked him to move out, where was *she* supposed to live? "Just because he couldn't keep it in his pants, *all* of us have to suffer?" she said. This was the same woman who wanted to disembowel my science teacher for destroying my homework. But she didn't bat an eye when I told her that my husband left me in a restaurant and took off with another woman.

CHAPTER 29

———————— ∽ ————————

CHARLIE DIDN'T COME home that night, or the next. By Monday morning, even my mother was starting to fume. I found the strength to go to a lawyer and file for divorce. Now it was real and, barring some incredibly embarrassing failure of will, there was no turning back.

As I drove to work after filing the paperwork, I wondered what it would be like to be single. I'd been married at thirteen and with Charlie since I was fifteen. Now I was thirty-two years old and had no idea what it meant to be single. Would I ever date again? If so, how do I go about it? Would anybody ever find me attractive? Was I, as Charlie had always told me, giving up the "best thing I could ever hope of having"? As I was juggling these thoughts, a very attractive man with a beautiful mass of dark hair pulled up next to me on the freeway. He motioned for me to roll down my window. After chatting back and forth across bumper to bumper traffic for a while, he asked for my phone number. I guess my look of shock prompted him to inquire, "You're not married, are you?" I glanced down at the divorce papers on the passenger seat and realized that, for the first time in my adult life, not to mention a portion of my childhood, I was *not* married. A smile came to my lips and I said in a loud, clear voice "No, I'm not married." My first day single and I'd been asked out already!

Charlie was there when I got home. I told him it was over and showed him the divorce papers. He really hadn't believed that I had a limit and, to be honest, neither had I. He was stunned. I told him that I was moving out with Tiffany, that the house was too much for me to manage and I didn't want to displace my mother (God forbid) or Melanie, who was now eighteen and had a boyfriend and probably wouldn't be at home that much longer anyway. He pleaded, he threatened, he bullied. But I held firm. "It's over," I said flatly. "We'll see about that" he said, threateningly. Furious, he threw some clothes in a bag and slammed out.

Later that night I was awakened by the sound of the sliding glass door in the bedroom being opened. I could see that it was Charlie and I figured he was there to try and change my mind, but then I saw the crazed look in his eyes and it scared the hell out of me. I jumped up to run out the other door but he grabbed me from behind and in the mirror I saw that he had a gun. He held it to my head and I froze in a strange, terrifying moment of disbelief. If I was about to scream, it never got that far. My mother had seen the automatic security lights go on and at that moment she marched into our room to see what the hell was going on. Without breaking stride, she crossed to Charlie and grabbed the gun out of his hand. "Oh, for chrissake, Charlie, *give* me that thing and get the hell out of here before I call the police." When I tell you that my mother was never in her life embarrassed and never experienced fear, I mean *never.* Charlie made a quick exit. After examining the gun, my mother said, "What do you know, it's loaded." Then she ordered me to go back to bed and get some sleep.

As if I could possibly sleep now? "What if he comes back?" I asked.

"I'll shoot him," my mother said with a smile. Then she added "I hope to hell he comes back."

As I lay there, not sleeping, I wondered if Charlie could have actually pulled the trigger? Most men bring flowers or candy if their goal is to woo their angry wife back into their arms. Charlie had put a gun to my head.

I rented an apartment for Tiffany and myself in Sherman Oaks a few days later and moved out of the house. I took only a few dishes, a couple of glasses, a TV, and a bed. I found someone to watch Tiffany after school and I threw myself into my new life and my new job.

Tiffany was not happy about the move. As a nine year old child, she didn't understand why I was leaving her wonderful father or why she had to leave her home, her friends, or her school. Of course I couldn't tell her the real reason; I wanted to protect her as much as I could. In retrospect, I wish I hadn't protected her quite so much; it made for a very angry child and a very combative relationship for a lot of years to come.

My new job title was Director of Advertising and Promotion for ABC network. Instead of physically designing artwork, it would now be my job to give out that work to some of the advertising agencies that I'd once worked for. The promotion part of my job involved traveling to locations where we were filming and supervising photo shoots and interviews with the cast. It was a whole new ball game with all new rules.

I was given an amazing office on the fifth floor of the 2020 building on Avenue of the Stars in Century City. It had floor to ceiling windows that looked out onto the plaza and was surrounded by thirty story towers that housed some of the most powerful and famous talent agencies, law firms, and motion picture production companies in the world.

The atmosphere was very corporate with lots of business people dressed in suits. Everyone seemed so important and focused and I still struggled with feeling out of place. There remained a constant voice that whispered in my ear that I didn't deserve any of this and that someone was going to snatch it all away. But each day I got in the car, drove to work, and put in the best day I could.

At home, on my own for the first time, I was discovering what kind of housekeeper I was. This may sound like no big deal, but my mother had always criticized me for being too neat; "It's not a fucking hospital," she would growl if I so much as emptied an ashtray. I was thrilled to find out I could actually keep my apartment clean all by myself without annoying anyone. I also found that I did just fine with a glass of wine or two at dinner; I no longer needed a dozen margaritas to get through a weekend.

But I wasn't getting any better with my parenting skills, and it was frustrating to say the least. I really expected that having been so much older (I was twenty-four when I had Tiffany) that I would feel confident. But I was terrified that I was going to ruin my child. I knew I couldn't look to my mother for modeling or guidance. You don't ask a fox how best to raise a happy chicken. And it only made matters worse that Tiffany was still angry with me for turning her life upside down "for no good reason."

If I had it to do over again, I would have found some age-appropriate way of telling her that I was leaving an unhappy, even dangerous relationship that included lies, and cheating, and abuse. She could have understood that, even at her age. But I didn't have those tools at the time, so I said nothing. There are many, many things I would do differently if given another chance to be a mother to my children. It was one of those "hidden costs" of having such a bizarre childhood with so little constancy. I guess I did better at finding my own way to housekeeping than I did to parenting. I wish it was the other way around, but it wasn't. And even though it took many years to get there, I think my daughters understand now how difficult it was for me to figure out the right thing to do back then.

My job at ABC was starting to get exciting. I was sent to Munich, Germany, where we were filming the mini-series "Inside the Third Reich." I was responsible for coordinating the "behind the scenes" interviews with the actors and overseeing cast photo shoots. Every second of the experience was thrilling to me from the moment I boarded the airplane. I may have been thirty-two years old chronologically but I was as excited as a ten year old kid going to Disneyland for the first time.

I'm sure my co-workers considered my wide-eyed enthusiasm a bit naive; there wasn't a task that I considered dreary or dull. I thought about all those times that I would sneak onto a sound stage to watch something being filmed when I was at Warner Brothers, and now here I was, actually being paid to be on one of those sets. In the many trips that followed over the years, I never did consider it work; it was much more like a continuing education. I was lucky enough while at ABC to be sent to Rome, London, Kauai, and many more wonderful places, in Europe as well as the USA. My first traveling experience had been when I ran away with Don and we made it only as far as a jail cell in Beloit, Kansas.

This was better.

A big part of my job depended on getting talented and sometimes temperamental people to pose for pictures and do promotional interviews even when they didn't particularly want to. And it turns out that I was pretty darn good at that. Perhaps it was because I had grown up with a very talented and sometimes temperamental father, and a less talented but always temperamental mother, and I had spent most of my childhood figuring out ways to get these two people to do things they didn't particularly want to do. Whatever the cause, I was good at my job and the network was happy with my work. And, of course, it didn't hurt that my job included the opportunity to work with some of the biggest stars in the world, icons such as Elizabeth Taylor, Sophia Loren, Clint Eastwood and Meryl Streep, to name a few. And nearly as famous were some of the photographers taking their pictures; creative masters like Annie Leibovitz, Matthew Rolston and Harry Langdon. I worked with some amazingly talented people. And to my utter amazement not one of them ever turned to me and said: "What the hell are *you* doing here?"

CHAPTER 30

⌥

TWO YEARS AFTER Charlie and I divorced, Tiffany and I moved into a wonderful little house in Studio City. We had the usual ups and downs that mothers and teenage daughters have, but it was a loving relationship and it was working. All that was missing from my life, all that I longed for, was a romantic relationship.

I got two dogs instead.

My dad would come over and stay many weekends. Even my mother would join in for a day by the pool. She was still Eve, but she was older and there was now a bit less force in the tornado. Eleven year old Tiffany, however, didn't see the improvement. It was around this time that the Sylvester Stallone movie "First Blood" came out. It was the one in which the tough-as-nails character of "Rambo" was first introduced and it inspired Tiffany to come up with a new name for her grandmother. Instead of "Grammie" as she'd always called her, she became "Grambo," which suited Eve just fine. Tiffany didn't much like Grambo and the feeling was mutual. I remember asking my mother once why she felt so differently about my two girls and she answered, quite matter-of-factly, that she just didn't have any feelings for Tiffany. The one thing you could always count on from Eve was an honest answer, no matter how cold it sounded. And the truth is that, while there's no excuse for not at least trying to connect with a little girl who happens to also be your granddaughter, my mother came from a background in which she was separated from her sister until they were in their teens. This may explain why Eve had no problem favoring me -- if you could call it that -- over Chris, and was now favoring Melanie over Tiffany. There might have been something in my mother that made it difficult to understand that it didn't have to be a competition. But whatever the source of the problem, the result was that Melanie, to this day, has much fonder memories of her "Grammie" than either me or Tiffany.

⁓

After three years at ABC I was offered a job with CBS as the vice-president of print advertising. This was an important job with a much higher salary. I went to my boss, Candace, for advice. I took her to lunch and she encouraged me to take the position. That lunch was memorable for two reasons; not only did I decide to take the job at CBS, but I accidentally got a lesson in just how big an impression my mother made in the world. During the lunch, Tom Selleck walked in and sat at a nearby table. The TV show "Magnum P.I." was a hit at the time and Tom was a huge star. Candace spotted him first and mentioned that she had dated Tom back when they both went to Grant High School. I shared the fact that I, too, knew him and had been related to Tom by marriage when we were kids. When Tom's lunch ended he stopped at our table.

"Candy? Is that you?" Tom said.

"Hey, Tom, nice to see you," Candace said as they pecked cheeks. Then Candace gestured towards me. "And of course you know Casey Clair; you used to be related," whereupon Tom just stared at me blankly. It had been well over thirty years since I'd last seen him so I wouldn't have expected him to remember me on sight. Trying to jog his memory, I said; "Remember, we used to play in the cul-de-sac? You and your brothers, and your sister and my cousins, John, Doug, and Gregg?" Nothing. And now people were staring. "My sister Chris and I were there, too." I rambled on lamely. "We were kind of chubby... We all used to play ball and hide and seek?" Still nothing from Tom. It was getting very embarrassing as more people in the restaurant stopped to listen. I seemed like a pathetic fan who had simply made up a story to create a connection to a celebrity. I wanted to crawl under the table and hide. All seemed lost, but then a faint glimmer of acknowledgment came over Tom's face. "Wait a minute," he said, the memories forcing his eyes wide open. "Was your mom Eve?! Eve Whitney, the *really* loud one?"

"Yes, yes, yes, yes!" I almost cried with relief. "That's her. Eve is *my* mother." Never have I been so glad to claim her as my mother, and, for once in my life, grateful that she was a big loudmouth. At least *she* had made a lasting impression, albeit a bad one. I could hear the silverware begin to rattle again as everyone went back to their business and I, happily validated, finally relaxed.

I took the job at CBS in 1984.

The Farmer's Market was right across the parking lot and many days I would go there for lunch. The Los Angeles Farmer's Market has been a popular landmark since the nineteen thirties. It's still there today and looks pretty much the same even though it is now surrounded by "The Grove," one of the most upscale outdoor malls in America. As I walked among the outdoor stalls of the market I would remember the trips I made here with my wonderful grandmother, my "Gummy." This was one of the places she would take me to shop and have lunch. And here I was, thirty years later, walking the same steps, missing her sweet, comforting smile. Many were the days I would have to slip on my sunglasses because it would've been difficult to explain the tears that were running down my cheeks for no apparent reason in the middle of the afternoon. Gummy's voice would always ring in my ears as I passed the same lunch stands I remembered from my youth. "Doesn't anybody *feed* you?" she would ask as I ordered something from this stall, or that stall. "Doesn't anybody ever *wash* you?" was another "Gummy" refrain. And she'd take me into the little girl's room and give my little hands a good scrubbing before I ate. She knew I wasn't getting the kind of care I needed, and she was "just sick" about being too old and infirm herself to be able to do much about it. But she did more than she knew, my dear, wonderful "Gummy." She cared. She noticed. In the brief amount of time we spent together she gave me more attention and love than I dared hope for back then. Gummy left me some wonderful memories, and how lucky I was now to be able to walk across the street to lunch and conjure up so many other afternoons spent with someone so singularly important in my life.

_6

I must say that, whatever else my parents were or were not in the way of good role models, they were both extremely proud of my success. When they saw my new office at CBS, they gushed with pride. I was so happy to get this acknowledgment from them, so grateful for the recognition, that it never occurred to me to look back with blame on how rough a road it had been. So deeply implanted was my belief that any difficulties along the way were strictly my own fault at worst, and just the way life was, at best, that I never once felt an ounce of resentment about the obstacles I had faced. I had a pretty positive disposition back then, and I have one now, and I recommend it as a way of facing life's challenges. But I also have come to believe that periods of relative calm in one's life are opportunities to take stock of what's true and what's not true about one's past. This would have been a good time to take a good look at what really happened during my childhood, but I didn't. "Why rock the boat?" whispered the small voice in my head. Why bring up the past when it's not a pretty place to visit? Why not enjoy this incredible gift of having your parents back in your life? And so I basked in the lighthearted nature of my newfound relationship with my parents. And my relationship with CBS continued to flourish as well.

All this good fortune would invariably trigger incredible guilt when I thought of my sister. She would never have the same opportunities I was having. We'd been born fifteen months apart to the same parents, and yet our lives had turned out totally different. Why me and not Chris? But I knew the answer to that one. Even though I hadn't had a normal life either, I'd been shown love by my father. He could be neglectful and moody, and he dropped out of sight when I needed him most, but that didn't negate the fact that, when he was in good shape, he was very loving to me --- and, compared to my mother, he'd been downright steady. My sister got nothing from either parent. Sometimes I would almost forget I had a sister and my parents barely mentioned her anymore. The world she lived in, the world of drugs and dealers and nights spent in jail, was light years away from mine. Sometimes I thought of myself as an only child with a sister.

CHAPTER 31

I HAD BEEN divorced from Charlie for almost five years and I did my best to make up for lost time when it came to dating. After all, during my teen years, when every other girl was going to parties, and out on dates, discovering boys and learning from their mistakes, I was married and caring for a daughter. It was the eighties and it was a good time to get an education about the opposite sex. Rules were being challenged and a girl could play the field without people labeling her promiscuous or worse. There were rich guys, poor guys, interesting guys, and dentists. Mostly, though, there were guys who *liked* me and pursued me. I figured that would narrow the odds of being rejected, which was, of course, my worst nightmare.

I felt as though I knew nothing about men or relationships, and I wanted to learn. My strictest rule was that Tiffany wasn't subjected to a parade of men in our house, so I made sure that my personal life was kept discreet. I'd be lying if I said I didn't have fun, but the "fun" of dating begins to wear thin after a while and I began to look for something more meaningful.

My head told me that I was ready to be vulnerable enough to fall in love and get married, but my heart had other ideas. With all the good fortune that had come my way during the previous few years it looked to all the world, and myself as well, that I had my life together and was ready to press ahead with joy and happy faces scribbled all over the page. But there were "things...." things that bothered me in the middle of the night. Thoughts and feelings that woke me up in a cold sweat and kept me pacing until daybreak. I couldn't quite get a handle on what was happening; after all, I had a terrific job, I was healthy, I had even been told that I was more attractive now that I no longer had that grim look of anger that was etched onto my face during the last years of my marriage. But there was still something hidden that I couldn't get to. Not by myself, anyway. I remember one incident in particular that shook me up. I was dating a wonderful guy named Steve and it was going well enough that he asked me to fly with him to meet his family in San Francisco. Everything seemed fine until Steve's father asked me if I had children. I was about to answer when Steve interrupted with "Casey has a fifteen year old daughter named Tiffany." I waited for him to add that I also had a twenty-five year old daughter, Melanie, but he didn't. I was about to say it myself thinking that he'd accidentally forgotten. But something in Steve's look stopped me; he didn't want me to tell his father about Melanie. It was a terrible moment and it sent me into a tailspin that was completely out of proportion to the offense. It probably wasn't Steve's most chivalrous moment, but it wasn't horrible for him to assume that my childhood pregnancy might be something to discuss at a later date. But I absolutely melted down. I felt he was ashamed of me, embarrassed by my past. I had spent my whole life feeling bad about myself and apologizing for my life, and I'd worked incredibly hard to overcome all that. If he was embarrassed by my past, then he was embarrassed by me. Or, at least that's the way I felt at the time. But my reaction was way over the top for a simple case of embarrassment or miscommunication. The moment triggered all the fears and insecurities I thought I had buried long ago. I would *always* be haunted by my past. I would *always* feel less-than everybody else in a group, *always* be unlovable, and unworthy, and, well… an embarrassment. At that moment I felt doomed and I took it out on Steve.

We broke up not long after. Unfortunately, the whole incident only served to validate my fears about relationships; that it wasn't worth the pain to risk actually caring for someone. And it would be many years before I'd risk feeling those emotions for someone again.

_ɕ_

At the end of the 1980's everyone was doing some belt tightening, including CBS. They brought in a team of bow-tied efficiency experts who determined that my entire department could be outsourced, so I was thanked for my good service and shown the door. For the first time in a very long time, I was unemployed.

I had a little money saved so I didn't panic immediately. But the free time made it difficult to avoid the fact that something important was still missing from my life. I filled the time with a series of flings with interesting but unavailable men that couldn't possibly go anywhere meaningful.

The truth was that, in addition to picking unavailable men, I was also going through a particularly insecure time in my life. I didn't have a job, I was doubting my talent, my purpose, and I was losing confidence that I might actually be an attractive woman. It's incredible how deep those messages go when you hear them as a child. "You're fat." "You're a pain in the ass." "Why would I spend the weekend at home with you when I've got a date?" That self-image went into the "wet cement" of my young psyche and now it seemed that it was stuck there; set solid as I became an adult. No matter how hard I worked, no matter how much I accomplished, no matter how many people told me how wonderful a job I'd done overcoming Himalayan sized obstacles, I still didn't feel deserving of love.

CHAPTER 32

————— ❧ —————

AT LEAST THOSE sleepless nights helped me come to a decision about my professional life. I had always wanted to be a writer, and if not now, when? I had grown up with a writer, and no matter how much heartache my father went through when things were tough, I never forgot the joy he experienced when he got a story, or a joke, or a song just the way he wanted it. I decided to enroll in several writing classes. I took courses and seminars for the mechanics and rules of writing movies and TV sit-coms. I learned how to pitch a story, how to get an agent, and how to organize a writing schedule.

And then I just started writing. I wanted to approach it like a real job, so I got up every morning and did whatever I needed to do to be at my computer by nine. My father had been a "binge writer," throwing himself into round the clock sessions, and then "crashing" for days at a time, all aided and abetted by drugs. I had seen what that did to his health and I knew I wanted something different. So I stuck to a schedule. I focused on television writing. Like so many kids growing up in the fifties, television had been my nanny. My first glimpse of the world was through the eyes of Ozzie and Harriet, Howdy Doody, Lucy and, of course, my favorites, Burns and Allen, and Jack Benny. Now I watched and studied every sit com on TV, chose about three shows that I really liked, and wrote "spec" scripts for all of them. I got good reaction but no sale. So I went back to the desk and wrote dozens more. Tiffany was seventeen now and doing well, so I could really take a chance on making this work. Maybe it was madness, chasing a dream like this at the age of forty, but I was enjoying it more than anything

I'd ever done before in my life. It felt like I had finally found my niche.

Once again, my parents surprised me. As distant as they had been in my childhood, they watched what was happening in my life now and they cheered me on. My father especially wanted me to do well and would read all my scripts and offer tips and support. I hadn't made penny one and the end of my funds were not far in the distance, but I just kept sitting down to that keyboard every day and putting words onto the screen. I had to refinance my home to keep myself afloat, but by now writing felt like home and there was no plan "B". If I didn't make it as a writer, at least it wouldn't be from lack of trying.

─⟲─

My father's health had begun to deteriorate over the last few years. One day my daughter, Melanie, and her girlfriend dropped by to visit "Poppa" and found him unconscious. He was rushed immediately to the nearest hospital. The doctors told us that he was in a coma and in critical condition.

Since my father didn't have a regular doctor at the V.A. and no one could give us a straight answer, I called a doctor I had met at a clinic when I'd gone in for a back problem. His name was Daniel Ruben and we had become friends; he had met my father socially on several occasions and had absolutely fallen in love with him. It turned out that "Dr. Dan" had recently opened up a practice of his own. He came right away when I called and, after examining my father, had him transferred to another hospital. He reviewed my dad's chart and requested a list of all the medications my father was receiving from the V.A. And then he set out to determine if they were helping or adding to my father's problems.

In the meantime, my father remained in Intensive Care, in and out of a coma, his health failing rapidly. In the end his prognosis was not good. Dan gave us the sad news that, while they still couldn't determine the exact cause, my father was dying, and we could lose him any day.

I couldn't believe it. I heard the words but I couldn't take them in. My breath immediately became labored as I struggled to process what I had just been told. How could this be happening? He was seventy-seven years old but only a year ago he had been absolutely the most vital human being in the world. And I had just been told that he was going to die, probably very soon.

How odd that my very next thought was of Chris. It had probably been months since I'd seen her, but now Daddy was dying and I thought I should get ahold of her and let her know. But mom didn't think it was such a good idea. She knew from Samantha that Chris and her addict boyfriend, Kenny, were completely strung out on heroin at the time. "What if Eddie does wake up?" she argued, "The sight of Chris could kill him." She had a point.

We called all of Daddy's friends and that night there were about fifteen people crowded into his room in the Intensive Care Unit of the Sherman Oaks Hospital. Everyone was telling stories, including my mother, and all of us were alternating from laughter to sobbing with grief. It may seem an odd thing to do, but stories were everything to my father and we told them now to honor him. My favorite story was one my mother told about when my dad was writing songs and comedy for "Spike Jones and his City Slickers." The group specialized in satirical arrangements of popular songs which were often punctuated with sound effects like whistles, cowbells, gunshots, and big, fat burps. My dad traveled all over the country with Spike and the guys on a private railroad car. The band not only recorded wacky songs, they also dressed outrageously. Spike and the band would wear brightly colored zoot suits which were eye-catching enough, but one of the guys, Frankie Little, happened to be a dwarf, and another, Junior "Locks" Martin, stood seven foot seven. One time when they were playing a small town in Indiana, Spike, Frankie, and Locks, all dressed in their outrageous get-ups, decided to walk into town and my dad, dressed normally, tagged along. As I mentioned earlier, my father was a very handsome man with a debonair mustache and Clark Gable looks. As they walked down the main street, everybody stopped dead in their tracks and stared at the sight of the oddly mismatched group. After a while Spike got annoyed and remarked, "What the hell is everyone looking at?"

"I don't know," said my dad, "Maybe they've never seen a Jew before."

Everyone in the hospital room laughed for five minutes straight. At that point Dr. Dan came in and asked us to keep it down because people were asking what the hell could be so damn funny in the ICU, I can't say that I blamed them, what could be so funny? I guess you had to be there.

For all my father's flaws, for all his ill-timed absences, I loved this man with all my heart. I couldn't bear the thought of losing him, especially this way, comatose in a hospital. And then my mother shocked me by saying "What the hell, I've got three bedrooms and I can take the man in a coma. Let him die at my house."

"You'd do that?" I asked, incredulous.

"He's your father," she said.

"Are you sure?" I asked.

"I'm almost positive," she said.

"I meant about taking Daddy to your house,"

"Sure, why not?" she said.

It was a generous offer and I was very grateful. *Until I saw my mother's house.*

It had been a nice place when she'd bought it a few years back but I hadn't been there in a long time. When I arrived, I was greeted with the all-too-familiar terrain of strewn clothes, the stench of stale cigarettes and overflowing ashtrays, dirty dishes and garbage spilling over everywhere. The coffee table was stacked with used plates and unopened mail. It was exactly what I had grown up with. Why should she be any different now?

But she had offered her home and so I bit my tongue and followed Mom to the bedroom where Daddy would stay. The hospital bed I'd ordered was already set up in the middle of the room amidst stacks and stacks of overflowing boxes that lined the walls.

"Geezus, Mom, it's a mess."

"I don't think Eddie will mind," she said.

"I mind," I said.

She was unmoved. On the upside, Dad's room had a nice big window that overlooked the yard. Eve agreed to let me move some of the boxes around so that it would it be easier for a nurse or a visitor to get to him. I offered to pay for a housekeeper but she declined. "No need," she said through a haze of cigarette smoke. "I already *keep* my house the way I like it. If you wanted a fucking hospital, you should've kept him where he was."

The paramedics arrived shortly after with my father. As if on cue, one of them shook his head as he entered and said, "Wow, I guess you've had a rough time of it. First your husband takes ill, then someone ransacks your house." They settled my father into the bed and hooked him up to an IV and monitors. As they were leaving, my mother gave each of them one of her business cards and tried to sell them a second trust deed. Grief can take so many different forms, can't it?

Now we had the daunting and achingly sad task of cleaning out my dad's apartment. He had been in the same place for over twenty years and had accumulated quite a collection of stuff. He had a huge weakness for gadgets, anything that had more than one function, like a pen that was also a radio, or a flashlight that was also a radio, or eyeglasses that were also a radio. The man liked radios. He *loved* Radio Shack stores and was rarely happier than when I would drive him to a nearby store and let him browse for an hour or two or three.

Because he would now be bedridden and unconscious until the end, I didn't think he'd need much. We packed up all his clothes; shoes, hats, tennis rackets and golf clubs. I gave a lot of his clothes to my mother's gardener; the rest went to the Goodwill. Dad had a couple of dozen bowling and golf trophies but my mother's house was so packed with junk that I didn't want to add to the mess. The only things I saved were his TV, several boxes of his writing, some photos, a few watches, a few radios, and of course, his cherished "Eve and Eddie" ring that my mother had given him years before when they were dating.

Over the next week we managed to make Daddy's room at Eve's house a little more homey. He also now had regular visits from a nurse who gave him sponge bathes and monitored his IV and vital signs. Dr. Dan still dropped by every few days, but there was nothing to do but wait.

It was excruciating.

"Well, Daddy," I would whisper in his ear. "Here you are, finally living with the woman of your dreams. All you had to do was fall into a coma. Why didn't we think of this sooner?" While I was sitting there at his bedside, I adjusted his blanket and noticed he was wearing a pink blouse of my mother's. I called out for my mother and she came running in. "What happened? Did he die?"

"No," I answered. "Why is Daddy wearing your blouse?"

"Oh," she said. "I spilled some coffee on him when I was adjusting his I.V."

"You spilled hot coffee on Daddy?"

"I don't think he felt it. He didn't complain."

Raising my voice, I said, "Couldn't you find something besides a pink blouse to put on him? I mean, for chrissakes, give a dying man a little dignity."

"Hey, don't yell at *me*," my mother yelled right back, only louder. "I'm not the one who gave away most of his clothes."

"What was I supposed to do?" I bellowed, "Bring everything here? There's no room!"

"There's plenty of room!" my mother snapped back.

"Could you keep it down?" came a weak whisper from the bed, "I'm trying to sleep."

"Shut up, Eddie!" said my mother and turned her attention back to me. It took a long second, but I think we both realized at the exact same moment that Daddy had just spoken.

Oh, my God! We both rushed to his side. His eyes fluttered open and he managed a weak smile. "Hi," he whispered. I shrieked with joy and hugged him for all I was worth. My mother stood by in complete shock.

This was the first coherent sentence my father had put together in well over a month. What did it mean? I called Dr. Dan and he came right over. He was amazed to see my dad conscious and lucid. He examined him and asked him a series of questions to determine his state of mind.

"What's the last thing you remember, Eddie?" he asked.

"A burning sensation, right here," he said, pointing to his chest.

"My mother spilled hot coffee on him," I told Dan.

"Not on purpose," she said.

"Maybe you saved his life," said Dr. Dan.

"What can I say?" my mother responded without missing a beat, "accidents happen."

"Eve... thanks for being here," my dad whispered.

"I'm not here. *You're* here. This is my house," said mom.

"You know, Eddie, you almost died," said Dr. Dan.

"Good, because I feel like shit," came his reply.

And that's how we knew he was okay. We all laughed, including the good doctor. He explained that he was going to run a lot of tests on Eddie over the next few days. His belief had always been that the coma had been brought on by the interactions of all the drugs my dad had been taking. Dr. Dan had slowly altered my father's drug intake and apparently it had worked. He had saved my father's life. Dan was nearly as excited as I was. Before he left he told my dad, "I'm ordering a nurse for this afternoon."

"Order me one too, and make her gorgeous. My life depends on it," said a fragile-voiced Eddie.

"I don't know if you could survive a beautiful nurse," I told my dad.

"Shows what you know," he whispered, "It just so happens I've survived several." He was weak but he was back, and *with* his sense of humor!

⟶

As the days and weeks went by my father continued to improve. I knew he was feeling better when he started asking me to take him to Radio Shack. As he grew stronger, dozens of friends dropped by to "kibbitz" and say hello, and once again I got a chance to witness the humor and charm of this man. He had come to within an inch of death and all he could do was laugh, and make other people laugh. And, as that laughter filled his "sick room," I began to realize what an incredible gift he had given me and how much it had helped me survive the many rough spots in my own life. The jokes and stories that we had shared all through my youth, during the best of times as well as the worst, turned out to have been a magical set of survival tools. And I was beginning to understand just how important those tools were, and continued to be.

Everyone was happy that Daddy was recovering except my mother. On one visit she told me that we needed to talk. "I said your father could *die* here, not *live* here," she said. "What are we going to do?"

Why was I surprised? Did I really expect that my mother would be suddenly and miraculously happy to have my father living there? "Okay," I told her. "I'll figure something out, but give me some time; he just got out of a coma."

"Just?" she said, "It's been a month. I'd like my life back."

My mother's unhappiness over spending time with my father was matched only by his joy of being with her. He thought he'd died and gone to heaven, she thought she was in hell. I guess things hadn't changed so much after all.

Or had they? Neither my mother nor I had a whole lot of extra cash at the time, so it wasn't all that simple to find dad another apartment right away. And he wasn't in good enough shape yet to be on his own anyway. The longer it took, the less my mother pushed for him to be out. The two of them were forced to spend time together under the same roof and this time around they were getting along pretty damn well. For a woman who had a history of restraining orders against this man, she sure was doing a lot of laughing at his jokes. When dad would break into a rendition of one of his songs, it was always Eve who would remember the lyrics word for word; proof that there was some hidden fold in her brain, if not her heart, that still remembered why she had married him in the first place.

CHAPTER 33

———— ✺ ————

IT WAS 1992 and I was still writing one spec script after another for love and no money when I finally got my first big break. A friend had gotten one of my scripts to a writer/producer on the Will Smith sit-com, "Fresh Prince of Bel-Air" and I made my first sale. I would actually get *paid* to write an episode. It was beyond exciting. The show was filmed before a live audience and the night my episode was shot, my mom and dad and my kids were there. Everyone was proud of me, but no one was prouder than my father. I'm so incredibly thankful that he lived to see me make it as a writer. That night he gave me a congratulatory gift, a new calculator from Radio Shack that was also…. a radio.

After "Fresh Prince" I did what a lot of writers do, I went right back to the unemployment line. But luckily, after only a few months, I got a staff writing position on a show called "Getting By" with Cindy Williams and Thelma Hopkins. It was about two divorced women, each with kids, sharing a house and trying to make a living. *I knew something about that!*

Being offered a staff writing position on a show changed everything. For one, it was much easier to get an agent once I had a job -- and two, by the time I was actually hired on the writing staff of a sit-com I found that it was much different than writing on my own. Instead of just me, there were now ten funny people working on one script, so it had the potential to be ten times funnier. It was also very validating. It's one thing when your family thinks you're funny, but to be pitching jokes to established comedy writers and making them laugh, well…that's the stuff that makes you think that maybe you can do this for real.

Unfortunately, the show was cancelled after the second season. It was disappointing to be unemployed again but I wasn't discouraged. If anything, I was even more sure than ever that being a writer was what I was meant to do, even if it was an unsteady life.

Happily I was offered a job on a sit-com called "Step by Step" with Suzanne Somers and Patrick Duffy. The show was about a blended but loving family unit, kind of an updated "Brady Bunch." The kids ranged in age from seven to about eighteen. Many of the episodes were about "typical" daily dramas that any "normal" family might face; a kid getting caught cheating on a test, one of the girls not being asked out to the prom, mom missing one of the kid's drama performances, and feeling *horrible* about it! Certainly nothing to draw on from my own childhood, yet here I was contributing sweet, innocent story lines just like all the other writers. It was family life as I had always imagined it could be. No wonder I had such a good time on the show.

~⧸~

When the earthquake of 1994 hit Los Angeles, it hit Northridge the hardest but the damage was felt all over the San Fernando Valley and my house wasn't spared. Block walls came down, windows were broken, television sets were thrown across rooms, entire sets of glasses and dishes were dumped and shattered onto the floor. When I finally got a contractor to assess the damage, he told me that if I was ever considering a remodel, now would be a very good time to do it since most of the "tear down" had already been done. And so that's what I did. I was making a good salary and decided to put it into my house. Because the work was going to be extensive, it would take many months to complete. I stayed in the house until the last possible minute, and then I took a deep breath and asked my mother if I could move in with her and dad until the job was finished.

She surprised me by offering to let me stay for as long as I needed. Eve even went so far as to clean the room that was to be mine. She had her rules, of course; "You can keep this room as clean as you want," she barked. "Just make sure it stays in here. I don't want the rest of house looking like this." Fair enough, I thought, and moved in.

My first night there, my mother made a real dinner: a beef stew. She even cleared the cat off of the dining room table and set out clean plates. She also put out an opened bottle of Chardonnay that I liked. I had brought the same kind a few years before and I was touched that she'd remembered the brand. I tasted it and about choked when I realized that it *was* the bottle I had brought before. It makes me pucker even now when I think of it, but it was the thought that counted and my mom had remembered that I liked a glass of wine with dinner. During the meal, mom and dad told one story after another and we all laughed for hours.

And then I cried.

"Do you realize," I said through my tears, "that I'm living in the same house at the same time with my mother and father? That hasn't happened since I was seven years old. All those years you guys weren't speaking to each other, this is what I missed out on. No school events together. No trips to the zoo. I don't remember one birthday party with both of you there at the same time. We didn't we do any of those things."

My mother was unmoved by my sentimentality. Her attitude had always been, and always would be, that her "toughness" was what had enabled me to become a successful person in the first place. It was a Catch 22 for me; the better I did, the more she took credit. "And what about Chris?" I would ask when I was looking for trouble in all the right places. "What effect did your toughness have on her?" Her response was always the same. "She made her own choices. She could have had a good life, but she threw her life away with both hands." So Eve gets all the credit for whatever success I had achieved, and none of the blame for any of Chris' failures. Ah, isn't narcissism just the best!

My mother was about to launch into a chorus of "waaah, waaah, waaah; poor you" when my dad interrupted with; "Well it's not too late; we can still do all those things." Then he added, "Hey, the Ice Capades are in town."

"Over my dead body," said my mom, and we were back to laughing and we didn't stop until the wee hours.

It was one of the best nights of my life. After dinner I did the dishes and cleaned up the kitchen and went to bed. As I lay in bed that night, I couldn't help thinking how strange it seemed to feel safe and warm *because* my parents were there. I was forty-five years old and this was the first time that I had ever felt that way.

⟿

The next few months were wonderful. Living with my parents was actually fun for the first time in my life. Working as a writer on the show was pure joy. Tiffany and Melanie were each happily married and working on families of their own, and that hum of anxiety finally seemed to be set on "low" in every area of my life.

Except one.

Depending on who you asked, my dating history had been either hugely successful (I'd had plenty of dates) or one hilarious disaster after another. I met some nice men, but I seemed to get involved with the wrong ones. There was the doctor who turned out to be a cross-dresser, the guy who lived three states away, the rich but penny- pinching pilot who only took me to places that had a happy hour, the CEO of a manufacturing company who regularly woke up sobbing in the morning, the actor who gave me his head shot and resume at the end of our date, the very handsome, extremely macho guy who turned out to be gay and would only take me to work-out dates at the gym, the famous singer whose apartment was painted completely and totally black.

All of this made for splendid material as the writing staff gathered around the table on Monday mornings. There was nothing quite like hearing about my latest Saturday night train wreck to get a group of comedy writers going. Truth be told, I used these misadventures in dating as a way to bolster my self-confidence at the table. Some of the writers I was working with were veterans of the business and competition could be pretty rough; a good story about a bad date was frequently my best way in and it helped me find the courage to start pitching jokes and ideas for episodes.

I thought I was making progress when I met Alan. He was a bright, successful entertainment lawyer for the studios. He took me to a Lakers basketball game one night and we went directly to one of those million dollar sky-boxes reserved for VIPs. I tried to enjoy the thrill of it all, but my head began to swim and my vision became blurry. I was having a first-class panic attack. It was all too much for me. I felt overwhelmed by the very real belief that I couldn't possibly fit in with all these attractive, confident and sophisticated people. I was convinced that I was going to be found out at any moment, and that every bejeweled finger was going to be pointing at me, casting out the girl who got herself knocked up at thirteen. That girl certainly didn't deserve to be here. Hell, *that* girl didn't deserve much of anything; not this man, not happiness, not a real relationship, and certainly not love.

After that, I hit an all-time low. I went from bad to worse when I began a relationship with a married man, something I swore to myself that I would never do. I was terribly ashamed of myself. After having had a husband who cheated on me and knowing the pain it caused, I don't know how I could have done that to another woman.

When it ended, I did some significant self-evaluation. I had become involved with this man who was not only married, but also condescending, duplicitous and obviously unavailable. So, why was I attracted to him? "Condescending" and "duplicitous" were never qualities I had listed in my diary of relationship hopes and wishes. So, that left "unavailable." Could *that* be what made him attractive to me?

I was sleeping a lot, I was lethargic, I had put on weight, and I was depressed. On the surface, this was the best my life had ever been.

So why did I feel so bad? On the recommendation of a woman I worked with, I went to see a therapist named Lynn. She was a kind, caring individual; unfortunately, she was also very heavy, probably near three hundred pounds. I was much too sensitive to *her* weight to bring up the issues I was having over my ten pound weight gain or my feelings of hopelessness and self-loathing over my negative body image. So, I didn't talk about *that* in therapy at all; but I kept going to Lynn because I didn't want to hurt her feelings. How's that for co-dependence? At least I could talk to her about my poor choices in men. But I still had this self-destructive body image, so I found *another* shrink who I could talk to about *that*. He turned out to be an attractive single man and this posed a whole new set of problems. I found myself trying to impress him with what a nice, normal person I was; so, of course, I didn't share anything negative or damaged about myself. So, for several months and thousands of wasted dollars, I went to two shrinks and got nowhere. You begin to see how wildly popular I became around the comedy table at work.

Underneath the obvious high hilarity of this situation was a woman who, despite scraping her way to a successful life in several areas, was still quite incapable of believing she deserved to ask for anything for herself, even if she was paying a hundred and fifty dollars an hour for it.

Don't get me wrong, I'm a big fan of therapy but I believe that it's really important for you to be honest in order for it to work; and I wasn't being honest with anyone, not even myself.

CHAPTER 34

IT WAS DURING this time, living with my parents and seeing them interact, that I began to realize that my childhood image of them and their marriage wasn't exactly accurate. It had always helped me to think of my father as the good guy and my mother as the villain; it was good casting and, for the most part, it was accurate. But now that my father was relatively healthy again, I could see how manipulative he could be. He would use any trick he could think of to get me to take off work and spend time with him. When I would make my way to the kitchen for coffee in the morning, he would be there with the paper opened to the movie section. He had our entire day planned out. When I would remind him that I was being well paid and that I had to, kind of…you know, show up at the studio, he would put on his sad face and implore me to play hooky.

"I almost died," he would say with a catch in his throat. "Don't you want to spend as much time with me as you can?"

"Daddy," I said, "I was with you every day when you were in a coma."

"That doesn't count, *I* wasn't there."

My father demanded a lot of attention. When I lived with him as a child, I was too young to see how life revolved around him and only him. It was never about me --- or my sister. Growing up with dad was certainly better than life with mom, but now I could see how sweetly narcissistic and manipulative he could be and how my mother was right; no matter how much time you spent with him, it was never enough.

At first it was dear, and cute, and flattering; my father begging me to spend time with him. But then the requests would be more insistent. It took me a while, somewhere in the vicinity of thirty years, I suppose, to figure out that my father was also a very self-centered man. While he was proud of my success on the show, he was not particularly interested in my work schedule. Nor, for that matter, was he interested in much of anything else going on in my life that wasn't good news. When I tried to talk to him about my growing anxiety about being forty-five and single, his response was to throw a couple of compliments my way and offer to make me a "Maxwell Special" --- one of the whipped cream and m&m peanut concoctions he used to make us for breakfast when I was eight years old.

My mother reminded me that my dad had always been like this. "He's the most wonderful, talented guy in the world if you just want to laugh and have a good time, but sometimes there's more that happens in life and, at those times, he's pretty useless." She pointed out that I had just gone to him for some fatherly advice and he had responded with whipped cream and m&m peanuts. "*You* were the one who turned him into a God," she said.

"At least he tried!" I snapped back defensively. "I don't remember you even doing *that.*" She just shrugged, but I wasn't finished. "I guess there were a lot of things you didn't do back then, like raise your own kids. You left Chris and me alone.... *All* the goddamn time! Who lets their kids sleep in a carport!?"

"So you slept in the carport a few times," she shrugged. "It was summer; it was an adventure. Makes you interesting."

"It wasn't summer, and it was pouring rain," I corrected.

"Waaah, waaah. waaah." she sang mockingly.

"And you sent us to Villa Cabrini, that awful, horrible place," I said.

"Okay, here we go. So, I wasn't exactly Mother of the Year."

"Mother of the Year?" I laughed. "I wouldn't even call you Mother of the Weekend."

"You don't know as much as you think you do," my mother warned.

"I don't think I know much at all," I said. "*You* certainly never told me anything."

It seemed as though Eve had something to say and then changed her mind, but I was in no mood to indulge her. "You got something to say, say it!" I challenged.

"You want to know why you lived with your father instead of me?" she barked. "Because *someone* had to go to work. You think I wanted to be a bookkeeper? Who do you think paid his rent? Bought his car? Kept food on your table?"

"What are you talking about? Daddy worked."

"The last time your father sold something was a very long time ago."

"But he was writing all the time," I argued.

"He started a million things, he just didn't finish them. Half the time he was composing hate letters to me. *Those* he finished."

"You gave Daddy money? Why didn't you tell me? Maybe I wouldn't have spent my whole life hating you."

"Better you hated just one of us. How would you have felt about your father if you knew? Besides, Eddie was a better father than I was a mother. Hell, he was a better mother."

That was more information about the nature of my parents' relationship than I had received in forty years, and it gave me pause. I was quiet for a long moment.

"You could've tried," I said, minus the fury that had been in my tone before.

"Yeah, I could've tried," she answered. "I'm trying now."

That was the closest thing to an apology that I'd ever heard from my mother. How different these people were from the parents I knew as a child.

Everything was different now because I didn't *need* them to be perfect anymore. After my dad kicked his drug habit he was never again that extreme, unpredictable person, staying up several nights in a row and sleeping for days at a time; he was sweet and charming most of the time. I would never have to put my life in his hands again, so it was easy to love him now. Same with my mom. She really couldn't hurt me the way she had when I was little; I didn't *need* her to stay home with me, or protect me, or tell me she loved me anymore. It was a choice I made consciously to look at these two flawed people and let my anger and resentment go; maybe not all of it but enough so that I could get on with my life.

_ₒ

So my father wasn't all good and my mother wasn't all bad. Finally, all these years later, I was beginning to see the truth of who my parents really were; complex, complicated, with elements of good and bad in each of them.

My mother was right. I *had* idealized my father into someone nearly perfect. And I had also idealized the nature of his love for her. I didn't see a damaged man incapable of accepting the truth, I saw an incurable romantic who so loved this woman that he devoted his life to finding a way, *any* way to stay near her. And as I began to realize this, I also began to see how it affected the choices I was making in my own life.

I was looking for something, for someone, who didn't exist. The father I imagined never *really* existed in my life, and I wasn't going to find him in the real world. So why not just choose one unavailable man after another so I would never have to face the disappointment of losing a fantasy that had nurtured me through a lonely childhood? I didn't want to give up the dream of who my father was because it was all I had. But now I had finally gotten a chance to understand the truth. And if I could see my father and my mother as they really were, then I had a chance of looking for, and maybe even finding, a real person with whom to share my life.

It all sounds easy as I write the words, but there were tears, and therapists, and stacks of self-help books, and bad choices, and more bad choices. The truth, as they say, may very well set you free, but it's rarely an entirely pleasant experience.

——✃——

The fact was that my father and mother, while incredibly brilliant, charismatic people, were not, and never would be, very good parents. I got a grim reminder of that when we received a phone call one day letting us know that my sister, Chris, was dying. She was in a hospital in Hemet, California, and the doctors needed my mother's permission to unhook Chris from life support. "We're going to see Chris," my mother announced to my dad and me.

"Like hell," my father said.

"She's your daughter. She's dying. You're going," she ordered.

And with that we were in the car and on our way to Hemet. Three hours later, we were in the ICU where my sister was on life support. I hadn't seen Chris in a long time. She still had a mass of long, dark hair. She looked old, much older than me. She'd lost more teeth, her skin was sallow and scarred. She was in and out of consciousness when we arrived. Her boyfriend, Kenny, was there and he told us that this was the first time in a week that Chris had shown signs of being aware of her surroundings. We found out that she had Phlebitis, liver failure, and a myriad of other ailments that drug addicts frequently battle. By now Kenny and Chris had been together for fifteen years. He told us that he and Chris had been trying to kick heroin and had been going to a methadone clinic, but with little luck.

While we were there Chris' eyes fluttered open. Amazingly, a soft, sweet smile came to her face when she saw her father and she called out "Daddy." She repeated it several more times and each time she regressed further and further into a child's cadence. "Dad-dy, Dad-dy." I had to fight back tears as I realized that even now, after a lifetime of neglect, Chris was still calling out for the "Dad-dy" she had always longed for.

I actually felt badly for my mother. It had always been Eve who had bailed Chris out of trouble and sent her money. Maybe there hadn't been a smile and a hug to go with it, but Eve hadn't completely turned her back on her. And who does Chris call out for? The father who never loved her, who barely acknowledged her existence. I can't imagine that didn't hurt my mother's feelings. But, of course, I never found out because my mother would rather choke on hot coals than admit to having any feelings other than righteous indignation.

Chris slid back into unconsciousness. We stayed and took turns talking to her. We reminisced about any sweet stories involving Chris that we could remember --- but there weren't many. I stroked her cheeks and hair and held her hand. She looked very peaceful. Maybe seeing her father would give her closure. After another week, with Kenny's permission, as well as the doctor's, my mom authorized the hospital to remove Chris from the machines that were keeping her alive. She also signed a DNR, a "do not resuscitate" order. I was overcome with deep sadness and regret over Chris' life. We drove home in silence, each of us lost in our own thoughts.

When the phone rang at my mom's the next day, we all assumed that Chris hadn't made it through the night.

But Chris did make it through. "What is it with this family?" my mother remarked with a look to my father. "Do they need to be told they're hours from dying before they can get better?!"

My mother and I made the drive again. This time my father stayed home. When we saw Chris, she really did look better; at least she was conscious and off life support. The nurse told us that Kenny hadn't been back to see Chris all week. Mom and I drove to their house but no one answered the door when we knocked. Chris would be released from the hospital in a few days and she certainly couldn't care for herself. It occurred to my mother and me that maybe Kenny had had enough of Chris. But why abandon your own house? And Kenny and Chris had been inseparable all these years; it seemed strange that he'd walk out on her now.

Three days later we got a call from the Hemet police. There had been a fire at Kenny and Chris' house and it had burned to the ground. Not long afterwards they found Kenny's body in the hills; he'd been shot and killed execution style.

Mom and I drove back to Hemet to make some arrangements for Chris because the hospital couldn't keep her any longer. My sister didn't seem to understand what they were telling her about Kenny; she seemed much more confused than devastated. "Kenny's not dead, he's coming to get me," she said repeatedly. We gently convinced her that Kenny was gone and that he wouldn't be back. "Oh," she said, "Then if Kenny's not coming, who will take care of me?" She didn't cry and she didn't seem too upset, except about what would happen to her. I don't know if she really understood what was going on, but that lack of awareness saved her from some very deep grief.

Somewhere in the damaged recesses of my poor sister's mind, she knew she couldn't possibly take care of herself. A life without love, a broken soul medicated by drugs, had turned her into a sad, needy woman full of fear and dependence.

My mother contacted a social worker and made arrangements to commit Chris to a mental health facility in Hemet. Chris had no belongings, she'd lost everything in the fire, but it didn't seem to bother her. She smiled at me. I don't know how, but there was still a sort of sweet innocence to my poor sister. Kenny's murder was never solved and I don't remember Chris mentioning him ever again.

CHAPTER 35

⎯⎯⎯⎯ ⌒ ⎯⎯⎯⎯

WHEN MY HOUSE was ready and it was time for me to move back home, I took my mother out to lunch to tell her that I would be willing to take Daddy with me; he could have my second bedroom and she could have her house and her life back; after all, she had done more than her share of taking care of him.

My mother listened to my news. "You don't need your father living with you. He's fine where he is. Go, live your life." Then, after a long pause, she said, "Besides, he makes me laugh, he still thinks I've got a great ass, and he likes my pot roast."

"But, you deserve a life, too," I said.

"Listen, Casey," she said, "Things change when you get to be my age."

"But he's not going to change, Mom. You even said that."

"I don't need him to change. I don't expect anything from him, so he can't disappoint me anymore. He is who he is. And I'm okay with that."

It was official: my mother and father, "Mommy and Daddy," after forty years of cat and mouse, stalker and prey, call it what you like, were back together.

In the time it took to finish our Caesar salads, my mother had calmly informed me that my most fervent childhood wish had just come true. So what if I was forty-five years old.

⌒

My judgment seemed to be improving and maturing in so many areas; work was going well, the show had been picked up for another season and I had been picked up with it. My relationship with food was getting better. I will probably battle my body image forever, but I wasn't obsessing about it as much. I had even developed a healthy interest in politics. My mother was so loud and obnoxious about her politics that I had been turned off to the subject for years, but I was taking baby steps back into that part of world affairs and finally enjoying it on my own terms. But still none of this growth seemed to have had any effect on my ability to make a healthy decision when it came to the relationships in my life. With each passing year, I spent more time wrestling with this problem, and more time waking up in the middle of the night in a cold sweat.

I also spent more time in therapy and learned the difference between "costs" and "hidden costs." Obviously a childhood like mine has very real, somewhat predicable costs. Bounced back and forth between a charming but drug addicted father and a strong-willed but unfeeling mother will, nine times out of ten, produce an insecure child who has trouble interacting socially. Add a pregnancy and marriage at thirteen and motherhood at fourteen and you've got a recipe for a less than successful life. Those are the costs of such circumstances. But I had, with help from many people over the years, managed to pay those costs and move on to a life that was successful in many ways. But there are also hidden costs contained in such a childhood and I was just now, after all these years, learning about these. In my case I was still living in fear of opening my heart the way I did when I was a child. My way of handling that fear -- by always being cheery and cute and just so nice that, gosh darn it, you *had* to like me – made it even harder for me to know my own true feelings. A therapist pointed out that perhaps I was so busy being cheery than I had forgotten how to be happy. Worse, perhaps I was afraid that happiness was something for everyone but me. And so the unavailable men, and the unavailable friendships, all orchestrated to spare me the pain of never finding a man like my father, or who I had *imagined* my father to be.

And who picks unavailable people over and over again? Someone who is unavailable herself. It was quite a little light bulb that went off when I tumbled to that stubborn piece of logic. As obvious as it seems, it had never occurred to me that *I* was the one who was unavailable to a real relationship. I had always thought I had just made interesting but unsuccessful choices. But now, heading towards my fiftieth year, I could see a pattern and it was both a caution as well as a comfort. What had been confusion now became somewhat clear. Friends, lovers, work relationships…. the common thread of co-dependence was me. The good news, I suppose, was that if I was the problem, then perhaps I could be the solution. And how would I go about doing that? I wasn't exactly sure, but my way of exploring the question was to write a book.

I put together a proposal for a book originally titled "Single and Unavailable." The publisher changed the title to "Still Single: Are You Making Yourself Unavailable When You Don't Want To Be? What to do about it!" --- available wherever books with extremely long titles are sold! After months of form rejection letters I finally got lucky and landed a literary agent who found a publisher, St. Martin's Press. Even though I thought I had a good idea, no one was more surprised than me that I actually sold a book on relationships without being in one myself.

CHAPTER 36

———— ⌒ ————

MY DAD'S HEALTH began to fail -- again. It had been ten years since he had awakened from his life threatening coma in my mother's house. He had lived, blissfully happy, with her ever since. Even in his older years he had a scampy twinkle in his eye that was youthful and vital and it was easy to pretend that he was going to defy the odds and live forever. But the twinkle was finally fading; he was very thin now and seemed to age overnight. He had a stroke that put him in the hospital and things didn't look good. Even though he was eighty-seven years old I hoped against hope that history would repeat itself and that he'd recover to live another ten years. He did rally a few more times and he still had his sense of humor, but he was very weak. He took a fall and had to be admitted to a nursing care facility near my home. My mom and I went to see him almost every day. His friends visited, my friends visited, and daddy still had the energy to charm the nurses and staff. But he was going downhill very fast and was in and out of consciousness. One evening his old doctor and dear friend, Dr. Dan, stopped by to visit Eddie while I was there. He sat with my dad and held his hand. Then Dan called me into the hallway and told me that, in his opinion, my father would pass in the next few days. I reminded Dr. Dan that he hadn't been right the last time; he assured me that, sadly, he wasn't wrong this time.

That weekend the whole family came to visit my dad. He seemed to revive a little when everyone gathered; he even managed to hold out his arms to Melanie and hug her. Tiffany had just had her first baby, Nina, three months before. She brought Nina close to my dad; he tried hard to keep his eyes open and stay connected but it was taking every ounce of his energy. We decided to let him get some rest and we would all come back the next day.

The next morning just before I went to see my father, I was sitting in my big, comfy chair in the living room; the one where I write with my laptop computer. It faces a set of sliding doors that overlook the swimming pool. I wasn't writing though, I was just staring at the pool and feeling deeply sad at the prospect of losing my father. Then my mother arrived and we drove to the nursing home together; it was less than a mile from my home.

Not long after my mom and I got there, my father passed away. No matter how prepared I thought I was for this news, the realization just stunned me. Amazingly, the male nurse who had been tending to my dad started to cry; he told me how special he thought my dad was. Some of the patients in the facility had been there for years, my father had only been there for three months, but this nurse was absolutely touched by his loss. Whatever rocky path I had taken to get to the truth of who my father really was, it never ignored the magic of his smile, the loving look in his eyes that beguiled every single person he ever met.

Less than an hour later I was back home. I sat in the very chair that I'd sat in earlier that morning. Again I stared out at the pool, only now my father was gone. How strange it felt. Nothing had changed, yet everything had changed. And then I noticed that there was some object floating in my pool and a voice in my head told me that I should go out and get it. But I thought; who the hell cares what's in my pool, my father's gone. I tried to forget about whatever it was that was in the pool and just feel the pain of my loss. But the sensation wouldn't go away; that voice in my head *compelled* me to go see what was floating in my swimming pool. I opened the sliding doors, crossed to the pool and pulled out a black plastic bag. I was about to throw it away when I straightened it out and saw that it was a large bag, almost two feet across, from *Radio Shack*.

I don't consider myself someone who is particularly invested in other realities. For the most part I live my life here on earth, but the sight of this simple plastic bag from Radio Shack knocked the wind out of me. I had to sit down to keep from falling. I looked around my backyard, trying to figure out *how* in the world this bag could've gotten here. I have eight foot fences surrounding my yard, so it couldn't have come over from my neighbor's yard. I hadn't been to Radio Shack in months so it didn't come from me. And in twenty-five years this was the first time I had ever pulled anything but leaves out of my swimming pool.

There was only one answer for me; and that's that it was my father letting me know, in a way that he knew I would understand, that wherever he was going -- he was going to be okay. You can think what you want, but you could never convince me otherwise.

There's one thing I do know; something changed for me that day. It's not that I didn't mourn my dad anymore because I did. But I felt a sense of profound peace come over me. His death was sad but it wasn't a tragedy. He lived a good, long life and he left me with a smile and a big Radio Shack bag. I still have the bag and the thought of my father still makes me smile. I'm old enough to know that that's more than many people get when a parent passes away.

A few days later, I asked my mom if I could keep the "Eve and Eddie" ring that had meant so much to my dad.

"Sure," she said. Then she added, "You know Eddie always thought that I had that ring made for him."

"Didn't you?" I asked, confused.

"I was dating a guy named Eddie Judson before your father. He was Rita Hayworth's ex-husband; he had it made for me. It was solid gold; what was I going to do, give it away? Who wants a ring that says 'Eve and Eddie' if your name's not Eve or Eddie?"

I was blown away. So, the ring that was my father's absolute *proof* that my mother had once loved him, the ring that he clung to, drew hope and strength from; it turns out that it wasn't even made for him. I'm glad he never knew.

_⌒⌒_

Instead of a traditional funeral; which no one in my family has ever had, we had a huge "Going Away Party"; A beautiful night of reminiscing and storytelling with family and friends. There were a lot of laughs and a lot of tears. Unfortunately, no one knew where my sister was at the time, but all four of *her* children were present. I was surprised that they all came seeing as my father was not only a negligent father to their mother, he also wasn't particularly nice to any of them either. I don't forgive him for the way he treated my sister or her children. It was wrong.

But I still miss him.

I expected my mom to be somewhat relieved that my dad was gone; he had been a lot of work for her, but I think she missed her difficult, charming, witty, irreverent friend. After all, she had taken care of him, cooked for him, and yelled at him for another ten years. *Now* what the hell was she going to do?

She was going to fall apart, that's what. She may have bitched and moaned about my father for forty years, but she never remarried and, now that he was gone, she seemed to lose the raging torrent of wind that had always filled her foul mouthed sails. She was ten years younger than dad but within a year she had lost her ability to drive, taken a couple of nasty falls, and finally admitted that she needed to be in an assisted living facility.

Now I faced one of the toughest challenges of my life: the daunting, discouraging, depressing, overwhelming, bacteria-filled, mold encrusted task of packing up my mother's house. Not only was she a slob and a world class packrat, she also kept important things in the same places she kept junk, so I was forced to go through every single thing myself to determine what to keep and what to throw away. I couldn't even hire anyone because they wouldn't know what was important and what was trash! The first few times that I went over there to begin the job, I'd just sit down and cry. I was angry, too. Yet another mess in my mother's life that she neglected to clean up. The job took almost three months of working five days a week, six or seven hours a day. For reasons I'll never understand, my mother kept every receipt, every frickin' magazine, every piece of junk mail she had ever received. But I couldn't find one school picture, not one report card or school project of mine or my sister's that my mother had saved. Not one.

CHAPTER 37

————— ❧ —————

IT HAD BEEN eighteen years since I'd divorced Charlie. Eighteen years of telling myself I wanted a real relationship, believing I wanted a real relationship, and then doing everything I could do to make sure I picked men with whom a real relationship would be almost impossible.

Creeping up on fifty, it was no longer amusing.

As I worked on my relationship book I did research, conducted interviews, and put together lists of questions that should be asked and qualities that should be looked for if a relationship with an "available" man or woman was the desired result. How fun and easy it was to put together that list, how difficult to follow it. It was all theory until I put it to use in my own life.

Exactly one week after I turned in the first draft of my book I met a man named Christopher Beaumont. He was having lunch with a friend of mine who invited me along. I immediately felt an ease as well as an attraction. He was a writer and, like me, his father had been a writer as well. His father, Charles Beaumont, had a brilliant reputation as one of the creative forces behind the Twilight Zone television series, having written twenty-two of the episodes. Both of Christopher's parents had died tragically when he was quite young and he had raised his sisters and brother by himself, so we had child rearing at a ridiculously early age in common as well. So far, so compatible. He was even age and geographically appropriate.

But he didn't ask for my number.

I was so accustomed to only dating men who chose me; this was a whole new deal. If I was going to get to know this man, it was clear that I was going to have to take the initiative and it scared the hell out of me. My friend Susan had always told me that until I was willing to "skate on thin ice" as she put it, willing to risk rejection, that I'd never meet the right guy. I decided that Christopher was worth the risk. I called him up and asked if we could meet to talk about a writing project. Okay, I didn't exactly ask him out but I did get the ball rolling. We met for lunch the next day and talked for three hours.

I made myself available for this remarkable new person in my life. We started to date and things went from good, to better, to best. I had paid attention, looked for signs that I had perhaps picked yet another unavailable man without knowing it. I didn't want to fall in love with him if he wasn't in the same place emotionally. I didn't want to spend two years, or four, or forever in my old pattern of trying to make something work that didn't have a chance. So I did one of the hardest things I've ever done in my life. After three months of dating I *asked* Christopher, in plain English, if he was available to be in a relationship. I made it clear that I wasn't pushing him to be in a relationship *with me* but --- was he a person who was looking to be in a committed relationship?

And he said "no," that, in fact, he *wasn't* available at this time.

There was no other woman, and it wasn't that he didn't like me, because he said he cared about me very much. Then he told me about his younger brother, Gregory. Chris had raised him from the time he was six years old. Gregory had been diagnosed with Cancer and it looked like he wasn't going to make it. Christopher was honest with me; he told me that his own experience with relationships was that they could be a lot of work and, frankly, he wanted to spend as much time with Gregory as he could. It certainly wasn't what I had hoped to hear, but I understood. We didn't really know each other well enough for me to be the one he leaned on during this time and, besides, he had made it quite clear that he wanted to go through this ordeal with his family and nobody else.

My head and my heart were filled with a mix of emotions. On the one hand, I was crushed. I didn't want to lose this man but, on the other hand, I was proud of myself for doing what I was advising others to do in my book. I had gotten a clear message that Christopher was unavailable for a relationship and I was willing to let him go in order to make room for someone who *was* available. In the past I would have held on to a fantasy, if only to avoid a real relationship that might actually make me happy. That had always been a risk I was unwilling to take. In my book I had written that it wouldn't be an easy thing to do, and now I knew it was true. There are, and always will be, dozens of reasons to avoid finding out what we suspect is true. I had gone a lifetime without opening my heart the way it was open now. To tell the truth, it didn't feel wonderful. It felt frightening. But it also felt authentic.

⸺ɕ

Christopher's concern for his brother made me think about my sister, Chris, and I had an overwhelming desire to see her. I called my niece, Samantha, and found out that Chris was in a hospital/mental health facility about an hour away from me. Even Samantha hadn't known her mother's whereabouts until the facility had called her about a week earlier. She told me to be sure to bring plenty of cigarettes when I visited Chris as they were the hot article of trade.

I went the next day and I brought a few things for Chris besides the cigarettes; some slippers, some pretty things for her hair. The administrator advised me not to give Chris the whole carton of cigarettes; something that valuable would surely cause a riot.

Chris was sitting in a wheelchair when I entered her room. This was my baby sister, she was forty-nine, and yet she looked like a sad, old woman. Her hair was long and wiry and part of it was pulled up and held together with a big pink bow. She was wearing ill-applied, garish make-up and bright fuchsia lipstick. Perhaps someone had helped her get ready to meet her "visitor." She studied me a long time and I was afraid she didn't know me, and then a big toothless smile came to her face.

"Casey," she said.

"Yes," I answered as tears came to my eyes.

"You're my daughter," she said, "or my mother."

"I'm your sister," I said.

"That's right," she said.

I asked what happened to her; why was she in a wheelchair?

"Nothing happened," she said. "I just like having a place to sit."

I gave her the slippers, the hair accessories, and a pack of cigarettes. She was very excited by the cigarettes. I had also brought pictures of us when we were little. She studied them.

"Do you remember these?" I asked.

"A little bit," she said.

I showed her a picture of the four of us; mom, dad, me and Chris.

"Daddy," she said. "I miss my daddy." And she started to cry.

I thought by her comment that she knew that Dad had passed away. But she didn't and I chose not to tell her. For whatever reason, Chris still had a warm spot in her heart for her father and I didn't think she needed to know the truth; it just would've made her sadder.

I couldn't help myself; I started to cry all over again. Chris saw the tears rolling down my face and she started to comfort *me*. I felt like such a horrible person, such a bad sister. How could Chris have ended up in this place? She wasn't born with a physical disability. She didn't suffer from some terrible disease. But she was unloved and neglected, and I guess that's a disease in and of itself. And it was heartbreaking to see how this disease had ravaged her so unmercifully.

"I'm sorry, Chris," I said. "I'm sorry I wasn't a better sister to you."

She paused a minute, thinking it over. "You could've taught me more stuff, but that's okay." And then she grinned at me. "Can you bring more cigarettes next time?" she asked.

I promised I would. I told her I loved her and then Chris wheeled herself off.

I sobbed the whole way home. I promised myself that I would visit her at least once a week, maybe find a way to get mom to come with me; anything to bring a sliver of warmth to what had become of her life.

Six days later my sister suffered a heart attack and died. When I spoke with the doctors they told me Chris had abused her body with drugs for so many years that the heart attack was just the culmination of all that mistreatment. I was very grateful that I'd gotten to see her before she died, but I was still devastated.

I felt an overwhelming urge to call Christopher. I hadn't spoken to him in several weeks but I knew he was dealing with some of the same feelings as me and I wanted to reach out to an understanding soul. I didn't call right away; I was afraid he would think I was trying to rekindle our relationship. But after a few days I picked up the phone and dialed his number. I told him about my sister and he shared that Gregory wasn't doing well. I apologized for calling but he told me that he, too, had thought of calling me as well.

Over the next few weeks he called, and I called, and we grabbed a bite of dinner here and a cup of coffee there. He was in a tremendous amount of pain knowing that his kid brother, thirteen years his junior, was fighting a losing battle for his life. I took it as a compliment when Christopher told me how much comfort it brought him to have our moments on the phone or over a coffee. We still weren't calling it a relationship, but we felt incredibly close to each other. And it certainly wasn't because the setting was romantic; hospital waiting rooms and cafeterias were a long way from flowers and candlelit dinners. But it didn't seem to matter. And I guess you could say that difficult times are a better test of what two people mean to each other than when everything's going smoothly.

One night I asked Chris if he wanted to join me on a trip to babysit my grandkids. He had been at the hospital every day and night for two weeks straight and I thought he could use a break, if you can call an evening with four children aged thirteen down to two months a break. And it was there, in yet another less than romantic setting, that we told each other "I love you." Because we were comfortable with each other, because we were excited by each other, because we "got" each other, because being with each other added energy to our lives instead of taking it, because I finally understood that I could ask for something real. For all those reasons and more we decided that we were, after all, both of us, "available" for a relationship.

I had beaten those "hidden costs" after all. I had broken away from the tapes in my head that told me I would never find another man who could love me the way my father had loved my mother. I had seen my father for who he was and loved him for the wonderful, flawed, brilliant, difficult man he was. And I had opened my heart to the last barrier that stood between me and happiness. I had let myself fall deeply, madly in love. And I had even managed to pick an available man capable of love, who felt the same way about me. It was delicious. It was real. And it changed everything.

And when I remember that it was my sister's passing that prompted that fateful phone call to Christopher, I let my mind wander to a spiritual place, and let myself think that maybe she had a hidden hand in bringing Christopher and me together. Was it just a coincidence or a sign that his name was also "Chris"? True or not, how nice to have thoughts of love and gratitude to my baby sister, even after she's gone.

─⁓─

Gregory passed away on Mother's Day that year. He was thirty-six years old. I was by Christopher's side as he and his family suffered through the grief and sadness of Gregory's passing. For Christopher, it was more like losing a son than a little brother; he had been the only "father" Gregory had known since he was six years old.

We had been there for each other, Christopher and I, through these difficult times. There's an Old Russian saying that "you don't really know a person until you've eaten a pound of salt together" – in other words, been through hell and back. We had gotten to know each other through all that had happened. And over the next year it was wonderful to discover that we were great together in the good times as well, the ordinary, day to day times, and all the moments in between.

Chris had even gotten to know my mother a little. Eve was fairly tame by then and not doing well physically; she'd had several strokes and was going downhill quite fast.

That Christmas, Chris surprised me with a ring and a proposal that we spend the rest of our lives together. We happily spent the next several months planning the big day.

My mother passed away that February. I was holding her hand at the time and was surprised by her quiet exit. She seemed... peaceful. Not a state of being that I would have ever used to describe her in life.

Chris and I were married October of 2002 in a remarkable wedding in front of a hundred and fifty people who seemed to sense not only the joy but the triumph of the occasion.

A blushing bride at fifty-three. How nice to know that good things do come to those who wait. Strange, for a girl who was married for the first time at thirteen years old, that I could still consider myself a late bloomer.

CHAPTER 38

⁓

I HAD ALWAYS felt displaced in my life. One night spent at my father's on a cot, another at my mother's, alone and anxious, a year at Villa Cabrini in the care of nuns whose idea of love was an eyebrow raised in judgment, a summer with total strangers in Blythe, another in the blistering heat of Hesperia with a different set of strangers, pregnant and married at thirteen, a mother at fourteen, living in an apartment that was anything but a home. The only constant in my life was that low hum of anxiety that seemed to accompany me wherever I laid my head.

And now? Loving, and in love with Christopher?

Home.

At long last a home, for me, for my heart, for us, for our hopes and dreams, our struggles, our failures and our successes.

Home.

⁓

My sister. I think about her often. And while I try to focus on the times we shared as children, there are moments when the questions won't let go. What happened? Why did her life turn out so very different from my own? We were only fifteen months apart, raised by the same parents, and yet she made such different choices and paid such a very high price. There is no single answer, of course, but the best I've come up with is "light." Call it light, or love, or nourishment, we all need it to build a life. Plants will go to almost unbelievable lengths, twisting and turning themselves in order to find the smallest speck of light that will keep them alive.

But my sister had no light at all. Or at least not enough to keep her soul afloat. It was all inside of her; the joy, the fun, the humor. I know, because I saw it with my own eyes. I remember her at four, and five, and six, and even ten, laughing, playing like any other child. I remember her singing. But I also remember watching helplessly as she grew up and was denied the love she deserved; seeing her twist and turn looking for anything that resembled light, and then, finding none, turning to drugs to medicate her aching heart.

I will always feel a pang of guilt knowing that I lucked into so much more "light" than my sister had. My head tells me that I did the best I could to be a good sister in a situation over which I had no control; but my heart still wishes.

THE END

P.S. Under the heading "Eve always gets the last word." I was going through some drawers in my office not long ago when I came across a tape recording of a phone message from my mother that I'd saved. Mom was calling me, but while she was waiting to leave a message she must have noticed that my father was eating something that she'd made for herself. The message went something like this: "Hi, Casey, it's your mother." That was funny enough because her voice was so deep and distinctive that you'd never confuse her with anyone else. In fact my father used to have a joke, "If you call and a man answers, don't hang up; it's probably my wife." So, my mother is leaving this message and after her pleasant greeting to me, she went off on my dad, screaming: "EDDIE!! You son of a bitch!!! You're eating my goddamn toast. Don't eat my goddamn toast. I asked you if you wanted toast and you said no. Then you go and you eat my goddamn toast!" She went on for another five minutes forgetting completely that she was on the phone leaving a message for me. Amazingly, when I listened to that tape I got misty. I know it's my crazy mother yelling at my precious father and that shouldn't tug at my heartstrings, but it does.

Light. It comes in so many different colors and hues.

$\backsim$

About The Author

CASEY MAXWELL CLAIR has worked in the entertainment industry for over twenty-five years. She began her career designing major motion picture campaigns and subsequently served as the Director of Advertising for Warner Bros. and ABC Motion Pictures, as well as Vice President of Advertising and Promotion for CBS Television Network. After that, she spent the next decade as a successful comedy writer and television producer for several hit sitcoms. Ms. Clair authored the well received ***"Still Single: Are You Making Yourself Unavailable When You Don't Want to Be? What to Do About It"***, a book on relationships in which she explored her own penchant for choosing unavailable men. She examined ways in which to change this behavior and promptly met an available man with whom she fell in love; they have now been married for fourteen years. Clair and her husband, producer and screenwriter Christopher Beaumont, live in Los Angeles and are currently at work on a feature screenplay.